MAGGIE CHRISTENSEN

Happy Ever After in Bellbird Bay

Copyright © 2024 Maggie Christensen

Published by Cala Publishing 2024

Sunshine Coast, Qld, Australia

This publication is written in British English. Spellings and grammatical conventions are conversant with the UK.

The moral right of the author has been asserted.

All rights reserved. No part of this book may be reproduced, stored in a retrieval system, or transmitted by any means, electronic, mechanical, photocopying or otherwise, without the prior written permission of the author.

This is a work of fiction. The locations in this book and the characters are totally fictitious. Any resemblance to real persons, living or dead, is purely coincidental.

Cover and interior design: J D Smith Design

Editing: John Hudspith Editing Services

Dedication

To Jim, with whom I found my own happy ever after

Also by Maggie Christensen

Oregon Coast Series
The Sand Dollar
The Dreamcatcher
Madeline House

Sunshine Coast books
A Brahminy Sunrise
Champagne for Breakfast

Sydney Collection
Band of Gold
Broken Threads
Isobel's Promise
A Model Wife

Scottish Collection
The Good Sister
Isobel's Promise
A Single Woman

Granite Springs
The Life She Deserves
The Life She Chooses
The Life She Wants
The Life She Finds
The Life She Imagines
A Granite Springs Christmas
The Life She Creates
The Life She Regrets
The Life She Dreams

A Mother's Story

Bellbird Bay
Summer in Bellbird Bay
Coming Home to Bellbird Bay
Starting Over in Bellbird Bay
Christmas in Bellbird Bay
Finding Refuge in Bellbird Bay
Escape to Bellbird Bay
Second Chances in Bellbird Bay
Celebrations in Bellbird Bay

One

Cass Marshall was eating a leisurely breakfast while scrolling through the news items on her iPad, when a headline caught her eye.

***Sudden death of Toni Morgan,
wife of popular breakfast host Ray Morgan.***

The article was accompanied by a photo of the couple at the Logies, the television awards ceremony held on the Gold Coast the previous year. Peering at the photo, Cass could see Ray had aged well, the dark hair she remembered now had silver streaks and his face was more lined, but otherwise he was the same Ray who had broken her heart twenty years earlier. The article gave an account of the couple's thirty-year marriage, their three children, now grown, citing it as one of the most successful of celebrity marriages. *If only they knew.*

They'd met by chance when the magazine Cass worked for sent her to interview the new host of the Channel Twelve breakfast show. Back then, Ray had been trying to make a name for himself and had been delighted to be interviewed by the rookie reporter. And Cass had been blown away by the handsome television personality, so much so that, despite knowing he was married, she'd agreed to have a drink with him afterwards. One drink led to another, then dinner, then, before she knew it, twenty-three-year-old Cass was in the midst of an affair with Ray Morgan who was fast becoming the darling of the early morning breakfast shows.

She sighed, remembering those heady days, days when she believed his lies. But instead of Ray leaving his wife as he'd promised, it had been Cass who left him at the news his wife was pregnant again, the news she learned from his proud announcement on morning television.

She remembered how she'd left the city, determined to put it and Ray behind her and she'd done just that. But the experience had made her wary of all men and prevented her from trusting anyone enough to form another relationship.

When she arrived in Bellbird Bay, Cass's parents greeted her with open arms, pleased she had joined them in the peaceful town they had chosen for their retirement. Since then, a lot had happened, most important of which was the establishment of *Sassy's*, the beachwear shop on the esplanade which catered for everything anyone would need to spend a day on the beach.

It had been Cass's intention to return to the city when she got back on her feet. But the success of *Sassy's* coupled with her dad's unexpected death two years later had meant she stayed. Now she couldn't imagine living anywhere else; this was where she belonged.

Feeling no need to read the article in any detail and pleased to discover she no longer felt anything at the sight of the man for whom she'd once been prepared to give up everything, Cass continued to scroll through the news till she was interrupted by a loud meow. Hector, her Siamese cat, wanted his breakfast. Sometimes Cass felt the cat owned her rather than the other way around. She opened a sachet of Hector's food, smiling as he purred and rubbed against her ankles to show his pleasure.

Once Hector was satisfied and lying in his favourite sunny spot by the window, Cass tidied away her breakfast dishes and set off.

It was Monday and *Sassy's* was closed as it was every Monday, so Cass felt more relaxed than usual as she drove through town on her way to *The Pandanus Garden Centre and Café* where she'd arranged to meet her friend, Greta, for coffee to discuss her forthcoming wedding.

It was a beautiful morning, the sun sparkling on the ocean, and the esplanade almost deserted at this time of day. Bellbird Bay's mayor, Will Rankin, was already at one end of the beach with the van from which he ran his surf school. A few early morning surfers were waiting to catch a wave, and a class of students from the local high school playing a game of volleyball. It was a typical morning in Bellbird Bay, the sort of day that made you glad to be alive and made Cass glad to be living here.

Cass made her way through the garden centre to the café which was almost hidden by a hedge of plumbago. It wasn't in bloom at the moment, but Cass could remember it covered with blue flowers last time she'd visited. Once there, she marvelled again, as she did each time she came, at how well the café was set out around the large pandanus from which the garden centre and café got its name, and how the small tables had been artistically placed among a series of small bushes and towering palm trees. Blinking in the bright sunlight, she saw Greta wave to her from one of the tables.

'Cass,' her friend greeted her, getting up to give her a hug. 'I already ordered. Skinny cap for you and I also ordered two of the yummy brownies. They're just as good as the ones Ruby used to make,' she added, referring to the old woman who, until recently had provided the café with its delicious selection of home-made cakes. Ruby Sullivan had been in an accident several months earlier and had called on a young friend from Sydney to help out with the baking. Sandy Elliot had been so successful she had now moved to Bellbird Bay and taken over most of Ruby's business.

'Ruby did make these ones.' Cleo, the manager of the café, appeared with two coffees and a plate containing two brownies. 'I couldn't help overhearing. Sandy makes the deliveries, but Ruby is still baking for us, though not as much as she used to. She'll be along shortly,' she added, referring to Sandy who, with her business, *Celebrations,* was to provide the wedding cake and catering for Greta's wedding. 'Bev and I will join you both when she arrives. Meanwhile, enjoy your coffee, ladies.'

'Thanks, Cleo.' Greta smiled. 'Isn't it lovely to have a free day? I love my business, but I don't know what I'd do without one day to myself.'

'It is,' Cass agreed, taking a sip of coffee. 'And this is such a lovely place to meet; a wonderful spot for your wedding, too.'

'Yes.' Greta gazed around. 'I'm so glad Leo agreed. At first, he wanted to have it in the hotel.' She grimaced.

Cass mirrored her expression. Greta's prospective husband was the new owner of a hotel on the outskirts of town which he'd recently renovated. *The Leonard Family Resort* was proving popular but wouldn't have provided the intimate setting of the garden centre and café.

They had almost finished their coffee, and only a few crumbs remained from the brownies, when an auburn-haired woman appeared, followed by a taller one, her faded blonde hair tied back into a ponytail. They were quickly joined by Cleo carrying a tray with five cups of coffee and another plate of brownies.

'You know Bev and Sandy, don't you?' Greta asked Cass.

Cass nodded. Both had been customers of *Sassy's*, and she knew Bev had been at school with Greta. It was a few years since Bev had expanded the garden centre to offer it as a wedding venue and *Pandanus Weddings* had taken off. Now Sandy, although relatively new to Bellbird Bay, had joined with her to provide the catering.

Cleo set the cups and plate of brownies on the table and took a seat. But before they could discuss arrangements for the wedding, Sandy said, 'Did you see the news headline this morning? Ray Morgan's wife? What a sad thing to happen. I loved him on the breakfast show, and he was a regular in the café I used to work in, when I lived in Sydney.'

They all made sympathetic noises. Then Greta turned to Cass. 'You lived in Sydney, didn't you? You must remember him. I saw the programme once, when I was there on holiday. He's quite a dish, or he was back then.'

They all chuckled, all except Cass who felt herself redden. Suddenly she was flooded with memories, images of times she thought she'd long forgotten.

'Cass?' Greta was looking at her strangely.

'Sorry, I just had a moment. Ray Morgan? I vaguely remember seeing him, but I'm not much of a morning television person. I prefer to catch up on news on the radio or my iPad.'

The others seemed to accept her response and began discussing the wedding as Sandy made suggestions for various dishes, and Bev took note of the music Greta and Leo preferred. But, for Cass, it all passed in a blur. She was glad no one asked for her opinion; she felt incapable of offering anything worthwhile.

'Are you all right? You were very quiet in there,' Greta said to Cass as they walked out to the car park together.

'Sure, I'm fine. You all seemed to be doing okay without my input.'

'Sorry.' Greta gave her a brief hug. 'You know I couldn't do without you on the day, and I wanted you to be part of the planning, too. It's not something I intend to do ever again.'

Cass squeezed Greta's arm. She was pleased for her friend but couldn't help envying her. Greta had not only been married to the handsome Mick Roberts, who owned the local whale-watching business, but was about to marry Leo, the new owner of *The Leonard Family Resort*. Greta would be the third bride Cass had been bridesmaid to, and she couldn't forget her mother's oft repeated saying, *three times a bridesmaid, never a bride*. She stifled a sigh and tried to hold on to the hope there was someone out there for her. If only he wasn't taking so long to appear.

Two

'Are you all right, Dad?'

Mick Roberts dragged a hand through his hair and smiled at his daughter. He was still becoming accustomed to the fact that, after so many years overseas, she'd finally returned to Bellbird Bay. 'I'm fine, sweetheart.'

Jo twisted a strand of hair between her fingers. 'I worry about you.'

'There's no need. I'm fully recovered.' It was true, but the heart attack he'd suffered a year earlier had scared him into drastically changing his lifestyle. 'You're not going to get rid of me for a good many more years.'

'I hope not, and I have big plans for your sixtieth.'

'That's still two years away, sweetheart.'

'You're okay about Mum and Leo, too? Their wedding is only a few weeks away.'

'Sure,' Mick said, although he still felt an ache when he thought of his ex-wife with the man she'd been in love with as a teenager. He'd been so sure there was a chance for them to get back together before Leo Carlson arrived in town. 'I'm glad she's happy.'

'Good. How's Grandad?'

Mick frowned. His dad had finally been forced to sell the fishing boat which had been his life, and Mick and his brother were trying to persuade him to move out of the large family home and into a retirement village. 'He's still being stubborn about moving, but I'm hopeful he'll see sense soon. Maybe he'll listen to your Uncle Pete. He won't listen to me.'

'Your charm not working?' Jo grinned.

Mick chuckled. 'Never did work on the old man... the women, now, that was a different story.'

'Dad!'

'Sorry!' Mick raised his hands defensively. 'Not something you want to hear and not something I'm proud of. It was what destroyed my marriage to your mum. But those days are long past; I'm a reformed character.'

'Not too reformed, I hope. I loved the old version.'

Mick gave her a hug and kissed her on the forehead. 'Don't let your mum hear you say that, though she loved the old version for a while, too.' He fell silent, remembering. 'Anyway, what about you? Didn't I hear you were going to have to move?'

'You heard right. I knew I could only rent Eddie's lovely house on the boardwalk while she was recuperating. Now she's well again, she's keen to move back.'

'So, what'll you do? You know there's always a place for you here.' They were seated on the deck of Mick's home behind the harbour, the one he'd bought when he and Greta divorced. It was really too large for one person, but he loved the location and the view of the harbour from the deck. It was almost like being on his boat.

Jo blushed. 'Bryan wants me to move in with him and Mia.'

'So that's the way the wind blows. I thought you were taking it slowly.' Since Jo had returned to Bellbird Bay, she'd started teaching in Bellbird Bay Primary and formed a relationship with the father of one of her pupils. Bryan Grant was a widower who had moved to Bellbird Bay with his father and daughter after his wife died. Jo had challenges of her own to deal with, and the pair had bonded over their common grief.

Jo twisted a strand of hair again. 'Bryan's dad's moving out – he and Bev have decided to live at her place – so it makes sense. It's only a few doors up from where I am now.'

'Right.' Mick was aware of the relationship between Bryan's dad, Iain, and Bev Cooper who owned *The Pandanus Garden Centre and Café*. He was surprised Iain hadn't made the move sooner, suspecting he had been loath to leave his son and granddaughter. 'I suppose the pair of you will be announcing your own wedding soon.'

Jo blushed again. 'It's not something we've discussed, but… I hope so. I'd like… Mia would like a little brother or sister, and I know Mum would love another grandchild. She already considers Mia to be her granddaughter.'

'I do, too,' Mick said huskily, surprised how fond he had become of the little girl.

'Anyway,' Jo said, 'all that's in the future. At this stage I'm only moving in, but…'

'Bryan's an honourable guy. He wouldn't have suggested it if he didn't intend to make an honest woman of you.'

'Dad! I didn't think you were so old-fashioned. No one talks like that these days, and not everyone gets married.'

'Your mum and I did.'

'And look what happened there.'

Embarrassed, Mick asked, 'Shall we go inside? It'll be warmer there, and dinner should be almost ready.' He didn't want to talk about his failures as a husband and father, especially not with Jo.

'Okay.' Jo picked up her glass. 'I can't get over what a good cook you've become.'

'Needs must. I didn't want to eat at the surf club every night when your mum and I separated. Though I must admit I did for a while, till I forced myself to learn a few recipes.' He remembered his first few weeks and months as a single man again. If he was honest, he'd also relied on the various women he managed to charm into cooking for him. He'd missed Greta more than he'd expected and had found comfort wherever he could. There had been plenty of women ready and eager to share his life and his bed, but none of them had touched his heart.

'You know, Dad,' Jo said, when they were enjoying the curry he'd served, 'you should find someone, too.'

'What sort of someone?' Mick grinned.

'A woman, someone to take care of you in your old age. Now Mum's marrying Leo, it leaves you on your own.'

'I've been on my own for a long time, honey. I've become used to taking care of myself.'

'But…' Jo pointed her fork at him, '… you know what I mean. I was pleased when I thought you and Mum… then Leo appeared on the scene.' She looked pensive for a moment then said, 'Now, Mum has Leo, and I have Bryan, but you're on your own. Maybe you could join a choir or something… somewhere you could meet someone your own age.'

Mick laughed. He'd never had trouble meeting women in the past, but those days were over. 'I'm not in my dotage, Jo. I'm perfectly capable of finding my own woman friend if I wanted to, and I don't. It would have been different if your mum… But that's life, and I've accepted it wasn't to be. You don't need to worry about me.'

Jo didn't reply, and the subject was dropped, but from his daughter's bullish expression, Mick knew Jo hadn't forgotten. Her parting words confirmed it.

'Love you, Dad,' she said as she hugged him goodbye. 'Don't think I've forgotten. I'll put my thinking cap on and I'll be in touch.'

Mick sighed as he watched the lights of her car disappear into the distance.

Three

The following Monday, Cass had just fed Hector and was about to take her own breakfast out into the courtyard which this morning was bathed in sunlight, when her phone rang. Glancing at the screen, she recognised the number of Rosebank Nursing Home, and she felt the now familiar tension headache begin to form. Since she'd been forced to move her mother there six months earlier, she dreaded these calls, fearful the next would be to tell her Jean had passed away or was about to.

She picked up the phone.

'Hello, Cass here.'

'Ms Marshall. Cass. I'm sorry to trouble you, but Jean…'

Cass listened, a frown creasing her brow. Her mother wasn't the easiest of patients, as she well knew, but at the rate the nursing home was charging, surely they were equipped to deal with her tantrums. Her mother had been going slowly downhill ever since Cass's dad died and had been diagnosed with dementia several years earlier. It had been a blow, difficult to accept when she could no longer care for her at home. Now, the dreaded calls had become more frequent. 'Thanks, I'll drop by as soon as I can.' Cass closed her phone, thinking of all the things she had planned for her day. She picked up her phone again.

'Good morning, Greta,' she said when her friend answered. 'I'm going to have to cancel this morning. I'm sorry.'

'Your mother?' Greta guessed.

'Yes.' Cass sighed. 'They found her wandering around the gardens again last night and want me to drop by. My presence seems to calm her… even though she rarely recognises me.'

'I'm sorry. If there's anything I can do…'

'Thanks, but no.'

'Maybe lunch instead? Leo's going to be tied up with some hotel business,' Greta said. 'We can chat about the wedding.'

After arranging to meet for lunch in the surf club, Cass tidied up the kitchen and set off.

Arriving at the nursing home, Cass didn't take time to admire the beautifully landscaped gardens as she hurried towards the entrance.

When she entered the room which was now her mother's home, Jean was sitting in an armchair staring out the window. Seeing Cass, she became agitated.

'Who are you? Where's my daughter? They told me Cass was coming to take me home.'

Cass swallowed. She hated seeing her mother like this. Jean Marshall had always been such an independent woman, ready to help others. Now she was a travesty of the woman Cass remembered.

'It's me, Mum.' Cass took her mother's hand, the contact seeming to calm her, but she continued to mutter under her breath. Then, suddenly, she peered at Cass. 'Cass? Is it you? Are we going home?'

'Not today, Mum, but maybe we can go for a walk? Would you like that?' It pained Cass to have to treat her mother like a child. Jean nodded, and they were soon on their way out into the gardens. Once there, Jean appeared more settled and Cass was able to enjoy her mother's company, to remember what the older woman had been like before the dreadful disease took hold.

All too soon, it was time to return to the main building, but now Jean seemed to have forgotten her desire to go home and was happy to be led into the room where residents were seated in front of a large television streaming the latest episode of a popular American soap. By the time Cass turned to leave, her mother had forgotten she was there.

Driving back into town, she had to wipe away the tears which were never far from the surface when she visited her mother. She hated how the disease had taken away the older woman's personality, turning her into either a fractious child, or a compliant creature.

It was a relief to reach the surf club and to see Greta waiting for her on the deck.

'You look like you could do with a glass of wine,' Greta said, when Cass took her seat. 'I'll get it. What would you like for lunch?' There was no need to look at the menu. They both knew it by heart.

'Chicken salad. Thanks, Greta.'

When Greta had gone inside to order, Cass stared out at the view of the beach and the ocean. Sitting here, it was easy to forget her problems, to convince herself her life was happy. And it was, she assured herself. Her mother was in good hands, her business was going well, and she owned her own home. What more could she want?

'Here we are.' Greta returned and placed two glasses of wine on the table. 'Isn't it a glorious day?' Then her expression changed and became more serious. 'How is your mother? It must be hard for you.'

Cas sighed, picked up her glass and took a sip before replying, the wine giving her a familiar buzz. It would be easy to drown her problems in alcohol, but she wasn't tempted to go down that route. 'No change there,' she said. 'She was pretty agitated when I arrived, but we went for a walk, and it seemed to calm her. The worst part is when she pleads to come home – even worse than when she doesn't recognise me.'

'Oh, Cass!' Greta placed her hand on Cass's. 'I can't imagine what that must be like.'

Cass sighed again. 'It is what it is, and I'm not the only person whose parent has succumbed to dementia. And she is happy most of the time – or at least that's what they tell me. I have to believe them.'

'How's Jo?' Cass asked, after a pause during which she sought to find a change of topic. 'Didn't you say she was moving in with Bryan Grant? You okay about it?'

'Yes.' Greta smiled. 'I know I wasn't happy about their relationship at first, but when I saw how happy they were together... and when little Mia started to call me Gigi, I changed my mind. Bryan has really helped Jo heal from losing the baby, and I think she's helped his healing process, too. I'm hoping...'

'The next wedding?' Cass raised an eyebrow.

'It's on the cards. I know Bev's hopeful, too.'

Cass nodded. Bev Cooper was Bryan's birth mother. She'd only discovered he was her son after they moved to Bellbird Bay, and Bryan started to work at the garden centre. It had been a shock for everyone at the time, but people soon became used to the idea – and to Bev and Bryan's father, Iain, becoming a couple, too. 'Stranger things have happened,' she said.

'So,' Greta said, 'all this talk about weddings. What about you?'

'What about me?' Cass blushed. Could Greta read her mind, know how much she wished it was her turn?

'No one on the horizon?'

'Come off it, Greta. You know you'd be the first to know if there was. There aren't a lot of options in Bellbird Bay.'

'I'm not so sure.' Greta seemed to think for a few moments. 'There's Finn at *The Bugle*,' she said, referring to the editor of the local newspaper, 'and there's a new principal at the high school, and what about…?'

'Stop!' Cass said. 'Just because you've rediscovered the love of your life, doesn't mean everyone else needs to pair up. I'm happy as I am… and with Mum the way she is, I don't have the time or energy for anything else.'

'Hmm.' Greta didn't seem convinced, but she let the matter drop, and Cass hoped that was the last she'd hear about it. Greta might have a man in her life, but Cass was perfectly capable of finding one for herself. She had no intention of allowing her friend to play matchmaker.

Four

Mick whistled to himself as he showered and dressed, ready to have dinner with Jo and Bryan. It was over a week since Jo had moved in with him, and the first time Mick had been invited to her new home. He hoped the new outfit of dark blue pants and pink shirt wasn't over the top, but he wanted to make a good impression, make Jo proud of him. As he checked himself out in the mirror, he considered he didn't look too bad for fifty-eight. Since the heart attack, he'd lost most of the weight he'd put on over the years, and his face was more lined than it had been in his twenties, but he still had all his hair even if the dark brown was now streaked with silver. Some might say it made him look more distinguished. Didn't they call men like him silver foxes? He chuckled to himself, then a thought struck him. Jo hadn't said any more about him finding a partner. What if…? No, she wouldn't. Suddenly, the invitation to dinner took on a more sinister note. He shrugged. No, there was no way his daughter would set him up… or would she?

Picking out a bottle of wine from his wine rack, he headed to the car.

A few minutes later, Mick pulled up outside the renovated beach shack. It was a part of town he'd often admired, wished he could afford. It seemed strange to think his daughter now lived here.

When he knocked at the door he heard footsteps, then Jo's voice saying, 'I'll get it, Mia,' but the little girl beat her to the door, opening it with a big grin.

'Hello, Grandpa Mick,' she said, reaching up for a hug. 'Jo said it would be you.'

'Hi, Dad.' Jo appeared behind Mia. She hugged Mick too. 'I'm glad you could come. We have a few friends here.' She took the bottle of wine and led him through the house to the back deck. It was this feature that made these houses so special, facing the boardwalk and the ocean. Tonight, the roar of the waves was particularly loud, almost drowning out the chatter of the group of people sitting there with glasses of wine.

'I think you know most of us,' Jo said.

Mick recognised Iain Grant and Bev Cooper, Rob Andrews who owned *Bay Bikes* with Sandy Elliot, owner of *Celebrations*, plus another couple who were strangers to him. He gave a sigh of relief – no single woman in sight. His fears were groundless.

'I don't think…' he began.

'Oh, of course. You don't know Andy and Brenda Collins. Brenda teaches with me, and Andy is…' She was interrupted by Mia pulling on the hem of her dress. 'Sorry, Dad.'

'Mick Roberts. I'm Jo's dad.' Mick held out his hand to each of them in turn. They were both closer to his age than Jo's, Brenda a short, curvy, blonde woman who had a lovely smile, and Andy taller, his sandy hair beginning to thin. They both smiled and shook his hand. 'How do you know Jo?' Mick asked.

Brenda spoke first. 'We work together. We moved here recently, and I was lucky to find a position. Andy works in the library.'

'Jo tells us you run the whale-watching cruises,' Andy said. 'Must be interesting. I sometimes wish I'd been more adventurous in my career choice.'

Smiling, Mick allowed himself to be drawn into a conversation about his experiences, enjoying being the focus of attention.

At the dinner table, Mick found himself seated between Brenda and Sandy, and discovered he and Sandy had a lot in common, both being small business owners. He knew she had come to Bellbird Bay when Ruby Sullivan had been laid up after being attacked by a magpie but hadn't realised her business now provided the catering for *Pandanus Weddings* and would be doing so for Greta's wedding. Unwilling to be caught up in a conversation about his ex-wife's nuptials, he turned to Brenda on his other side. 'How are you enjoying living in Bellbird Bay?' he asked.

'I love it,' she responded with a smile. 'We moved here after our parents passed away. Andy was offered a position at the library, and I decided to try my luck with the education department. So far, it's worked out well.'

Mick thought it strange to speak of *their* parents, not hers or his, but decided to let it pass. He knew some married couples treated both sets of parents equally and assumed this was the case with them. It hadn't been with him and Greta. While he had got on okay with her dad, he always felt her mum didn't approve of him, although she had always liked his folks and vice versa. And his parents doted on Jo. They had been really upset when he and Greta divorced, though, to give her credit, she'd never tried to stop Jo seeing either him or her grandparents. They were the only ones she had left as Greta's parents died in Bali just before the divorce. He often thought Greta used their death as an excuse to end the marriage, although he knew his affairs with other women were the real cause.

The evening passed pleasantly, confirming Mick's opinion of Bryan as being right for Jo. He had a strong suspicion he was the reason she'd decided to stay around in Bellbird Bay – him and the job at the primary school. Whatever the reason, he was glad about it, and he hoped he was right in thinking Bryan had marriage in mind. As he'd told his daughter, her mother wasn't the only one who'd like to have grandchildren.

By the time Mick reached home, he was feeling tired. It had been a long day, and he had an early start next morning. Now the whale-watching season was in full swing, he was rushed off his feet. There had been reports of large pods off the coast, and people were lining up to take advantage of his cruises. It was good to be busy but some days he wished he had two pairs of hands – or more boats. Maybe, if he could swing it, he could buy another before next season. It was certainly worth considering. Meanwhile, he'd see if he could find a youngster willing to earn a few extra dollars by helping out on *Bay Whale Cruises*, not the most imaginative name, but it worked; everyone knew what it was.

Now Jo was more settled, he was enjoying seeing more of her

and before he left, they'd made arrangements to meet for a drink the following Wednesday. It had been Jo's suggestion, and she'd winked at him as she spoke. Mick wasn't sure what that was about. Maybe she had something to tell him about her and Bryan. He looked forward to finding out.

Five

The phone call from her sister took Cass by surprise. Vi, christened Viola, Cass's younger sister, had left Australia over twenty years ago after a whirlwind courtship when she married the handsome Englishman she'd met at a student party. He had been in Australia on a working visa and, when it expired, she had returned with him to make her life in his hometown, leaving Cass to cope with their aging parents and now their mother's failing health.

'Vi. It's been a long time.' Too long. Although she kept in touch with her sister's life through Facebook, it was rare the pair spoke; their lives had gone in such different directions.

'Sorry, you know how it is with Roger and Justin. I don't seem to have a minute.'

No, Cass didn't know how it was. She'd have dearly loved to be in her sister's position with a husband and family. But it hadn't happened, and there was no use in wishing for something she didn't have. 'Are you calling about Mum?'

There was a pause, then, 'How is she? I wish there was something I could do to help, but…' Vi let her voice trail off.

'She's not good. I try to see her as often as I can. It's not easy for me either, Vi.' Cass didn't want to sound plaintive, but she did sometimes wish Vi was here to share her load. Her sister didn't respond. 'That's not why you called, is it?' she asked. She knew her sister so well and was sure Vi had an ulterior motive.

'No, it's not. I wanted to ask a favour.'

Cass sighed, reminded of when they were growing up together. Despite the fact Cass was the older sister, Vi had always managed to be the one to make demands – and to get her way. But what could she possibly want of Cass now?

'It's about Justin.'

Cass racked her brains, trying to remember how old her nephew was. 'Justin? He must be about…'

'He's nineteen,' Vi finished for her. 'He's got into a bad crowd, and we don't know what to do. Roger suggested we could send him to Australia for a bit, to…'

'To Bellbird Bay?' Cass couldn't believe her ears. She'd never met her nephew. The few times Vi had returned to visit she'd come alone, citing the cost of bringing him with her and the impossibility of Roger leaving his law practice.

'Where else?' Vi chuckled. 'I know it's a lot to ask, but we're at the end of our tether, and Roger thought, in a different environment, maybe Justin would be able to sort himself out, realise how good life is for him here, make him appreciate what he was missing. Please, Cass.'

Cass didn't reply immediately, thinking of the disruption it would be to her life. She knew nothing about teenage boys, and Justin was almost a man. What would he do here in Bellbird Bay? If it had been a girl, she could have helped out in *Sassy's*. But a boy… and one who was already presenting difficulties for his parents…?

'Please, Cass,' Vi said again. 'I wouldn't ask if we could think of another solution.'

'What does Justin think about it?' It was all Cass could think to ask.

'He thinks it'll be an adventure. He's seen some movies set in Australia and…' she hesitated, '… he may have a romanticised view of it.'

'We're not in the outback.' Cass tried to think what movies he might have seen and could only come up with *Crocodile Dundee*, *Rabbit-Proof Fence* and *Picnic at Hanging Rock*.

'I've told him you live in a small coastal town, that there might be surfing. He'd like that. He enjoys it when we visit Roger's brother in Cornwall. They go sailing.'

So why couldn't they send Justin there?

Vi's next words gave the answer. 'We'd suggest he went there, but his so-called friends would find him. We only want what's best for him, Cass. If you won't help, I don't know what we'll do.' She started to cry.

Cass sighed. The one thing she'd never been able to resist was Vi's tears. As a child, her sister had been able to turn them on and off at will, but this time, Cass could tell they were genuine. How difficult could it be to have a nineteen-year-old around? It might even be interesting.

*

Cass was still thinking about it when she popped into *Birds of a Feather* with two takeaway coffees next morning.

Greta knew immediately something was up. 'What's happened?' she asked, accepting her coffee.

'My bloody sister.'

'The one in England?'

'The only one.' Cass had often sounded off to Greta about how Vi managed to escape any responsibility for their mother, how she'd swanned off to the other side of the world without a care, how she could easily afford to visit more often, how...

'What's she done now?'

'Just talked me into having her problem son to stay.' Cass grimaced, but she knew she only had herself to blame for agreeing. By the end of the conversation, she'd actually found herself feeling sorry for the poor kid.

Greta's eyes widened. 'Wow! How old is he?'

'Nineteen.' Cass took a sip of coffee, keeping her eye on the esplanade outside her shop in case any potential customers arrived. 'Seems he's got into bad company and they – for they, read Vi's husband – think a change of scene is the answer.'

'Oh!'

'Yes. It's probably drugs. What the hell have I let myself in for?'

'When does he arrive?'

'In two weeks. He's finished school and has dropped out of uni. As if I didn't have enough on my plate with Mum. I guess I'd better prepare myself. You have experience with teenagers. I may call on your help.'

'Only Jo. Boys are different. You'd be better off speaking to Will Rankin… or Ted Crawford. His grandson is close to that age.'

'I might do that. I have no idea what to do with a nineteen-year-old boy.'

Just then, the door opened, and one of the women from Cass's book club walked in. Grace Winter was Ted Crawford's partner, young Zack's grandmother, even if she and Ted weren't married.

'You can advise Cass about teenage boys,' Greta said, before Cass could speak.

'What?' Grace looked from one to the other.

'Sorry, Grace. Ignore Greta,' Cass said, embarrassed. 'I should be going before I have a queue at the door of *Sassy's*.' Cass picked up her paper cup and started for the door even though she could see the path outside was empty. She and Grace had belonged to the same book club for years, but she didn't feel she knew her well enough to ask for her opinion, though it might be useful. As she was leaving, she heard Greta ask, 'How can I help you today, Grace?'

Glad to be in her own shop, Cass set about preparing for the day. There weren't many customers but setting up a new window display helped take her mind off her promise to Vi. She should have asked more about the boy she realised, when she took time to consider what she had let herself in for. What did teenage boys like to eat? How did they spend their time? There were plenty of activities here in Bellbird Bay, but which ones might appeal to him? Then she grasped onto one thing Vi had said. Surfing. Well, that was easy. Will Rankin was the local expert on surfing. He ran the surf school and as Greta said, he had a son. She tried to remember how old Owen Rankin would be… older than nineteen. He had his own business now, designing and making surfboards and was a surfing champion in his own right. But talking with Will would be a good place to start. She didn't know him well either, but as he was the local mayor, their paths had crossed on a few occasions, and she'd been impressed how approachable he was.

On reflection, it was good of Greta to suggest Grace, but the older woman – she must be more than ten years older than Cass, maybe twenty – always seemed so confident and was always so elegantly dressed, Cass felt in awe of her. She was one of a group of Bellbird residents who lived in a row of renovated beach shacks on the boardwalk looking out onto the ocean, a far cry from Cass's own home on the edge of town and the sort of place Cass could only dream about.

So when, at almost closing time, Grace walked into *Sassy's*, Cass did a double take.

'I've been thinking about what Greta said this morning,' she said, 'and I don't want you to think I'm interfering. After you left, she did mention your nephew was coming to stay and you weren't accustomed to young people. I'm no expert, but I can remember what my son, Ben was like at that age, and, since Ted and I got together I've had a lot to do with Zack, so if there's anything…'

Damn Greta. Why did she have to interfere? Why had Cass even confided in her in the first place? But she knew why. Greta was her friend, and that's what friends did. She took a deep breath. Grace was only being kind. 'Thanks, Grace,' she said. 'It's good of you to offer. Can I get back to you on that? At this stage I'm not sure what sort of advice I may need… not until Justin actually arrives.'

'Sure, but you know where I am if you do want to chat.'

'Thanks,' Cass said again. She had no idea what Justin would be like, how he would react to being sent here as what he might deem to be a punishment – even though Vi said he saw it as an adventure – and how much help and advice she might need.

Meantime, she would stock up on the sort of food a teenager might like, prepare her spare room for him, and hope she wouldn't regret her rash decision to agree to her sister's request.

Six

As he'd predicted, Mick was run off his feet for the next few days. By the time Wednesday came around and his planned drinks with Jo, he wished he could stay home, put his feet up with a glass of beer and have an early night. Instead, he found himself grabbing a pizza on the way home which he wolfed down between showering and getting dressed in an outfit Jo would approve of. He didn't normally bother about what he wore but, since Jo returned home, he found himself caring about her opinion.

They'd arranged to meet at the surf club but when he reached the top of the stairs and entered the restaurant there was no sign of her. Seeing Will Rankin at the bar, chatting to the barman, he sauntered over. 'Hey Will,' he said.

'Mick! We were just talking about you.'

Mick raised an eyebrow.

'Nate mentioned seeing a few pods of whales travelling up the coast. Must be good for business.'

'It is.' Mick exhaled. 'Can barely keep up with demand. Wish I could clone myself.' He chuckled.

'Know how you feel. I sometimes feel the same way in holiday season when I'm swamped with tourists all wanting surf lessons. Guess you could do with another boat?'

'You're not wrong. Maybe next year. I'm thinking of taking on an apprentice. If you know of anyone…'

'No one comes to mind, but I'll keep my ears open.'

'Thanks.'

'Did you see the article in this week's *Bugle*?'

'No, haven't had a moment to scratch myself never mind reading the local paper. Something interesting?'

'You might think so. I've managed to persuade the council to isolate some funds – a couple of thousand – from the budget to put towards the purchase of a mobility scooter for Ruby Sullivan. The old woman is having trouble getting around since the accident with the magpie last year. It was the least we could do. She's an institution in Bellbird Bay.'

'Ruby Sullivan? That name takes me back.' Mick remembered how, as children, they used to tease the old woman, knocking on her door, then running to hide and laughing when she came to see who was there. 'How old is she now? She seemed old when we were kids, but I guess she might have been younger than we are now.'

'Must have been. No one knows how old she is, and who'd dare to ask? Even Sandy Elliot doesn't know, and she's known her since she was a kid too.'

'So, she'll be able to keep bothering people with her weird predictions. Does anyone believe them?'

'She was spot on with Cleo and me,' Will said with a chuckle. 'May have been a coincidence, but I'm not a fan of coincidences.'

'Hmm.' Mick couldn't understand a man like Will believing the sort of claptrap he'd heard was peddled by Ruby Sullivan. He glanced across at the entrance to the restaurant, pleased to see Jo standing there. 'Sorry, mate. My date's here.'

Will looked across, then grinned when he recognised Jo.

'I know,' Mick said. 'Sorry state of affairs when the only date I can get is with my daughter.' But he didn't mean it. He was happy to be spending the evening with her. It wasn't often they had the opportunity to spend time alone, now she and Bryan were a couple.

'Hi, Dad.' Jo gave Mick a kiss on the cheek.

He returned her greeting. She was so like her mother had been when she was younger, he felt a pang of regret for what might have been, then he smiled. 'What'll you have?'

'A glass of chardonnay please, Dad. Hey, Will,' she said to his companion. 'Did I hear you plan to do sessions for the primary kids?'

'You did. Not all the youngsters belong to Nippers, and we thought it would be good to give them some basic water safety lessons.'

Jo laughed. 'Mia is telling everyone about Nippers and boasting you'll be teaching her to surf.'

'That's as maybe.' Will chuckled. 'She's a good kid, keen too. She'll do well.'

Jo glowed with as much pride as if Mia was her own daughter.

When their drinks had been served, they took them out to the deck where they could talk without interruption. Mick was keen to hear what Jo had been doing and how she and Bryan were getting on, hopeful she might have some news for him. He was surprised when his daughter asked, 'What did you think of Brenda?'

'Brenda? I thought she and Andy seemed a nice couple. Why?'

Jo laughed. 'They're not a couple, Dad. Not in the way you mean. They're brother and sister. I know Brenda through school, and she and her brother don't know many people here as yet.' She fixed Mick with her eyes. 'I wanted you to meet her.'

Mick recalled Brenda referring to *their* parents. He'd thought it unusual at the time. Now he knew why.

'Dad?'

It took Mick a moment to realise what Jo was saying. He shifted uncomfortably in his chair, took a gulp of the low alcohol beer he'd ordered. 'I don't need you to throw women at me. I'm fine as I am. I told you that. It would have been different if your mum and I… But she chose Leo. I'm happy for her, and I'm happy on my own. If that's all you wanted to talk about…' He drained his glass and made to rise.

'No, Dad.' Jo put a restraining hand on his arm. 'There's no need for you to get into a snit. I'm not trying to run your life for you. I just want to see you settled.' She gazed at him with such a pleading expression, Mick immediately melted. Ever since she was a small child, he'd been putty in his daughter's hands, but this time, she may have gone too far. 'I'll forgive you this time,' he said, 'but promise me you won't try to set me up again.'

'I promise,' she said, 'if you promise me something, too.'

'Anything,' he said, glad she'd given in so easily. It was unlike her.

'Promise me,' she said with a wicked glint in her eye, 'you'll arrange to see Brenda again. No,' she said, when he started to object. 'Just once. She's new to town. Do it as a favour to me. Then I'll leave you alone to get on with your life. I won't interfere again.'

Mick sighed. He wouldn't do it for anyone else, but this was Jo. 'Just once. Okay?'

'Thanks, Dad.' She leant over to give him a kiss on the cheek. 'I knew I could count on you. She's a nice woman, and I think…'

'Steady on. Just once, I said.'

Jo grinned.

'Now, what's happening with you and Bryan? You seemed very comfortable together when I came to dinner.'

'Things are good… very good.' Jo's eyes softened. 'It's different to what it was with Damien,' she said, referring to the man she'd lived with in London before returning to Bellbird Bay. 'I can't believe I wasted so much time on him. Bryan loves being a dad. I love seeing him with Mia, and Mia loves her dad. I'm so lucky to have met them, both of them.'

'It's not just because…' Mick hesitated, wondering if he dared to ask, but he had to know, '… because of Mia?'

'No!' Jo sounded shocked. 'Though… maybe at first. She was such a sad little soul when she joined my class. She'd lost her mother… and I'd lost my baby. Then I met Bryan. I could tell he was grieving, too. It spoke to me and… well, here we are. I love him, Dad. I don't know what I'd do if anything happened to spoil it.'

'Nothing's going to happen, honey, I won't let it.' Though what could he do if Bryan decided to end the relationship? 'I'm looking forward to walking you down the aisle.'

'Oh, Dad!' Jo's eyes misted. 'I hope you're right.' She wiped her eyes. 'Now,' she said, taking a sip of her wine, 'What's happening with you? I heard there are more whales than usual travelling north this year.'

The remainder of their evening was spent with Mick recounting various episodes from his recent cruises. Mick thought Jo had forgotten about her request about her friend. But when she left, Jo asked for his phone.

'Now you have no excuse,' she said, as she entered Brenda's phone number into it. 'Don't forget. I'll be checking with her.' Seeing his expression, she added, 'I love you, Dad. I only want you to be happy.'

Driving home, Mick reflected that it was what all of them wanted – for their loved ones to be happy. And if he could make his daughter happy by contacting Brenda and inviting her out, he'd do it, even if it was the last thing he wanted to do.

Seven

It was Greta's wedding day. Cass knew she should be feeling happy for her, and she was. But she couldn't dismiss the tinge of envy. This was Greta's second time as a bride, Cass's third as a bridesmaid. If only…

Cass swung her legs out of bed, determined to put her own feelings aside and be pleased for her friend on her special day. Both their shops would be closed today as it was Monday. The wedding wasn't till early evening, but there was a lot to do before then. Greta's daughter, Jo, had arranged for the three of them to have breakfast together, then had booked them into the spa in *The Leonard Family Resort* for pampering, followed by lunch at *The Beach House*. The afternoon was to be taken up with hair and nail appointments before they met at Greta's to dress for the wedding.

Dressing in a pair of jeans and long-sleeved tee-shirt, Cass headed to the kitchen where she fed Hector and filled his water bowl.

As she'd expected, breakfast was a lot of fun, Greta and Jo reminiscing about when Jo was small and had loved dressing up as a bride, and Cass recalling her sister Vi's wedding when she'd been forced to wear a dress she hated. Fortunately, this time, her bridesmaid's dress, a long, pale green gown with three-quarter sleeves, suited her so well, and was a perfect foil for Greta's ivory outfit. For once, her friend had chosen simplicity over the bright colours she normally favoured. Jo was to wear a dress similar to Cass's in a pale blue.

The day passed quickly, and all too soon it seemed, they were getting decked out for the big event. Cass was surprised to see Greta was a bag of nerves.

'I know I love Leo,' she said, 'and I'm doing the right thing, but I loved Mick, too.' Her eyes moistened. 'You don't think I'm crazy marrying again at my age, do you?' she asked Cass.

'Of course not.' Cass just wished she was in Greta's place, not with Leo, of course, but with someone she loved and who loved her. It must be wonderful to feel so sure of someone, to agree to spend the rest of your life with them.

'Ready?' Jo appeared in the doorway. 'Bryan's here with Mia.'

In the living room, Mia was waiting, more subdued than usual, her eyes glittering with excitement. She was carrying a basket of rose petals to scatter as Greta made her way towards the wedding arch. She'd seen her friend, Clancy, do this at Libby and Adam's wedding and pleaded to be allowed to do the same at Greta's.

They all piled into Bryan's car and drove to the *Pandanus Garden Centre*.

Once there, Greta clutched Cass's hand tightly. 'This is it,' she said. 'I didn't believe it would ever happen, that Leo and I would be getting married.'

Jo gave her mum a hug, as they heard music coming from the garden centre. 'Ready, Mum?' she asked again.

Greta nodded, and the three women followed Mia through the centre and up a pathway to where Leo awaited them under an arch covered with flowers.

Cass had tears in her eyes as she listened to the celebrant saying how marriage was a public declaration of Greta and Leo's love. Then, suddenly it seemed, the ceremony was over, Leo kissed the bride, the music started up again, and the guests all made their way to the café, leaving the bridal party to have their photographs taken by Martin Cooper.

In the café, Sandy of *Celebrations*, had outdone herself with nibbles to accompany the champagne, then a cold buffet comprising a selection of seafood and salads, followed by an exotic-looking wedding cake.

When it came time for Greta to toss her bouquet – a small posy of rosebuds – it was no surprise to anyone when she threw it directly at Jo, who blushed and glanced towards Bryan. Mia hopped up and down in delight.

'Looks like we might have another wedding soon,' Bev said to Cass, as Bryan gave Jo a hug, and she handed the posy to Mia.

'Mmm.' What was it about this town, Cass thought. Ever since Bev started up *Pandanus Weddings*, it seemed as if almost everyone she knew had decided to get married.

'No one on the horizon for you, Cass?'

Cass turned to see Grace Winter smiling at her. Grace was one local who had decided against marriage, but she had found new love since moving to Bellbird Bay. If there was something in the air here, as many said, it had missed Cass completely. She started to reply, only to be interrupted by Ruby Sullivan. Cass hadn't noticed the old woman earlier, hadn't realised she was among the guests.

'Your turn will come,' she said to Cass. 'Everything may not be what it seems, and there may be a few crests and troughs along the way, but you'll get your wish.'

How did she know? And what did she mean? Cass was aware many people called Ruby a witch. Not only did she bake delicious cakes – which made Cass think of the witch in Hansel and Gretel – but she had the reputation of predicting the future. Cass shivered.

Clearly seeing Cass's confusion, Grace said, 'Don't let Ruby spook you, but don't dismiss her out of hand, either. She told me a few things when I first arrived… and she was surprisingly accurate. Maybe we'll be celebrating your wedding here, too, someday.'

Cass looked at her as if she was mad, but somewhere, deep inside, a seed of hope took root.

Eight

During the two weeks after Greta's wedding, Cass was bombarded by emails from her sister. Vi seemed worried Cass might change her mind. And she almost did. But a promise was a promise, even if it wasn't the pinkie promise she and Vi used to make to each other. Now the day of Justin's arrival was here.

Cass checked the house before leaving for the airport to ensure she had everything ready. The fridge and pantry were stocked with the sort of food she imagined a teenager might enjoy, the bed was made up in the spare room with the navy bedcovers she'd bought specially, deciding he might not appreciate the floral ones she favoured. She'd even had a quick chat with Will Rankin who had suggested she enrol the boy in his surf school. He hadn't been able to offer much more advice, telling her that every nineteen-year-old was different and warning her he'd probably want to spend time in his room and would no doubt be addicted to computer games. Cass had sighed when she heard that, and wondered how, if that was the case, she could redirect his energies to more outdoor pursuits. To that end she'd visited *Bay Bikes*, and bought a second-hand bike from Rob Andrews, on the understanding he'd buy it back when Justin returned home.

On that topic, her sister had been remarkably reticent, merely saying they'd work something out.

Cass could see the plane coming in to land as she pulled into the airport car park and hurried into the terminal. Once there, she joined the crowd of people waiting for the passengers to alight, wondering if she'd recognise the nephew she'd only met on Zoom up till now.

A line of travellers began to straggle out into the building, many immediately greeted by loving friends and relatives. Among them was one solitary youth, a computer bag slung over one shoulder. He looked familiar. It was Justin. Cass moved forward.

'Justin?'

He looked up and pushed a lock of blond hair out of his eyes which, seen close up, were exactly like Vi's. 'Aunt Cass?'

Cass pulled him into a hug, from which he wriggled out. 'You look so much like your mother,' she said, gazing at him in surprise.

'So I'm told.' He pushed back the lock of hair again, clearly a nervous habit.

'Welcome to Bellbird Bay. I hope you'll enjoy your visit.'

'I hear there's surfing.'

'You're right. We can organise lessons if you like.'

'Awesome.'

'Let's find your luggage and we'll get on home.' He seemed a nice kid. Maybe this would work out okay.

'Mum said you have a shop,' Justin said as they drove back to town. 'What kind?'

'Beachwear – for women and children. Not something you'd be interested in.'

'Hmm.' Justin was silent till they reached the road along the cliffs. 'Wow! The ocean. It's huge.' He twisted around to get a better look. 'It's different to what I'm used to. Is your house near the beach?'

'Not exactly. I'm on the outskirts of town but there's a bike you can use if you want to.'

'Cool.' He fell silent again.

By the time they reached Cass's small house and settled Justin and his luggage into her spare room, it was almost lunchtime. 'Why don't we go over to the beach and have lunch at the surf club?' she said, unsure how to spend the rest of the day with the teenager who was still a stranger, a stranger who looked so familiar. It was odd.

'Sounds good. There's a lot of surfing here?'

'Most people I know surf. They're older now, but a few were local surfing champions in their day.'

'Really?'

'One of them – Will Rankin – runs the local surf school.'

Justin's eyes lit up.

Cass began to relax. Maybe Will would be at the club, and they could organise lessons for Justin right away. It would be a weight off her mind if she knew he had something to keep him occupied when *Sassy's* opened again next day. She had no idea what Vi thought she was going to do with him while she was at work. She couldn't keep her eyes on him 24/7, and he was too old to treat like a child. She thought back to their last conversation.

'You will make sure he doesn't get into trouble, won't you? We're sending him to you to get him away from bad company. You need to see he stays away from the sort of people he got embroiled with here.'

Cass had promised, while not being entirely sure what she was promising. Vi had been very cagey about the *trouble* Justin had found himself in, only saying it was a bad crowd. Looking at the boy, his eyes bright at the thought of learning to surf, Cass couldn't imagine he was the same one Vi was so worried about.

*

Being Monday, the club was fairly empty. Justin seemed impressed by the large surfing wall mural as they walked up the stairs to the restaurant, even more so when Cass told him she knew the man who it featured.

'Do you know all of them too?' he asked, pointing to the honour board.

Cass chuckled. 'Not all of them. Many died before I was born, but I do know several of them.' She read out the names of Ted Crawford, Will Rankin, Rob Andrews and Owen Rankin.

'Some of these names are there more than once. Does that mean…?'

'Yes, Ted, Will and Owen were champions several times.'

'Wow! And this Will guy… he's the one you said I could get lessons from.'

'He sure is.'

'Cool!'

To Cass's delight, when they reached the top of the stairs, she saw Will standing at the bar with his good mate, Martin Cooper.

'Hey Will,' she said, walking up to the pair.

'Cass. So, this is the young fellow who's come to stay with you. Welcome to Bellbird Bay,' Will said, holding out his hand.

'Uh, thanks.' Justin took the outstretched hand. He seemed bowled over by the sight of Will in his shorts and tee-shirt, the latter emblazoned with the words, *Bay Surf School*, his fading blond hair tied back in a ponytail.

'Cass tells me you might want to learn to surf. Done any?'

'Tried a bit when I was visiting my uncle in Cornwall.' Justin shrugged. 'Didn't do very well. I didn't learn properly. Uncle Vic wasn't keen. He's more of a sailor. I like the ocean.'

'Well, if you're interested, we can soon sort you out. Get Cass to bring you down to the beach and sign you up. I guarantee you'll be surfing like the best of them in no time.'

'Really? I'd love that.' Justin said.

A young man looking very like Will appeared at his side. 'Touting for business, Dad?' he asked with a grin.

'Hey Owen. This is Justin who's come to visit. Justin, my son, Owen, who designs and makes the best surfboards on the coast if not the whole of Australia.'

'Why stop there, Dad? Did I tell you we're exporting now? Started with the online shop Bronte set up for the surf gear – now surfboards.' He turned to Justin. 'Welcome. You could do worse than take lessons from my dad. He taught me all I know about surfing.'

'And young Owen here has taken out the championship more times than his dad,' Martin put in. 'I'm Martin Cooper, Justin. Can I welcome you to Bellbird Bay, too.'

Justin stared at the tall man for a moment, then, 'Martin Cooper? *The* Martin Cooper? Wow! I've seen your work in the travel magazines. You won the Atlas award three times,' he said, mentioning the prestigious photographic award. 'You've been to some amazing places.'

'Not any more,' Martin said with a smile. 'I've settled down now, come back home where I belong. I'm too old to traipse around the world, climbing mountains and struggling through the jungle. Talking of which, it's time I went home for lunch. See you all later.' He placed his glass on the bar and headed off.

Justin stared after him. 'This is amazing,' he said. 'Mum didn't tell me…'

'Your mum wouldn't know,' Cass said. 'On her brief visits, she never took time to come here, to meet any of the locals. I think she considered they were beneath her. So, you're interested in photography, too?'

Justin looked sheepish. 'I got a camera for my eighteenth, but Dad isn't impressed I want to spend time with it. He wants me to be a lawyer like him. Thinks anything else is a waste of time.'

They were seated out on the deck by this time, having ordered burgers and chips with a glass of wine for Cass and a Coke for Justin, who refused the offer of beer, saying alcohol had caused him enough problems back home.

'Why exactly are you here, Justin? Your mum was very vague about it, and if you're going to share my house for however long you're here, I need to know.'

Justin stared out at the ocean.

Cass waited.

'I suppose Mum told you I got into bad company?' he said at last.

Cass nodded.

Their drinks arrived.

Justin took a gulp from the can of Coke.

'That's not how it was... well, I guess it's how they saw it. I dropped out of uni at Easter. Hated studying law, but Dad refused to countenance my changing to another course, said if I did, he'd stop my allowance.' He shrugged. 'He thought I just needed a break, that I'd pick it up again. I bummed around the house for a bit, got bored, met up with a couple of guys I'd known at school, but not been good mates with. They weren't working or studying either.'

Cass was beginning to understand where her sister was coming from. She knew how class-conscious she and her lawyer husband were. They wouldn't approve of their son going around with a group of no-hopers.

'I guess we did some stupid things... but nothing illegal. We weren't criminals. We didn't steal cars or break into shops. We might have smoked a bit of weed, but nothing more serious. But when Dad found out, he read the riot act. Then Mum thought of you. Didn't the English used to send their crims here in the old days?' He gave a chuckle.

Cass stifled a grin. The boy had a sense of humour.

'It came to a head when Mum and Dad went away for the weekend.

I had a few of my mates round, we got into Dad's liquor cabinet, made a bit of a mess. I meant to clear up before they got back but… I got drunk and fell asleep.' He looked sheepish again. 'That was it… and here I am.' He glanced up at Cass. 'I'm not about to repeat that performance.'

'I hope not.' Cass tried to sound censorial. 'And you'd be hard-pressed as I only ever keep the odd bottle of wine in the fridge. But Vi will expect me to report back to her, so…'

'I promise I'll behave.' He gave her the boy scout salute. 'You've no idea what a relief it is to get out from under Dad's expectations for me.'

'I think I have.' Cass thought of the strait-laced man her sister had married. Athough she'd only met him a few times, she could see how rigid his thinking was. 'What'll you do when you go back, and he expects you to resume your law studies?'

'I'll cross that bridge when I come to it. Meantime, I plan to learn to surf and enjoy life in Bellbird Bay. Thanks for agreeing to have me to stay, Aunt Cass. You saved my life.' He put one hand on his heart.

'Get away with you. But less of the Aunt Cass. It makes me feel like an old woman. Call me Cass.'

'Okay, Cass.'

Their meals arrived, and Justin's eyes widened at the size of the burger. 'Wow! This looks great. Dad wouldn't approve of this either,' he said, picking it up with both hands. 'He'd expect me to eat it with a knife and fork. I'm going to like living here.'

Nine

Mick had finally taken the plunge and called Brenda to invite her to dinner. It had taken him almost two weeks – and several reminders from Jo – to pick up the phone. By the time he did, he could barely remember the woman and was pleasantly surprised by her well-modulated voice on the phone. He had sensed her hesitation when he gave his name and wondered if she felt she was being manipulated into this by Jo too. But she had agreed, and they were to meet at *The Bay Bistro* that evening. He'd chosen the bistro as there was less likelihood of them being seen there by any of his mates. He didn't want the teasing which would no doubt ensue if they met at the surf club.

Dressed more formally than usual in a pair of black slacks with the blue and white striped shirt Jo had given him for Christmas, Mick checked himself in the bathroom mirror. He scrutinised his face, not something he normally did, to see the fan of wrinkles etched beside his eyes and mouth. *Signs of a misspent youth and too many years in the sun.* He wondered how he would appear to the woman he was about to meet.

It wasn't something he'd ever worried about before, in the years when he had ricocheted from one woman to another with no thought for the hurt he might be causing them – and to Greta while they were still married. But those days were long gone and, if it hadn't been for Jo, he wouldn't be meeting this one. Instead, he'd have been holding up the bar in the surf club or settling down in front of the telly with a can of beer to watch whichever channel was showing sport.

As he approached the entrance to the bistro, Mick could see Brenda was already there, looking as unsure of herself as he felt. It immediately made him feel better and determined to put the woman at her ease. After all, he'd invited her to dinner. The least he could do was try to make it as pleasant for her as possible.

Brenda looked up at his approach. 'Good evening. It was kind of you to invite me.'

'No worries. I'd do the same for any new face in town.' As soon as he spoke, Mick realised he'd said the wrong thing. He was more out of practice than he thought. 'Sorry.' He drew a hand round the inside of his collar. To his surprise, Brenda laughed.

'This was Jo's idea, wasn't it?' she asked. 'I've caught her giving me strange looks ever since the dinner party. It's okay, you know. You don't have to go through with it. I'm perfectly happy to go home again.' Her eyes twinkled with amusement.

'No… I mean, yes, it was her idea, but no, you don't need to go home. I'm looking forward to getting to know you better.' As he gazed across the table at her, Mick knew it was true. This whole dinner thing might have been Jo's idea, but Brenda was a good-looking woman who clearly had a good sense of humour. The evening might not be an entire waste. It was a long time since he'd spent any amount of time with a woman other than Greta or Jo. It was probably time he did, and Brenda might prove to be an interesting dinner companion.

At his words, Brenda seemed to relax and, as her expression softened, Mick could see from the network of lines around her eyes, that this was a woman who had suffered. The realisation immediately brought out his innate sense of chivalry and a determination to discover what had caused them.

Once the bottle of semillon – Brenda's choice – had been served and poured, Mick said, 'I'm sorry I didn't realise you and Andy were brother and sister when we first met. I thought…'

'*I'm* sorry. It's a natural mistake. We've lived together since my husband died around the same time as our parents. Andy lived with them, and I worried he'd be lost on his own.'

'I'm sorry about your husband and your parents. Was it sudden?'

'Jeff died in a work accident, and our parents from pneumonia.' Her eyes glistened from unshed tears.

'I'm sorry,' Mick said again, unsure how to continue.

'Thanks. It all happened over eighteen months ago. The move here was to provide us with a fresh start.'

'Your brother never married?'

'Not his scene.'

'Right.' Mick felt awkward, wondering how to retrieve the situation.

'What about you?' Brenda asked gently. 'Is Jo's mother still around? I've never liked to ask her.'

'Greta. She's very much around and recently remarried her childhood sweetheart,' Mick said, hoping he didn't sound too bitter. He had been for a time, but hoped he'd got over it. As he'd told Jo, he was happy for Greta.

'And how do you feel about that?'

Wow, this woman knew how to get to the jugular. 'Good…. now. It was difficult to accept at the time. I had hopes we might get back together, but… it wasn't to be. Too much water under the bridge. I'm pleased to see her happy.'

'That's very noble of you.'

Noble? It wasn't an adjective Mick would use to describe himself, remembering the bitterness he'd felt when he discovered Leo Carlson was the man Greta had been pining for when they first got together. But he liked the sound of it. 'Thanks,' he said. 'Jo was only young when we divorced. It was a long time ago.'

Their meals arrived – a pasta dish for Mick and salmon for Brenda – and the conversation took a different turn.

'Tell me more about your whale-watching cruises,' Brenda said, 'It must be interesting. I've heard there are more of them travelling north than usual this year.'

'There are.' Mick was glad of the change of topic to one he was comfortable with and spent the next few minutes talking about how he'd set up *Bay Whale Cruises* and how much he enjoyed his business. 'I love being outdoors,' he said. 'I grew up working on my dad's fishing boat and couldn't imagine being stuck inside in an office all day.'

'I think I know what you mean. I love teaching but there are some days when I just want to run away. Especially here in Bellbird Bay where the ocean is so close.'

'You've always been a teacher?'

'When I left school, in the small country town where I grew up, the choice for a girl was teaching or nursing. I loved books so chose teaching. Andy loved reading too, and he'd often help out in the local library so chose to study librarianship. I've never regretted my choice. It worked well when I was married, when we hoped for children. But the children never eventuated and by the time we accepted they never would, I felt it was too late to make a career change. Coming here has been a big change in itself.' She laughed, and Mick was struck by how her face lit up when she did.

The remainder of their evening passed quickly.

'Thanks for a lovely evening,' Brenda said when they rose to go.

'Thank you. I enjoyed it too.' Mick was surprised how much he'd enjoyed Brenda's company. She'd been a relaxing companion; one he'd felt no need to try to impress. She was different from the women he'd been with in the past. Maybe he was getting old, but he relished the feeling he might have found a friend.

'Can I drive you home?' he asked as they stood outside the restaurant.

'Thanks, but I have my car.' Brenda pointed to a neat blue Honda Civic sitting by the kerb a little way off. 'Thanks again for dinner.'

Before he realised what he was going to say, Mick blurted out, 'Let's do it again. I'll be in touch.' Then he watched her walk to her car, before heading across the road to where his was parked. He shook his head, wondering what had possessed him, but at least Jo would be pleased.

*

Mick was barely awake when his phone rang next morning. Bleary-eyed, he checked the screen. It was only six o'clock. It was Jo. His heart lurched. He hoped nothing was wrong.

'Morning, Dad.' Jo's voice was way too bright for this time of the morning. 'You had dinner with Brenda last night. How did it go?'

Mick blinked and sat up in bed.

'It's six in the morning,' he said. 'And you're calling to ask about Brenda? You gave me a scare. I thought something had happened.'

'Sorry,' Jo said, 'I was itching to find out, didn't even consider the time. So, how was it?'

Mick sighed. 'It was okay,' he said cagily. 'She's a nice lady.'
'And…?'
'What? Do you want a rundown of what we ate and what we talked about?'
'No. Are you going to see her again? I really think…'
'I'll tell you anyway,' Mick said, 'pasta for me, Brenda had salmon. She didn't say much, but that was probably because she couldn't get a word in as I told her all my best jokes.'

Jo gasped.

Mick grinned.

'Dad, you didn't!'

'Scared you, did I?' Mick laughed.

Jo huffed. 'Touché. Now, answer my question, are you going to see her again?'

Mick sighed again, feeling his life wasn't his own. 'I may call her again.'

'Good. I thought you two would get on. She's very different from Mum, but…'

Jo was right. Greta and Brenda were like chalk and cheese. She was very different from the other women he'd dated in the past, too. Maybe that was a good thing.

Ten

To Cass's surprise, Justin was already in the kitchen when she walked in next morning. After his long flight, she'd expected him to sleep late. Wasn't it what teenagers did? Hector was rubbing himself around his ankles.

'Oh, you've met Hector,' Cass said. 'He wasn't around when you arrived, or when we got back yesterday. I should have asked if you liked cats.'

'I've never had much to do with them,' Justin said, fondling the creature's ears as the cat emitted a soft purring sound. 'Dad would never let me have a pet. He's a big cat. How old is he?'

'Twenty. I got him soon after I moved here. He's old for a cat and is great company. I'd be lost without him.' As if understanding she was talking about him, Hector turned his head towards her and gave a loud meow.

Justin laughed. 'You said I could come into town with you, Aunt… sorry, Cass.'

'I did.' But she hadn't expected him to take her up on it so soon. 'What would you like for breakfast?'

Justin flushed. 'I helped myself to cereal. I hope that was okay. The Weet-Bix. It's like what I have at home. We call it Weetabix.'

'Oh, good. I'm glad you like it.' Cass had bought several cereals not knowing which he would prefer, if any. She rarely had more than a slice of toast for breakfast, then coffee – and sometimes a croissant – with Greta when she arrived at work. 'Coffee?' she asked, going towards the coffeemaker.

'Can I have tea?'

'Of course.' She remembered now, her sister's predilection for tea, something she'd developed since moving to England. 'But you'll find we have lots of varieties of coffee here. It's worth giving it a try sometime.'

'Okay.'

'I did warn you I'll be tied up all day. I have to work, so I won't be able to show you around. I have next Monday free. *Sassy's* is closed on Mondays. I can spend time with you then. What do you plan to do with yourself?'

'I thought I'd go to the beach and see that guy we met at the surf club, maybe see if I can book a lesson with him, then...' he shrugged, '... look around.'

'Sounds like a plan. We have a good library, too, and we could have lunch together. There's a café near *Sassy's*, and I sometimes take a break there around lunchtime.'

'*Sassy's*, is that your shop? Awesome name.'

'Thanks, it's a corruption of Cass, short for Cassandra.' She grimaced.

'Yeah, Mum said how both of you got names out of Shakespeare – Cassandra and Viola. Guess it's lucky you didn't have a brother. Imagine being called Hamlet?' He chuckled.

Cass did, too. She'd always hated her name but she and Vi had got off lightly.

*

Cass parked her car in the usual spot behind the esplanade, and she and Justin walked towards the shops, stopping at *The Bay Café* for Cass to buy her usual two takeaway coffees. 'This is me,' she said, stopping when they reached *Birds of a Feather* next door to *Sassy's*.

'You only sell beachwear for women?' Justin asked, gazing into *Sassy's* window. 'Where would I get some new swimmers? I probably need new shorts and a couple of tee-shirts, too. Looks like everyone is much more casual here.' He glanced down at the long pants and shirt he was wearing and grimaced.

'You're right. We can go to the shopping centre after I close on

Thursday. It's open late then. There's a men's outfitters there… and a City Beach store which might suit you better.' She'd often considered stocking men's beachwear but hadn't had the confidence to make the move. Maybe Justin could advise her.

'Will's van is over there.' She pointed in the direction of the beach. 'Do you need any…?' She wasn't sure how to ask if he needed money.

Justin understood. 'I'm good. Dad is continuing my allowance while I'm here, and I have some savings. But thanks, Cass.'

'No worries.' There was something pleasant about having a teenager – this teenager – around. It was a bit like giving birth to a fully grown child. Although Justin had only been with her since yesterday, it felt as if she'd known him for ever, probably because he looked so much like her sister.

'See you, then.' With a wave of his hand, he was off, jogging across towards the beach, a beach towel over his shoulder.

'That him?' Greta gestured to the back of the young man who was now on the other side of the road and making his way towards *Bay Surf School*, when Cass entered *Birds of a Feather* and handed her friend her coffee. 'How's it going?'

'Surprisingly well.' Cass grinned. 'We had dinner at the surf club last night and he met Will and Martin, then Owen dropped in. Justin's eager to take surf lessons and he's also a keen photographer.'

'Did you discover why he's been banished to Bellbird Bay?'

'I did, and if he's been truthful, he's not a bad kid. He dropped out of uni because he didn't want to follow in his dad's footsteps. I don't blame him. If you knew his dad, you wouldn't either. And the bad crowd Vi mentioned just sounds like a group of normal teenagers with no real goals.'

'Well, sounds as if you've taken his side.'

'There are no sides, but I like him. I think we're going to get on. It should be interesting having a young person about the place.'

'Don't speak too soon. He could turn out to be a nightmare.'

'I don't think so, but I'll bear it in mind.' Cass laughed. 'Now, I'd better go and open up, or there will be a nightmare waiting for me.'

'See you for lunch?'

'You will. I've told Justin he can meet us then, so you'll be able to meet him and form your own opinion.'

'Look forward to it.'

The morning flew past, and Cass was ready for a break by the time she got a text from Greta to say she was about to close for lunch. At the same time, she saw Justin loping across the road.

'Hey, Cass,' he said, pushing open the door to *Sassy's* and entering the shop. 'Wow! You have a bit of everything here,' he said, his eyes scanning the display of ladies and children's swimwear, cover-ups, rashies, beach bags, shorts and tee-shirts and shell jewellery – even a few beach toys. 'Mum didn't say.'

Cass smiled. Vi had never expressed any interest in her business which had started small and grown over the years. 'Not your mum's style.'

'You're right there.' He grinned at Cass as if sharing a secret.

'How did you go at the beach? Did you catch up with Will?'

'Yeah. I booked some lessons and went for a swim. I realised I need better gear when I saw what the other guys were wearing. And I met a kid called Zack. He's close to my age and reckons he's going to be the next Bellbird Bay surfing champion. Awesome!'

'I know who he is. I know his parents and grandparents. His grandfather is a former champion, too.'

'So he said. This place is sick.'

Cass chuckled. 'Are you ready for lunch?'

'Sure.'

Cass shut down the computer and put the *Closed* sign on the door. Then they joined Greta who was waiting outside.

'This is my friend, Greta,' Cass said. 'We often lunch together.'

'Hi Justin, welcome to Bellbird Bay,' Greta said. 'You'll find it very different from what you're used to.'

'Better. I've already made a friend and booked surfing lessons,' Justin said. 'Are you the lady who owns the shop next to Cass's?'

'That's me.'

When they reached *The Bay Café*, they chose one of the sun-bleached tables outside, and Greta went into the café to fetch menus.

'This is sick,' Justin said, gazing across at the beach where a game of volleyball was in progress. 'Mum and Dad would never have sent me here if they'd known how mad it was.'

Cass smiled, knowing he was right. For some reason, Vi considered

Bellbird Bay was the back of beyond. On the few occasions she'd returned home to visit, she'd acted as if she'd come to the end of the earth, which, Cass supposed, wasn't far off the mark. But it was a beautiful spot, and for her it was home.

Greta returned with the menus, and the two women ordered panini with avocado and turkey, accompanied by skimmed milk coffee, while Justin chose a ham, cheese and tomato sandwich and a banana smoothie.

'Justin wanted to know why I don't stock men's beachwear,' Cass said while they waited for their meals. It had been on her mind all morning.

'And…?'

'I may look into it. Maybe you can help me out,' she said to Justin. 'We can check out City Beach on Thursday when we get you kitted out.'

'Really?' Greta asked. 'I didn't know you were thinking about it.'

'I wasn't, but it's a good idea. I stock everything for the little kids, but when the boys grow older, they have to go to the shopping centre. We're right by the beach so it makes sense.'

'You'll be suggesting I stock menswear, too, next.' Greta chuckled.

'No, you're fine as you are, but for me, it makes sense.'

'Oh-oh,' Greta said, as a well-built man with greying hair came walking towards them.

'Greta's ex,' Cass explained to Justin who appeared bewildered. She tried to stifle the tremor of attraction she had always felt towards Mick Roberts. But he was her best friend's ex and, as such, off-limits, even if he didn't have a history as a womaniser.

Eleven

Mick was walking along the esplanade, intent on reaching *Bay Books* where a special book he'd ordered was waiting for him, when he saw Greta and her friend sitting outside *The Bay Café*. Tempted to turn around and walk the other way, he forced himself to continue along the path that would take him right past where they were seated.

'Greta.' He nodded at her. 'Great day for it.'

'Mick.' Greta smiled.

Mick steeled himself for the pang of regret he normally felt when he met his ex. But today, it wasn't there. There was only the faint remnant of affection for the woman who was Jo's mother. *Had he been imagining his feelings all this time? Had they finally been extinguished by the knowledge she had married Leo Carlson?* Whatever the reason, it was a relief, as if a weight had been lifted from his shoulders. He walked on with a spring in his step. Maybe at last, he could move on with his life.

Mick went into the bookshop and picked up his book, taking a few minutes to chat with the owner. Neil Simpson had recently taken over the management of the shop from his father who was suffering from Parkinson's and had made a few improvements. The old man still came to the shop a couple of days each week, but it was easy to tell that he had given over all the decision-making to Neil. There was a fresh feel about the place, a sense of anticipation.

'Didn't you get your own copy?' Neil asked as he popped the book into the bag bearing the *Bay Books* logo.

'I did. Martin was very generous. This one's for Dad. He doesn't get out much these days and I thought he'd be amused to see what I get up to.' The previous season, Martin Cooper had spent several days with Mick, taking photographs, not only of the breaching whales, but of Mick at the wheel, and speaking to passengers. At first, he'd been embarrassed to be the focus of the camera but had soon become used to his old friend pointing the lens at him. The results – especially of the whales – were extraordinary, but only what was to be expected of such a talented photographer.

'You heard he's mounting an exhibition of the best shots?' Neil asked.

Mick scratched his head. He had heard some mention of it but hadn't paid too much attention. Art exhibitions and their like weren't something he normally attended, though maybe this one would be worth checking out. 'It's at the *Bay Gallery*, isn't it?'

'That's right. There's an article in this week's *Bugle*.'

'Thanks, I'll check it out.' *Maybe it would be something Brenda would enjoy.*

He was leaving the bookshop when his phone rang.

'Pete,' he said, seeing his brother's number on the screen, 'what's up?'

'It's Dad. He's had a fall, Mick. It's not good.'

Mick felt his stomach drop. 'How did it happen? Where is he?'

'He was lying in the yard when I called round this morning. He'd fallen off a ladder. The old fool was trying to clean the gutters. He should have known better. He knew one of us would do it for him. I'm at the hospital with him now. He…'

Mick's lips tightened. He didn't wait to hear more. His dad had been an accident waiting to happen ever since he sold the boat. 'I'll be there as soon as I can,' he said, before closing his phone and running to where he'd left the car, giving Greta a perfunctory wave on his way past. Luckily, he didn't have a cruise that afternoon.

When he'd parked, Mick hurried towards the Emergency entrance of the lowset brick building set among stands of palms and pandanus trees, his heart in his mouth. This is what he and Pete had been afraid of, why they had urged their dad to move. But the old man had stubbornly refused. Maybe now he'd see sense… if he survived.

He found Pete in the waiting room staring at his phone.

'Pete, where is he?'

'Dad's been taken off for an x-ray. Looks like he's broken a hip. It can be dangerous at his age.'

'Hell!' Mick dragged a hand through his hair.

'Sorry, Mick. I need to make a call, let someone know where I am.' Pete gestured with his phone before going outside.

Mick sighed. Trust his brother to have business to attend to when their dad was lying on a hospital bed. But at least Pete had found the old devil. He had to give him credit for that.

A doctor in blue scrubs appeared in a doorway. He peered at Mick. 'Mick, Mick Roberts?' Mick recognised him as someone who had taken one of his whale cruises a few weeks earlier. He remembered him because one of his children had been so enamoured with the whales, he hadn't wanted to leave.

'Yeah. Hi. How's my dad?'

'It seems we were right. He has broken his right hip. He's going to need surgery, most likely a total hip replacement. He's being taken up to the orthopaedic ward now. You can see him there.'

'Thanks.' Not waiting for Pete to return, Mick headed off in the direction the doctor had indicated. Once there, he found his dad lying in bed in a single room which overlooked the garden.

'Mick, there was no need to…' The old man let out a groan of pain. 'Where's Pete?'

'He'll be here soon. What were you thinking, Dad? You know I promised to do those gutters for you.'

'I wasn't going to wait till you got round to it. The rain wouldn't wait, and if they overflowed…'

Mick rolled his eyes. His dad had always tried to make him feel guilty and this time he'd succeeded. Mick had put the job off, telling himself it could wait a few weeks. How could he have known the old man would take it into his head to get up on a ladder by himself? 'You could have killed yourself,' he said.

'But I didn't. Maybe you'd have been satisfied if I had.'

'Dad! You know that's not true.'

'Oh, son, since your mother died, there have been some days when I haven't cared if I lived or died. Maybe it would have been for the best.'

'Don't talk like that. You know we love you. Pete, me, Jo. She'll be getting married one of these days. You need to be here for that.'

'Maybe.' He gave another groan. 'They say I may need a new hip,' he said with a frown. 'Bob Lennon got one. Took a long time to recover. It's no picnic, surgery like that at my age.'

'We're here for you… me and Pete.'

'Hmm.'

Mick flinched. Maybe he hadn't been there for his dad as often as he might have in the past few years, too caught up in his own issues. But no more, he vowed. If… when his dad got over this, he'd make sure to visit regularly, keep his eye on the old man. And surely this would make him change his mind about moving into somewhere that was easier to maintain?

Pete arrived at that point, followed by the surgeon.

'We want to operate as soon as possible,' he said. 'With someone of your dad's age, it's a fairly serious operation, requiring a lengthy period of recuperation. I have to ask if you've considered how you'll deal with it.' He looked from Mick to Pete and back again.

'I'm not going to be reliant on either of them,' Mick's dad piped up from the bed. 'They have their own busy lives to lead. I'll manage. I've managed to look after myself till now… ever since Glenda passed.'

'Mr Roberts,' the surgeon turned to address Mick's dad, 'it's customary for us to advise our patients' families of their requirements during recovery from surgery, and in this case…'

'We'll work something out,' Mick said hurriedly, seeing his dad was becoming agitated. 'Let's get the surgery over first, eh, Dad?'

His dad seemed to relax somewhat. 'Okay, son.'

'Now,' the surgeon said, 'I must ask you to leave, to allow your father to be prepared for surgery.'

'See you later, Dad,' Mick said.

'We'll be back,' Pete confirmed as the pair left the room.

'Doesn't sound good,' Pete said as the two walked down the corridor, having made sure they'd be informed as soon as the surgery was over, and they were able to visit again.

'No.' Mick shook his head. Despite the fact he was often annoyed by his dad, he'd never considered losing him. The old man had always seemed indestructible. Now, the thought of his mortality hung over both him and Pete. 'What'll we do if…' He couldn't imagine life without the irascible comments his dad threw at him when he was displeased with something he'd done or said. But he had supported Mick's decision to start his own business, even helping out with the purchase of the boat which was now his pride and joy. Mick sometimes thought his dad enjoyed their occasional disagreements… a sign he was still alive.

Mick farewelled his brother and drove back into town, thinking about his dad, about all the good times they'd had working together on the fishing boat. Would things have been different if he'd continued to work there? He'd never know. At the time, when he and Greta divorced, he'd needed something of his own to take his mind off the break-up of his marriage. *Bay Whale Cruises* had filled the space in his life, and for that he was grateful. He'd never considered how his dad might really feel about what he now saw as his abandonment of the older man.

He needed to talk with someone. Checking his watch, he saw it was after three. Jo would be finished teaching. She'd be home by now. He headed back in the direction of the esplanade, parked, and began to walk up the boardwalk. The fresh air helped to blow away his fear that maybe his dad wouldn't make it, that Mick wouldn't have time to make up for all the times he'd chosen to ignore his messages and requests, to delay attending to the tasks he'd promised to take care of for him.

'Dad, what are you doing here?' Jo and Mia were sitting on the deck, Jo with a cup of one of her herbal teas, and Mia with a glass of milk. A plate of scotch finger biscuits was on the low table alongside a notebook and a bunch of coloured pencils.

Mick dropped into a chair. 'It's Grandad,' he said to Jo in a low voice, one eye on Mia.

Jo's eyes widened. 'Mia, why don't you take your milk, notebook and pencils into the kitchen. You can sit at the table there. I'll be in shortly. Careful you don't spill it,' she warned as the little girl picked up the glass in one hand.

'Now, tell me what happened,' Jo said when they were alone. 'Would you like tea or coffee?'

'Later. Your Uncle Pete called me to tell me Dad had a fall. The damn fool was up on a ladder. It's his hip. He's in surgery right now.'

'No!' Jo's hand went to her mouth. 'Not Grandad! But he's going to be all right?'

'We hope so. It'll be a long road to recovery. At his age…'

'Oh, Dad, we're just getting over your heart attack last year.'

'That was nothing.' Mick dismissed what had been his second heart attack with a wave of the hand. 'Your grandad's a lot older. Even if he comes through this, he's going to need a lot of care to recover… more than we can probably provide. And he can't stay in that big house.' Even as he spoke, Mick wondered how they were going to persuade his dad to move.

'Isn't that what the nursing home is for?' Jo asked, 'For people who need round-the-clock care?'

Mick scratched his head. Jo was right. Bellbird Bay had a top-class facility in Rosebank Nursing Home. If they had a place for him, and if only his dad would agree, it would be a good temporary solution.

Twelve

'Where did you say we were going?' Justin asked as they drove away from the house on Monday morning. It was a week since he had arrived and so far, Cass had been visiting her mother on her own.

'I need to visit my mother – your grandmother,' Cass explained. 'I must warn you, most days, she's not very...' she bit her lip, '... she doesn't recognise me. So, don't be surprised if she acts a bit odd.'

'But she knows about me?'

'She did... before she became ill. She used to love talking about you, showing off the photos your mum sent her. She kept one of you in your school uniform in a prime position in her living room.'

'Oh, that one!' Justin grimaced. 'The one Mum likes, too. I hate it.'

'It's a good photo, but you've changed a lot since it was taken.'

'I should hope so. I was only eleven at the time. And always top of my class.'

'You're a bright kid, Justin. You say you don't want to study law. What would you like to do?'

'I don't know... something I could do outdoors, maybe Sports Science or Personal Training, but Dad would go mad if I suggested it.' He frowned.

'Couldn't your mum talk him round?'

'No chance. She always gives in to him.' He gave an exaggerated sigh. 'I think my coming here was the only time she made a suggestion he agreed with. Lucky for me.' He grinned.

'You're liking it here?' Cass was worried there wasn't enough for

Justin to do in Bellbird Bay. He went off each morning on the bike she'd bought for him, and reported he'd spent the day on the beach – swimming and surfing. But surely that would soon pall. He'd become bored. And wasn't that how he got into trouble back home?

'It's cool. Will says I'm making good progress with surfing, and Zack's promised to show me some special beach where a group of them go to chill. It's called Dolphin Beach and there's some story about dugongs. I'd never heard of them before.'

'Hmm.' Cass hadn't known the local youngsters had taken to going to Dolphin Beach. It was a special place with pristine white sand located between two rocky headlands. She hoped they were giving it the respect it was due. But Justin would be fine with Zack Crawford. He was a good kid, from a local family she was familiar with.

'Isn't Zack at university?'

'In first year. He's studying Sports Science. But he manages to spend a lot of time at the beach. He won the surfing championship last Easter. Will says he has a good chance of winning again next year.' Justin sounded impressed. 'His uni sounds cool,' he said enviously.

'We're here,' Cass said unnecessarily as they turned into the long driveway leading to the nursing home. As always, when she came here, Cass felt as if the place was closing in around her. Despite the fact it was a beautiful building with carefully maintained grounds, Rosebank Nursing Home wasn't somewhere she'd like to end her days. She regretted the circumstances which had forced her to put her mother here, but it had become too difficult to keep her at home.

They entered the building, Justin gazing around at the pastel painted walls, his nose turning up at the pervasive odour of furniture polish mixed with stale urine, to which Cass had become accustomed. When they reached her mother's room, they met a staff member coming out. 'Good morning, Cass. Jean's having a good day. Who is this handsome young man?'

'My nephew, Justin. So, Mum will recognise us?'

'Should do. She's just had breakfast and might enjoy a trip out into the garden.'

'Thanks. Ready, Justin?' she asked the boy who was looking a tad nervous.

He nodded.

Cass pushed open the door to see her mother seated in her usual chair, gazing out the window. She turned around.

'Good morning, Mum.' Cass went forward to give her mother a kiss on the cheek, noting how fragile her skin had become. 'Look who I've brought to visit you.'

Her mother peered at them for a moment, looking puzzled.

'It's Justin, your grandson, all the way from England.'

Her mother peered at them again. 'Vi's boy? Come and let me have a good look at you.'

Justin moved nervously towards her.

'My, you look just like your mother. Do you remember, Cass? Your sister looked just like that, the same blonde hair.'

'Hello, Grandma.' Justin smiled and kissed her cheek.

'Where's Vi?' Jean looked around the room as if Vi might be hiding somewhere. 'What have you done with her? Has she come to take me home?' Suddenly agitated, the older woman began to tremble.

Justin stepped back, his eyes widening in dismay.

'Where is she?' The older woman's voice became more strident. 'Where is she hiding? And who are you?' she shouted, pointing at Cass. 'What have you done with her?'

Oh, dear. Cass had hoped to prevent Justin seeing his grandmother like this.

The sound of shouting brought a staff member to the room. 'It might be best if you left now,' she said. 'I'm sorry. She was calm and quite lucid earlier.'

'It's okay. We'll leave. I'll come back later in the week.' Cass led Justin out of the room and into the corridor. 'Sorry, Justin. There's no way of predicting how Mum will react. At least she recognised who you were before she lost it again.'

'It's so sad. Mum didn't tell me she was like this.'

Cass pressed her lips together to prevent her from saying something she'd later regret. Vi knew exactly what their mother was like, but chose to ignore it, preferring to let Cass take full responsibility, her only contribution to her mother's care a monthly bank transfer to assist in the payment for the nursing home.

Cass's eyes were blurred with tears as they made their way back to the car, Justin trailing behind her. She'd had such hopes for this visit, hoped Justin would be able to see his grandmother on one of her good days, on a day when she'd be capable of carrying on a conversation. And it had started out so well, until… Damn Vi. She hadn't been there, but she might as well have been.

Cass was so upset, she failed to see the man walking towards them and cannoned into him.

'Steady there.'

Suddenly, Cass felt her arms gripped firmly. She looked up to see Mick Roberts gazing down at her.

'Are you all right?'

'Yes… no… sorry, I wasn't looking where I was going.' She looked around to see where Justin was. He was strolling along the path, unaware of what was happening.

'It's Cass Marshall, isn't it? You're Greta's friend. I'm…'

'I know who you are. I'm sorry,' she said again, feeling foolish and wishing the ground would open and swallow her up. Mick Roberts was the last person she expected to see here, the last person she wanted to see her in this state.

'You have a relative here?' he asked in a gentle voice.

'My mother. She has dementia.' Saying it aloud brought a tear to Cass's eyes.

'I'm so sorry,' Mick said.

'Do you have someone here?' Cass asked.

'Not at the moment, but my dad's had hip surgery, and my brother and I are looking at somewhere for him to spend a few weeks while he recovers. Neither of us is in a position to look after him at home and…' He spread his hands in despair. 'Are you happy with the care here?'

'It's a nursing home. They do what they can. It's not like home.' It was the first time she'd met Mick properly, had a conversation with him. This wasn't the sort of conversation she'd envisaged having when they did meet. She'd dreamt of this moment so often, but not here, not like this.

'Cass?'

She'd forgotten about Justin. 'Justin, this is Mick Roberts, he's…' Cass was at a loss as to how to introduce him – Greta's ex, or… 'He runs whale-watching cruises,' she said at last.

'Whales? Wow! Can I go on one?'

'And you are?' Mick asked in an amused tone.

'Justin's my nephew, my sister's boy. He's visiting from England, staying with me.'

'Well, if you turn up at *Bay Whale Cruises* and book into a cruise, I'll make sure you get to see some whales.'

'Wow!' Justin repeated. 'Where?'

'Mick's cruises run out of the harbour at the far end of the esplanade,' Cass said, having managed to pull herself together, and hoping Mick didn't consider her a fool.

'Your aunt is right. The cruises run morning and afternoon most days. I look forward to seeing you on one of them. Meanwhile, I should…' He gestured towards the entrance to the nursing home.

'Of course. Thanks for…' Cass stopped, embarrassed. What was she thanking him for? Catching her before she knocked him over? Being kind to Justin? All of the above? But she needn't have bothered. He had already left, walking smartly towards the pale brick building.

All the way back in the car, Cass mentally berated herself. Had she even expressed her sorrow to hear about Mick's dad? She couldn't remember. She had been so overcome to meet him like that, to feel his hands – firm and strong – on her upper arms, she'd completely lost the plot. What had he thought? What had Justin thought? She glanced sideways at the teenager.

He was busy on his phone. He looked up. 'I just checked out *Bay Whale Cruises*. They're awesome. Cass, did you know…?' He proceeded to read out the facts about whale migration, which Cass was familiar with, though she'd never had the courage to book herself onto one of Mick's cruises, too worried she'd let her attraction to him show.

No one knew how her heart had leapt the first time she'd seen Mick Roberts, then, to learn he was Greta's ex, and to hear the gossip about the women he'd dated both during and after his marriage. It was clear he was someone to give a wide berth to, and she had. So why had meeting him this morning caused her heart to flutter like the heroine in one of the regency novels she secretly loved to devour?

And why was her heart racing all over again just thinking about it?

'This is amazing,' Justin said, still engrossed in Mick's website. 'Zack spoke about dolphins and dugongs, but he never mentioned whales.' He went back to his phone and was silent for a few minutes, then, 'It says here there's to be an exhibition at the *Bay Gallery* of photographs by Martin Cooper… all about whales and *Bay Whale Cruises*. Can we go?'

'Oh!' Cass had read about the exhibition in *The Bugle* but hadn't considered attending. She wasn't in the habit of attending the gallery openings, though she had gone to a few with Greta over the years. But now Greta and Leo were a couple, Greta was rarely free to socialise so much with Cass. What if Mick was there? What if…?' She gave herself a mental shake. 'Of course we can, Justin,' she said. She couldn't keep avoiding Mick, and even if he was at the opening of the exhibition, there would be a lot of other people there, too. She had no reason to believe they'd bump into each other again. She remembered the warmth of his hands on her and wished things could be different.

Thirteen

Mick entered the nursing home in a trance. Cass Marshall, why hadn't he noticed her before? He'd seen her with Greta, been aware of her shop, *Sassy's*, right next door to his ex-wife's, known they were friends. But he'd never really seen her… till now, never noticed how delicate she was. She'd felt like a little sparrow, her arms fragile under his hands, as if she might break if not handled carefully. She was cute, too, with her mass of black curls, deep blue eyes and pale skin – unusual in a town where almost everyone sported a tan. If her mother was a resident here, she probably visited regularly. He suddenly became aware of a tall woman with iron-grey hair pulled back in a bun and wearing a navy uniform staring at him.

'Can I help you?' she asked.

'Sorry.' He pulled himself back to the present, remembering why he was there. 'I wanted to check if you had any vacancies. My dad's recently undergone surgery, had a hip replacement, and needs some place to recuperate until he can manage at home again.'

She smiled. 'Why don't you come into the office, and I'll see what we can do.'

Mick followed her into a spacious room looking out onto manicured gardens.

An hour later, having been shown around the nursing home, with a brochure outlining the rates and services offered, and the information there was a room currently available if he and Pete made their decision within twenty-four hours, he was back in the car park. He took out his phone and pressed his brother's number.

Mick conducted the afternoon cruise on autopilot. He was glad he had an easy group of passengers, and the whales played ball. His mind was in a whirl between thinking about Cass Marshall and wondering if the nursing home was the right place for his dad. How would the old man react to the institutionalised nature of Rosebank Nursing Home? Would it be better to see if they could arrange for someone to provide live-in care at home? But the house was so large, and the bedrooms were all upstairs. It was a big ask of anyone, without the added complication of a grumpy invalid.

He'd arranged to meet Pete at the surf club for dinner, kill two birds with one stone. They both had to eat. As he showered and changed, he tried to dismiss the image of the dainty woman who'd forced herself into his consciousness, aware Brenda was a much better option, one with no links to his past. Heaven knows what Greta had told Cass about him – nothing good, for sure. In an attempt to convince himself, he texted Brenda with an invite to the gallery opening on Friday. There, that should do it.

Smiling at his foresight, Mick let himself out and drove to the esplanade to park close to the club.

Mick had just ordered a beer when he felt a hand on his shoulder. He turned. 'Pete, what's yours?'

'Same as you.' Pete pointed to Mick's glass. 'How did you go at the nursing home?'

'Let's order food and find a seat first.' Mick picked up his beer and they headed over to order – roast lamb and chips for Pete, but Mick chose the grilled chicken with a salad. 'Doctor's orders,' he said with a grimace when Pete raised an eyebrow.

'But you're fine now?'

'So they say, as long as I take care. Jo makes sure I do. She's always interrogating me on my diet.'

'How is my favourite niece?'

'She's good. You knew she moved in with Bryan?'

'I'd heard.'

Mick smiled. They weren't the closest of families, but in a place as small as Bellbird Bay, word got around.

'Right,' Pete said, when they were seated out on the deck with the sound of the ocean in the background. 'What's the story?'

'The short version is they have a space for dad. The longer one is whether we want to put him into an institution.'

'Surely it's not that bad?'

Mick dragged a hand through his hair. 'Not really, but… I don't know… I wouldn't like to spend any time there myself. I got the impression they do their best, but the staff seem to be run off their feet. I don't know,' he repeated.

'What other option do we have? I can't take time off work, and I don't imagine you can, either.'

'No.' Mick sighed. 'We have to let the nursing home know by tomorrow.'

'Why don't we ask Dad?'

After only a moment's hesitation, Mick agreed, and they arranged to meet at the hospital next morning.

Mick was walking in the door to his house when his phone buzzed with a text. Brenda would be delighted to go to the gallery opening with him. He felt a tinge of guilt at the thought he might be raising her hopes but quickly stifled it. It was only a gallery opening. Half the town would be there.

*

Mick was feeling nervous as he approached the hospital next morning, unsure of how his dad would react to their suggestion. The old man could be cantankerous at times, and this might be one of them.

Pete was waiting for him at the entrance. 'Ready?'

It was as if they were eight years old again and about to face their dad after having trashed their bedroom.

Mick nodded.

'Dad!' Mick went across to the bed to kiss his dad on the cheek. He was very pale and hooked up to several pieces of equipment, a far cry from the strong fisherman who had been one of the best on the coast – *the* best if you were to believe all his stories. 'How are you?'

'In pain,' his dad grumbled, 'and they're feeding me rubbish.'

Mick hid a smile. 'Pete and I have been talking about what's to happen when they discharge you from hospital.'

'I suppose you're going to tell me I can't look after myself, that I have to go into a nursing home?'

'Well…' Mick looked at his brother who was studiously looking away. Trust Pete to leave it to him. 'It is a possibility. Shall we see what your doctor has to say?'

'I suppose. He should be here soon. They said, "after breakfast" and that was hours ago.'

The door opened and the same doctor they had spoken to the previous day walked in. 'Good morning, Fred, how are we feeling today?'

Mick's dad grunted.

The doctor turned to Mick and Pete. 'Your dad's surgery went well. We're pleased with the result. Of course, at his age, there is always the possibility of complications. About half the people who have a hip fracture aren't able to regain the ability to live independently, and when hip fractures prevent movement for a long time, there can be other complications – blood clots in the legs or lungs, bedsores, pneumonia and further loss of muscle mass, increasing the risk of more falls and injuries. I understand your father lives alone?'

'He does. We were wondering about… when he's discharged… if time in a nursing home would be a good idea.'

'An excellent idea. It would provide him with the ongoing care he'll need till he's able to walk unaided again… which should be in around three to six weeks.'

'Hear that, Dad?' Mick turned to his dad who was listening intently, his mouth turned down. He was a shadow of his former self, and Mick felt sorry for him. 'The doc says it would be a good idea. We can get you a room in Rosebank Nursing Home for a few weeks… just till you're mobile again.'

'I'd rather be in my own home.'

'We know that, but we can't take the risk of having something happen to you. Pete and I both have to work. You'd be all alone in that big house.'

'Hmm. I suppose… but only till I'm on my feet again. I'm not going in there to die.'

'Of course not, Dad. Just for a few weeks.' Then they'd have to have the next conversation about him moving into a retirement village, but that was for another day. Mick gave a sigh of relief. 'I'll call them, then.'

'Good job,' Pete said as they left the hospital.

'Yeah, thanks for your help,' Mick said sarcastically.

'What? I thought you were doing okay. You got the old man to agree to it, didn't you?'

'Mmm. I wish there was another way.'

'Well, unless you're prepared to cancel your cruises for the foreseeable future and move back home, I don't see what else we could do.'

'No.' But Mick still felt guilty. He thought about all the possible complications the doctor had listed, and his dad's fear of dying in the nursing home. Then, the image of Cass Marshall slipped into his mind. Her mother was in Rosebank, suffering from dementia. She was definitely going to die there. He wondered how Cass felt about it.

Fourteen

By the time Friday came around, Cass was wishing she hadn't agreed to go to the gallery opening with Justin. Mick was sure to be there, and she didn't know if she wanted to see him again so soon after bumping into him at the nursing home. The memory of his hands on her arms still made her shiver. But Greta would be there too, with Leo, along with many other locals she knew. And Justin was really excited about it. He was gradually finding his way around town, and on Wednesday had booked himself onto one of Mick's whale-watching cruises. He hadn't stopped talking about it since.

Once she'd showered and changed into a pair of her dressiest jeans and a colourful tunic she'd bought from *Birds of a Feather*, Cass was feeling better. She'd ordered pizza to be delivered and she heard the doorbell as she was finishing her makeup. 'Can you get that, Justin?' she called, pulling a comb through her hair before pushing it into shape with her fingers, glad she'd never been tempted to grow it. The sleek style she'd allowed to curl naturally when she broke up with Ray had served her well for over twenty years, though these days she needed a little help with the colour; she wasn't ready to embrace the grey just yet.

'Thanks, Justin,' she said when she entered the kitchen to see he had opened up the pizzas and set the table with plates, cutlery and napkins. He was such a help around the house. Cass had no idea why Vi and Roger had seen fit to banish him, but their loss was her gain. She was really enjoying having him around. 'Where's Hector?' She looked around for the cat.

'I fed him. Hope that was okay. He went out after.'

'That's fine. He knows he can come and go as he pleases through the cat flap, though I do like him to stay in overnight to protect the local wildlife.'

While they were eating, Cass was conscious of Justin continually checking the time.

'I emailed my mates back home,' he said. 'They're so envious I'm surfing every day and have actually seen whales. I can't wait to see the photographs Martin Cooper has taken. I bet they'll be awesome. He's a legend.'

'Do your parents know you're having such a good time?' Cass asked, to see Justin turn red.

'I may not have mentioned it,' he muttered. 'They think this is a punishment… staying in a small, insignificant town at the other end of the earth. Dad would die if he knew. Mum says she couldn't wait to leave, and Dad thinks everyone here is like that guy in Crocodile Dundee.'

Cass almost choked, but she wasn't surprised. Nothing about her brother-in-law would surprise her. 'Well, better not tell him,' she said with a grin.

*

People were streaming into *The Bay Gallery* when Cass and Justin arrived. As they walked in, Cass accepted a glass of champagne from Mel who worked in the gallery and was one of Cass's good customers, while Justin took a glass of orange juice. She was pleased to see he was keeping to his vow to avoid alcohol, but wondered if it was only for her benefit, and if he would behave differently with his friends.

Cass looked around, immediately seeing Greta and Leo. She glanced at Justin who was staring wide-eyed at the exhibits. 'I'm going over to speak to Greta,' she said, gesturing in her friend's direction. 'Will you be okay?'

'Sure.' Justin barely glanced at her. He was too intent on the display of photographs.

'Catch you later.' Cass patted him on the arm and made her way through the chattering crowd to where Greta was standing in one corner.

'Phew, what a crush,' she said when she reached her friend.

'Martin's work always attracts a crowd, but I doubt Mick expected this many,' Greta said. 'Have you seen the shots of him at work?'

'No, we just got here. Justin is checking them out now. He's in awe of both Martin and Mick – his new heroes… after Will Rankin.' She laughed. 'I'm not sure what Vi would say if she could see him now.'

'He seems like a good kid. I suspect your sister underestimates him. It's easy to do. But she'll be sorry if he decides to make a life here.' She bit her lip, and Cass remembered how Greta's daughter, Jo, had spent many years overseas.

'Oh, I don't think…' But was it a possibility? It was early days, but Justin certainly appeared to love it here. Before she could say more, there was the squeal of a microphone, then the voice of John Baldwin, the owner of the gallery, called for silence.

The chattering gradually ceased, and John began to speak, reminding everyone of Martin's reputation, to congratulate him on returning to his native Bellbird Bay where he had become a valued member of the community, and on providing this excellent and innovative exhibition. He then turned to where Mick was standing and proceeded to praise him for his work with the whale cruises, and for agreeing to be featured in many of the shots.

When Cass followed his eyes, she saw Mick standing with… she blinked… a short, curvy, blonde woman dressed in pale ivory. To her dismay, her heart dropped. What had she been thinking? Hadn't she decided he was off limits… for all sorts of reasons, one of then standing beside him? So why did the confirmation of her decision upset her so much? She felt Greta nudge her.

'I see Mick's up to his old tricks, though I guess I shouldn't complain when *I* turned him down.' She squeezed her new husband's arm and gazed at him with affection.

Cass attempted a smile of agreement.

John Baldwin finished his speech, and everyone applauded, a sign for the champagne to begin flowing again.

'Mum!' Greta's daughter bowled up to them, hand-in-hand with a tall man Cass recognised as Bev Cooper's son. She was grinning.

'Did you see Dad? The woman he's with teaches with me. I introduced them. I told him it was time he got over himself and found someone.'

Cass flinched.

'I'm sure he's perfectly capable of finding his own women, Jo. He never had much trouble in the past.' There was a hint of bitterness in Greta's voice.

'Mum! You know how much he wanted to put all that behind him, for you two to get back together. Sorry, Leo,' she said to her mother's companion, 'but it's true. Anyway, I thought it was time to give him a bit of help. Seems it worked.' She grinned again.

'I should go to see what Justin's up to.' Cass took the opportunity to slip away, too disturbed by Jo's comments to stay and hear any more. She picked up another glass of champagne and made her way across the room to where she could see Justin and Zack Crawford admiring the exhibits. She slowed down just before she reached them, at a group of photographs showing Mick at work. He was wearing a singlet which revealed his broad chest, muscular arms, and made him look like Bellbird Bay's answer to Brad Pitt. Cass swallowed.

'Hey, Cass!' Justin joined her. 'Aren't these amazing? I've asked Martin if he'll show me how he manages the perspective, and he says he will. I've to ring him. I can't believe it. Martin Cooper, the famous photographer, is going to show me how to improve. I wish Dad...' He looked down at his feet.

'Your dad doesn't share your passions?'

Justin raised his eyes. 'No, you're right. He never will. And he'll never understand me. I realise that now. I didn't before.' He went silent, then, 'Is it okay if Zack and I head off. He knows of a party and...'

'Off you go. Just make sure you're home by midnight and don't waken me or Hector when you come in.'

'Thanks, Cass.' He gave her a mock salute.

Cass watched the two boys leave, jostling each other as they made their way through the crowd who were now intent on examining the photographs, many of which already bore red SOLD stickers. The gallery and Martin were doing well tonight. She idly wondered how Mick felt about all this, about having his life laid bare in photographs. Laid bare in a singlet, the breeze blowing his hair... For a moment she considered buying one of the prints, then gave herself a shake. It seemed Mick Roberts hadn't waited long to find a replacement for Greta. She just wished it didn't hurt so much.

Fifteen

Mick saw Cass Marshall across the room and cursed his decision to invite Brenda to the gallery opening. Cass was looking particularly attractive, wearing a pair of tight black jeans and a bright top that looked like something his ex might have sold. Her hair was as untidy as last time he saw her, giving her the look of a woman half her age and making him wonder if she sported a tattoo. When he started *Bay Whale Cruises*, he'd had a small image of a whale tattooed above his right hip bone, which he now regretted.

'You look great in those photographs, Mick,' Brenda said, bringing him back to the present. 'The photographer has really caught your macho quality.'

'Hmm, don't know about that.' Mick pushed back his hair, wondering if he could slip away and talk to Cass. Probably not. Brenda wouldn't know anyone here except him and Jo.

Just then, Jo joined them, her glass raised. 'Hey, you two. Glad you took my advice, Dad.' She grinned. 'What do you think?' She waved her glass around sending drops of champagne everywhere. 'Oops,' she said.

'How many of those have you had?' Mick asked, as Bryan came to rescue her.

'Sorry, Mick. We had a few wines over dinner and… Maybe we should go home now, honey?' Bryan said.

'If you insist,' Jo said with a wink and then drank the rest of her champagne. 'Have fun, Dad,' she added as Bryan led her away.

'So, that's Jo's Bryan,' Brenda said. 'She talks about him a lot… you, too.' She smiled at Mick over her glass, making him hot under the collar.

This had been a bad idea. She was a nice woman, but… there was no spark. There had to be a spark. He remembered the frisson he'd felt when he took hold of Cass's arms outside the nursing home, and felt himself turn red. 'It's hot in here,' he said, running his hand around the inside of his collar.

'Oh, look!' Brenda pointed to the far side of the gallery, to where Cass was standing with Greta and Leo. 'Isn't that Jo's mum, your ex?' She glanced sideways at Mick. 'Jo says you're still good friends. Is that right?'

'Pretty much.' Mick remembered how Greta had stepped up to help care for him a year earlier when he had his heart attack. That had been when he still had hopes they'd get back together, before she and Leo teamed up.

'It takes a very special sort of man to remain friends after a divorce,' she said admiringly.

Mick flinched. This was getting worse.

'Mick!' Mick turned, relieved to see Martin Cooper.

'Hey, Coop.' He turned to Brenda. 'This is the man of the moment, Martin Cooper. Brenda… she teaches with Jo.'

'Hi, Brenda.'

'I love your photographs,' Brenda said. 'I have one of your coffee table books, the one featuring Bellbird Bay. My brother gave it to me when we arrived here.'

It was Martin's turn to redden.

'I see a good few red stickers,' Mick said. 'A successful evening.'

'John always puts on a good show,' Martin said, seemingly unwilling to take credit for his success.

'Will you excuse me, Mick? I see my brother over there.' Without waiting for a reply, Brenda wandered off.

Mick gave a sigh of relief, and Martin raised an eyebrow. 'Not your usual type,' he said with a grin. 'Fighting above your weight?'

'Jo's attempt at matchmaking. She's a nice woman, but…'

Martin nodded. 'Now, the dainty bird talking with your ex… that's another story.'

Mick gazed across to where Cass was engaged in conversation with Greta. 'I'm not looking for a woman,' he said, 'and even if I was, do you think I'd choose my ex's best friend?'

'Hmm, maybe not.' Martin stared across the room at the woman who now held Mick's full attention. 'But I agree with Jo. It's time you moved on. You don't want to be one of those sad sacks, growing old alone. Now Greta's remarried, there's no hope for you there, mate.'

Mick winced. His friend knew him so well. 'You may be right, but we can't all be as fortunate as you,' he said, referring to how Martin had met his sister's best friend when he came back to Bellbird Bay and was now happily married.

'You can make your own luck.'

'Hmm.' Mick wasn't sure about that.

'Sorry, mate, John's signalling for me. Catch you later. Don't go away. I think the guy from *The Bugle* wants to take shots of us both in front of one of the exhibits.'

Mick didn't reply. Wasn't it enough that he appeared in many of the photographs gracing the gallery walls? But he supposed it would be good publicity. He stopped a passing waiter and exchanged his now empty glass for a full one.

'So, you're famous now, too.'

Mick turned to see a small, elderly lady peering at him. He hadn't expected to see Ruby Sullivan here, but since the council had provided her with a mobility scooter, she appeared to be getting around better than ever. 'Ruby, I didn't know you were a fan of Coop's.'

'I like to keep my eye on what's going on around town. I read about the exhibition in *The Bugle* and decided to take a look for myself. It's impressive.'

'It is.' Mick glanced around, wondering how soon he could move away without being rude, but there was no sign of either Brenda or Jo, and Cass was still talking to Greta.

'You don't want to spend your evening talking to an old woman,' Ruby said, chuckling, 'but mark my words, your future is in this room. Don't let the past get in the way of what fate has in store for you.' Nodding her head, she walked off stiffly, making Mick wonder if her accident had caused more damage than was first thought. Hadn't it been her eye that was injured? And what had she just said about his future and his past? She was a strange old bird.

Seeing Cass was now on her own, Mick made his way across to where she appeared to be admiring a particularly good shot of a mother and baby whale. He cleared his throat.

Cass turned with a start and blushed.

'What do you think of the exhibition?' he asked.

'They're all amazing. Justin, who you met with me at the nursing home, went on one of your cruises this week and can't stop talking about it. You really made an impression on him.'

'The young fellow with the English accent?' Mick recalled the boy, young man actually, who had plied him with questions on one of the mid-week cruises. It was unusual for anyone to come on a tour alone, the usual passengers being couples or families.

'That's him. His parents sent him here as a punishment, but he's having the time of his life, sees it all as one big adventure. Though I expect him to get bored soon. There's not a lot for him to do here other than swim and surf.'

Mick made a sound to indicate his agreement, but his mind was working overtime. 'He's not looking for a job, is he?'

Cass's eyes widened. 'A job? Oh, I don't think so. You have one available?'

For a moment, Mick found himself unable to speak, stunned by the intense blue of her eyes. It was like gazing into a deep pool. Then he said, 'I've been thinking I need an assistant, but it'd be pretty basic stuff. I don't expect your nephew would want to spend his holiday on a whale-watching boat. It can be dirty work.'

'I can ask him.'

Mick ferreted around in his wallet to find one of his business cards. He didn't often have cause to use them. 'If he's interested, ask him to give me a call.'

'Mick!' Martin was back. He gave Cass a speculative look. 'The newspaper guy's ready for us.'

'Right. Sorry,' he said to Cass. 'I've got to go. Maybe…' But whatever else he was going to say was lost as Martin dragged him away, and he was conscious of her eyes following them.

By the time the press photographs had been taken, people were beginning to drift off, and there was no sign of Cass. Brenda had returned to Mick's side, along with her brother who had lots of questions about Mick's whale-watching cruises and was keen to book one.

'I'd love to come on one, too,' Brenda said. 'I'd love to see the whales for myself, not just in photographs, regardless of how good they are.' She smiled apologetically at Martin.

Mick felt a tinge of guilt at his earlier thoughts about Brenda. She didn't deserve them. It hadn't been a mistake to invite her to the gallery opening. He was glad she was enjoying the evening, even glad of her interest in whale-watching. 'Of course you must,' he said, to cover his guilt. 'You and your brother will be my guests. Let me check my bookings for tomorrow and Sunday and let you know.'

'Thanks, but we're quite willing to pay.'

'Not at all.' Providing them with a free tour would go some way to assuaging his guilt.

Mick drove Brenda home, giving her a friendly kiss on the cheek before they parted, and renewing his promise to let her know about the cruise. As he drove away, he wished life wasn't so complicated. As he'd decided earlier, she was a nice lady, why couldn't she be the one who made his pulse race, instead of Greta's best friend?

Sixteen

The house was empty apart from Hector, when Cass returned home. The cat immediately let out a loud meow to express his displeasure and ran to stand over his empty food bowl.

'You were fed before we left, Hector,' Cass said, but topped up the bowl, even as she reminded herself *she* was supposed to be the one in charge here. Sometimes it was easier just to give in to the cat. Feeling the need to have something warm to drink and trying to forget how many glasses of champagne she'd consumed, Cass made herself a mug of hot chocolate and took it through to the living room where she curled up on the sofa. Seeing her settled, Hector jumped up beside her, purring loudly until she began to stroke him, at which point the purrs became softer.

What were the chances, she thought to herself, as she sipped the warm drink, of bumping into Mick Roberts twice in the same week, after years of only seeing him in passing? When she arrived back in Bellbird Bay, Greta and he had already divorced. Was the universe trying to tell her something? She laughed at herself. She was beginning to sound like Ruby Sullivan. She'd caught sight of the old woman at the gallery but had managed to keep out of her way. She could do without another dose of her homespun wisdom, though others swore by it. Even Greta had succumbed to her so-called prophecies, telling Cass the old woman had been right with her prediction about her and Leo.

But what did it matter? There had been a woman with Mick – a very elegantly dressed woman, not like Cass who preferred the sort of casual gear she sold at *Sassy's* and whose hair often resembled a brush. But the sight of Mick in those photographs had send her blood pressure racing. She'd never gone on one of his whale-watching cruises, aware her friend's ex was a no-go area. So, she'd dreamt about him in private, wishing she didn't feel so loyal to Greta. She'd even encouraged her friend to get back together with him when it was clear it was what Mick wanted. That's what a sad case she was, putting everyone else's happiness before her own.

The front door banged, and Hector jumped down from the sofa and ran off.

'Hey, Cass,' Justin said, poking his head through the open door just as Hector shot out of the room.

'Hi.' Cass checked the time. It was only eleven o'clock. 'You're back early. Wasn't the party any good?'

'They started smoking weed, so Zack and I decided to split. It's not his scene… and not mine any longer.'

Cass smiled inwardly, glad Zack appeared to be a good influence. 'I'm having hot chocolate. There's probably some warm milk left, if you'd like some.'

'Thanks. How was the gallery thing after we left?'

'Make your hot chocolate first, then I'll tell you all about it.'

'Great.'

While Justin was gone, Cass thought back over the evening, about the amazing photographs, and her conversation with Mick. Had he deliberately sought her out? What had he been about to say when Martin dragged him off? And why had she felt so deflated when he left?

'Thanks, Cass.' Justin plopped down on the floor, pulling a cushion from the sofa to lean against. 'Now, did we miss anything?' he said as if he didn't expect they had.

'Not really. People wandered around chatting, drinking more champagne, then they began to drift off. The photographer from the local paper took some publicity shots. Oh,' she blushed, 'I had a chat with Mick Roberts.'

'Mmm.'

Cass could tell Justin had lost interest.

'He asked if you'd like a job.'

The boy's eyes widened. 'A job… on his boat? Wow!'

'Would you want to do that? He said he needs an assistant. I don't think your parents…' She bit her lip. She probably shouldn't have mentioned his parents, but she could imagine Vi and Roger's reaction. They'd blame her for getting their precious son involved with someone they'd definitely not approve of.

'They're not here, and they did send me to Bellbird Bay. Did he really offer me a job?'

Cass fished Mick's card out of her pocket and handed it to Justin. 'He said to call him if you're interested. Are you sure it's something you'd want to do? He said it's pretty basic stuff and can be dirty work. I don't know what his boat's like, but you've been on it.'

Justin's eyes lit up with excitement. 'I'd love it, being outdoors all day, on the ocean… with whales.' He grinned.

'Maybe you should find out what's involved before you agree. You may not get a chance to sightsee if you're working.'

'It doesn't matter. Wow, just imagine!'

'So, you'll call him?' Cass didn't know why she felt so conflicted about Justin working with Mick. It didn't mean *she'd* be spending time with him.

'First thing tomorrow. Maybe I can even go out with him again this weekend.' His eyes glowed.

'Your…' Cass began.

'You don't need to tell them, do you?'

'No…oo.' Cass couldn't hide the suggestion of a smile at the thought of keeping this secret from her sister, just as she used to keep her own activities secret from her when they were teenagers, and the younger Vi wanted to be included in everything Cass and her friends did. 'No,' she said more definitely, 'I don't.'

*

Next morning, Justin was up before Cass again.

'I've fed Hector and he's gone outside,' he said, when she walked into the kitchen to the aroma of coffee and…

'Are you cooking breakfast?' she asked.

'Bacon and eggs. Hope it's okay to have helped myself from the fridge. I know Mick's first cruise goes out at nine-thirty and thought I'd try to catch him before that.' He grinned. 'Would you like some?'

'Thanks, but no. I can never eat much in the morning. I'll have a peppermint tea and a slice of toast, then I may pick up something on my way to work.'

'Okay.' Justin turned back to the stove.

'When did you learn to cook?'

'I just picked it up. Mum and Dad had often gone to work by the time I got up, so…' He grinned again.

'You weren't such an early riser back home?'

'There was nothing much to get up for.' Justin shrugged. 'Not like here. Have you spoken to Mum lately?'

'No.' Cass realised she hadn't spoken to her sister since she called to let her know Justin had arrived safely – nor had Vi called her. It was as if, having sent their son to Australia, Vi and Roger had washed their hands of him.

The pair ate breakfast together then Cass checked on Hector and prepared to leave. As she walked out the door, she could hear Justin speaking to Mick on his phone.

*

'Morning, Greta.' Having made her usual stop at *The Bay Café*, Cass handed Greta a takeaway coffee and placed the bag of almond croissants on the counter at *Birds of a Feather*. 'The gallery opening went well last night.'

'Didn't it. Leo bought a couple of pieces for the hotel. He likes to support local businesses and let his guests see more of the area. What did you get up to when you disappeared? Did I see you chatting to Mick?'

Cass swallowed. Not much got past Greta and, although she was happy with her new husband, Cass thought she detected a note of something – maybe a hint of jealousy? – in her friend's voice. 'He wanted to sound me out about offering Justin a job.'

'Wow!'

Cass laughed. 'That's what Justin said. He was ringing Mick when I left.'

'Huh, I expect he wants a dogsbody, someone to serve the snacks and clean up between groups of passengers. Trust Mick. But you say Justin's interested?'

'He sure is. You should have seen his eyes light up when I told him about it… and he was up at the crack of dawn to catch Mick before he went out this morning.'

'Well!'

'I think he was getting bored. There's only so much swimming and surfing he can do, and it's a bit cold for either this time of year. He was very taken with Mick and the whales when he went on the cruise a few days ago. It may come to nothing,' she added. 'You know what teenagers can be like.'

'And I know Mick. You're still getting on well with your nephew?'

'Yes. He's easy to have around… even cooked breakfast this morning, though I didn't have any,' She bit into her croissant, sending pastry flakes over the counter. 'Sorry.'

'No worries.' Greta brushed them off. 'So, when will this job with Mick start?'

Cass shrugged. 'No idea.' Her phone buzzed with a text. She opened it up and read it quickly. 'It's from Justin. He's setting off now to meet Mick at the harbour. He's going to join this morning's cruise to get a taste of what Mick wants him to do.' She frowned. This was all happening too fast.

'That's Mick for you. Never one to miss an opportunity. But it's a good idea for your nephew to get a feel for working with Mick. He'd be a fair boss but won't put up with any nonsense.'

'Hmm. Well, I'd better get going. Have a good day. See you tomorrow.' Saturday was usually a busy day for both shops, so they didn't arrange to meet for lunch.

'You can tell me all about it then.'

*

Mick closed his phone, wondering if he'd been too hasty in suggesting Justin come out with him today. He was booked to capacity for both the morning and afternoon cruises, and he wouldn't be able to spend much time with him. But it would be a good test of the boy's work ethic and his ability to take orders. And the extra pair of hands would be most welcome. Mick had been finding it more and more difficult to manage on his own since his heart attack. He was fully recovered, but the instructions to take things easy were difficult to follow when he had a boatload of passengers to take care of, in addition to maintaining his boat. He also had the faint expectation that offering work to Cass's nephew might help him get to know her better.

He was still debating the merit of his decision, when Justin cycled up to the wharf and locked his bike onto the railing.

'Hey, Mick!' Justin said, his eyes bright with excitement. 'Thanks for this opportunity. What would you like me to do?'

It took Mick back to the first time his dad let him help out on the fishing boat. He remembered the excitement he'd felt at being given responsibility for taking on the simple tasks, and the sense of achievement at the end of the day, when he knew this was where his future lay. But he hadn't stayed with it, choosing instead to set up his own business after he and Greta divorced. It hadn't occurred to him at the time, determined to make his own way in life, but he now wondered how much of a disappointment it had been to his dad. Pete had never been interested in the fishing boat, choosing instead to go into real estate.

Swallowing his doubts, Mick welcomed Justin and showed him around the business end of the boat, before setting him up to greet the passengers as they arrived and checking them on. Once they were in the bay, he could manage the snack bar, saving Mick that task. Without an assistant, he sometimes felt as if he needed at least two pairs of hands.

Then he checked the computer to work out when he could offer spots to Brenda and her brother. Discovering the only free spots were on the following weekend, he decided to wait till he returned to shore before contacting her.

The day passed quickly, his passengers catching sight of enough whales to satisfy them, and Justin proved a useful pair of hands. The teenager seemed willing to take on every task Mick asked of him without complaining. This was going to work out.

At the end of the day, Mick dug into his pocket before handing Justin a couple of fifty-dollar notes. 'Thanks, Justin. You were a big help.'

The young man stared at the notes, then at Mick. He reddened. 'Thanks, but I didn't expect. I thought… Don't you want me to come back?'

Mick slapped Justin's shoulder. 'Of course I do. You've earned that and more with the help you've been today. We need to work out a proper salary for you if you want to continue for the season. I know it's pretty menial work, probably not what you're used to.'

'It's sick. You really mean it? You want me to work for you?'

Mick chuckled. 'As long as your aunt approves… and your parents. I know you're of age but you're a long way from home, and I'm sure they'd want to have a say in what you plan to do.' He wished he'd known more about Jo's life after she left home.

There was a slight pause before Justin replied, 'It's okay with Cass. How long's the season?'

'Normally through September, though I continue the cruises throughout the year. But I don't expect you to keep with it. I presume you'll be going back home?'

Justin's face fell. He kicked the deck with one foot. 'I guess.' Then he brightened. 'So, what time do you want me here tomorrow?'

Once they had made arrangements for next day and agreed on a wage which suited both, Justin headed off on his bike, leaving Mick remembering what it was like to be nineteen and have all his life ahead of him. It made him feel old to see the energy of the younger man and to realise he'd never be like that again. He thought of Martin's words. Maybe he already was the sad sack his friend had referred to.

Too dispirited to go home, to face the empty house that awaited him, Mick made his way to the surf club where he knew he'd find some company.

Ordering a beer from the barman, he looked around, but couldn't see anyone he knew well enough to want to talk to. Suddenly, the thought of another solitary meal here lost its attraction. He downed his beer and headed home, stopping on the way to buy a takeaway pasta dish from the local Italian restaurant.

Once home, he took his meal through to the living room and turned on the television, prepared for another evening's viewing. By the time he'd eaten and switched channels several times, it became clear nothing was going to keep his attention. With a sigh, he picked up his phone to keep his promise to Brenda.

After arranging for her and her brother to come on next Sunday morning's cruise, he stared at the phone for several minutes. Then he pressed the number he'd asked Justin for, on the pretext of having to get Cass's approval.

He held his breath as he waited for Cass to answer.

Seventeen

Cass was relaxing in front of the television with a glass of wine, ready to watch the latest episode of Shetland.

Justin had arrived back from his day with Mick in high spirits, buoyed up with the news Mick wanted him to work on the boat for the rest of the season.

'You enjoyed it?' Cass had asked.

'It was amazing!' He'd burst into a detailed description of his day interspersed with "Mick did", and "Mick said", till Cass began to wish she had never passed on Mick's message. It was going to be difficult to put the man out of her thoughts with Justin working with him and so full of what he did and said.

They'd eaten the chicken casserole Cass had heated up, then Justin had dashed out to meet Zack and some of his friends, eager to share his news with them.

She took a sip of her wine, then her phone rang.

Cass didn't recognise the number on the screen so her 'Hello?' was somewhat guarded.

For a moment there was silence at the other end, as if the caller regretted making the call, then she heard a familiar voice.

'Cass? It's Mick, Mick Roberts.'

Cass's heart began to flutter. She took a deep breath. 'Hi Mick. Yes, Cass here. I must thank you for offering Justin a job. He's been singing your praises since he got back, and now he's off to share the good news with his friends.'

She heard Mick chuckle. 'He did well. I wanted to make sure you were okay with it, and to ask if I needed to check with his parents. I know he's over eighteen, but he's in a foreign country and...'

'No.' Cass swallowed. 'There's no need to check with my sister and her husband. They... well, let's say they might not understand. I'm very happy to give my permission, though I'm sure Justin would take the position even if I wasn't.'

'Right... well... I just thought I should check.' There was a long pause, during which Cass wondered if Mick had hung up, then, 'You said you hadn't been on one of the cruises. It's a good year for whale sighting. Why don't I book you on one? It'll give you a chance to see Justin in action too,' he added hurriedly.

'Oh!' Cass didn't know what to say. She remembered the photographs in the exhibition, the images of Mick in his singlet, his muscles... She swallowed again, glad he couldn't see her blushing.

'No cost to you. You'd be my guest.'

'It's not...' Cass realised how foolish she must sound. The man was offering her a free whale-watching cruise, her nephew was working for him... and she'd been dreaming about him for years. 'Thanks,' she said, 'it's very kind of you, but I'm happy to pay.'

'No, I insist. Call it a condition of your nephew's employment, so you can check out his workplace.'

Cass thought she'd be checking out more than that as the image of Mick in that singlet floated through her mind.

'Cass?'

'Sorry, yes, I was just thinking,' she said, now blushing furiously, 'it would have to be on a Monday. I work every other day. And not next week.' Cass had promised to spend the day with Greta who was anxious to make up for the days they'd missed spending together since her marriage. The two were planning morning tea at *The Pandanus Café*, followed by a pampering session in Leo's hotel.

'The following one?'

'Sounds good.'

'Great. I'll book you in. We leave the wharf at nine-thirty so you should arrive before that. I look forward to seeing you then.'

'Thanks, Mick.' *I look forward to seeing you, too*, she thought.

The call ended, Cass sat looking at the phone. *What had just happened?*

*

Next morning, Cass was still flustered at the memory of Mick's call, almost too confused to reply to Justin's comments at breakfast.

He had to repeat himself twice when he told her how Zack and his mates had been envious of his luck at snagging the position on the whale-watching boat. 'But they're all tied up with uni, so wouldn't have been able to do it,' he said with a grin when he finally had her attention. 'This could never have happened at home,' he said, 'Just wait till…' His voice trailed off as he realised he couldn't tell anyone back home if he wanted to keep the news from his parents. 'Oh, well,' he said. 'They'd be envious, too, if they knew.'

Once Justin had left, Cass fed Hector, made sure he had enough water, then headed to the car, trying to work out what to tell Greta. How would her friend react to the news Mick had called her, had invited her on one of his cruises… for free? Even though Greta had shunned Mick's attempts to reignite their relationship and was now married to Leo, Cass suspected her friend still felt some sort of ownership of her ex-husband. It was why Cass had never revealed her attraction to Mick. She valued her friendship more than the faint possibility Mick might ever be interested in someone like her.

*

'Well, how did Justin go with Mick?'

Cass had barely walked into *Birds of a Feather* when Greta started to quiz her.

Cass handed Greta her coffee, then said, 'He loved it. Looks like Mick's going to employ him for the whole season.' She took a sip of her coffee, glad of the hit of caffeine it provided.

'When will he be going home?'

'It's not clear. Vi didn't say, and we haven't been in touch.' Cass made a mental note to call her sister. If for no other reason, she needed to keep her informed about their mother. Jean had been quite lucid during her last visit, but days like that were few and far between. Justin wasn't keen to visit again, and Cass didn't blame him. But Vi was Jean's daughter. She ought to be interested in her mother's health. 'But Justin seems happy here and I enjoy his company… when he's home. He was out with Zack and his mates again last night after he got back, and off at the crack of dawn this morning. I hope it lasts.'

'Well, if he enjoys working on the boat with Mick… I wouldn't fancy it myself, though we did have some good times together on the fishing boat in the early days, when Mick worked with his dad.' Greta's eyes glazed over. Then she stared at Cass. 'There's something else. What are you not telling me?'

Cass shifted uncomfortably. This was what she'd been hoping to avoid. 'Mick called me last night.'

Greta's eyes widened. She put down the cardboard coffee cup which she'd been raising to her lips.

'Oh, it wasn't important,' Cass hurried to tell her. 'He wanted to check I was okay about Justin working there.' She paused. 'And he invited me on a free whale-watching cruise, to check out his workplace,' she quickly added.

There was a loaded silence, during which Cass cursed her warming cheeks.

'That was very generous of him.'

'I thought so. When we were chatting on Friday, he discovered I'd never been on one. He says it's a good year for…' She saw a strange expression in her friend's eyes. Why shouldn't she go on one of Mick's cruises? But it was proof, if she needed it, that she should keep away from Mick Roberts.

'So, when will you go?' Greta seemed to have recovered from whatever had fazed her.

'Next Monday. It's the soonest I could make it. I told him I already had arrangements for tomorrow.'

Greta raised an eyebrow.

'We planned a girls' day out.'

There was a pause. 'Of course,' Greta said, back in a normal tone. 'I'm looking forward to it. It's been too long since we had one.'

Cass heaved a sigh of relief. For a moment, she'd been afraid she'd inadvertently offended her best friend. Mick's invitation was nothing compared to her and Greta's longstanding friendship.

'I think I see someone at *Sassy's,*' Greta said, peering out the window.

'Oh, better go then. See you for lunch?'

'If I'm not snowed under.'

'Right.' Cass picked up her cup ready to leave. Sunday was a strange day. The shops could be busy or not. It all depended on the number of tourists in town. But she and Greta normally found a few minutes to catch up. Had she upset Greta more than she thought? Damn Mick Roberts! She shouldn't be thinking of him like that. If her friend was annoyed with her, it was all down to him.

Eighteen

When the following Sunday came along, Mick was already regretting his offer to Brenda and her brother. It had been a good week business wise. Almost every cruise had been filled, and Justin was pulling his weight. Mick didn't know how he'd managed without him. And the young fellow appeared to be enjoying it, taking on more and more of the hard work from Mick. And he'd be seeing Cass again tomorrow. The thought gave him a small thrill, though he counselled himself not to put too much store on her acceptance of his invitation. She was coming along to see the whales and to check Justin out, not to see him.

Seeing the enthusiasm in Justin's eyes when he came aboard, ready for another day, was enough to make Mick smile. It was good to have some young blood around the place. He missed Jo's younger days when she'd join him and his dad on the boat in her school holidays, safely lodged in one corner of the wheelhouse for a trip around the bay.

'Ready for another busy day?' Mick asked, to be greeted by a grin.

'Cass says she's coming out with us tomorrow,' Justin said. 'I told her she'll love it.'

'I hope so.' Mick busied himself with preparing for the day's passengers to hide his expression.

The day's passengers began to arrive, stepping onto the boat in twos and threes. Brenda and her brother were almost the last to arrive. Today, she looked as elegant as usual. She was wearing a pair of smart jeans with a pale blue sweater and a puffer vest in a darker shade of blue. She had a cap over her blonde curls and looked good enough to eat. But she left Mick cold. He sighed inwardly. If only he could turn on the feelings for Brenda that he felt when Cass was around, life would be much simpler. Jo would be pleased, and he would have no worries about the risk of getting involved with the best friend of his ex.

'Good morning. Welcome aboard. I hope we can produce some whales for you.' Mick kissed Brenda on the cheek and shook hands with her brother.

'Thanks.' Brenda smiled.

'Good of you to invite us,' Andy said. 'We'd have been happy to pay.'

'Not at all. What are friends for?' Mick said. 'Now, if you'll excuse me, I need to get things going. Young Justin here can answer any questions you have.' He gestured to where Justin was standing, ready to help pull up the gangplank. In the week he'd been working here, the young man had found a tee shirt printed with the emblem of *Bay Whale Cruises* and a cap with the similar logo. Over the tee shirt, he wore a loose jacket which he'd remove as the day became warmer. He really looked the part, as if he belonged. Mick had to keep reminding himself that it was only a temporary position for Justin.

They were lucky. Once they were out on the ocean, Mick grabbed the microphone. He had just begun his commentary, explaining how each year at this time, the whales migrated from Antarctica to Australia and travelled northwards up the coastline to breed, when a pod of whales came into view causing lots of oohing and aahing from his passengers. Sending a happy grin in Justin's direction, Mick continued his commentary as they watched the magnificent underwater mammals breach, splash and spy hop. The latter movement occurred when the whales rose and held a vertical position partially out of the water, exposing their entire rostrum and head. Mick compared it to a human treading water, and everyone laughed. It was as if the whales were watching the humans instead of the other way around.

When the show was over, Mick turned the boat around and chatted to several of the passengers, while Justin provided snacks to those who wanted them. When they were tied up at the wharf, Andy shook Mick's hand again. 'That was magnificent,' he said. 'I never imagined we'd get such a close look at them. They're amazing creatures.'

'I second that,' Brenda said. 'You must find it so rewarding to do this every day.'

'All in a day's work.' Mick reddened. 'It was a good day. The whales aren't always so obliging.'

'As a thank you, we'd like to invite you to dinner this evening,' Brenda said. 'I hope you're free.' She smiled.

Mick winced. It would be rude to refuse, but... He looked at her pleading expression and weakened. 'Thanks, it's kind of you.'

'Seven? I'll text you the address.'

'Thanks,' Mick said again, feeling as if he'd been forced into accepting the dinner invitation, when of course he could have refused.

The afternoon cruise proved to be equally successful, and by the time Mick returned home he was wishing he'd had the guts to say "No" to Brenda. Even more so when he received a call from Jo.

'How did it go today? I know Brenda and her brother went out with you this morning. I hope you managed to conjure up some whales for them.' She chuckled.

'The humpbacks put on a good show,' he said. 'Nothing to do with me. I think they were pleased.'

'And? When are you seeing her again?' Jo didn't give up.

Mick sighed. 'I'm having dinner with her and her brother tonight.' Jo would find out soon enough so he might as well tell her now and get it over with.

'I'm so pleased, Dad. I knew you two would hit it off. She...'

Mick didn't want to hear any more. He hated to disappoint Jo, but there would never be anything more between him and Brenda. 'Steady on, Jo,' he said, 'there's nothing happening there. She and Andy came on a cruise. They invited me to dinner as a thank you. She's a nice woman, but...'

'Da...ad! You can't just start seeing someone, then dump them for no reason.'

Mick bit his lip. He remembered Jo's hurt when she came back to Bellbird Bay after a shattered relationship. He should have been more sensitive to her feelings.

'Jo, I've only seen Brenda a couple of times. I doubt she thinks there's any more to it than I do,' he lied. He was pretty sure Brenda was interested in him and would like their friendship to lead to something more. It wasn't that he was conceited about this, but he'd been with enough women over the years to recognise the signs. He vowed to let this one down lightly.

'So you say,' Jo replied. 'I know what it feels like.'

Mick was swamped with guilt. It had been a mistake to ask Brenda out in the first place, but he'd done it as a favour to Jo… Well, not entirely. He'd been curious to see if he could find a connection with her but had soon realised his interest lay elsewhere. 'Sorry, sweetheart. I know she's your friend, but I can't manufacture feelings when they aren't there.'

'She'd be good for you, Dad.'

'I don't doubt it, honey.'

Jo didn't reply.

'No hard feelings?'

'No, Dad. I only want you to be happy.'

'I am happy, honey. I'm happy just as I am.'

'Hmm,' Jo said, her tone doubtful.

'Let's catch up again soon, okay?'

'Okay.'

But as Mick finished the call, hoping he'd managed to pacify his daughter, the image of Cass Marshall flitted through his mind.

Nineteen

Cass was excited as she prepared for her very first whale-watching cruise, unsure whether the butterflies in her stomach were due to the prospect of seeing whales, or to seeing Mick Roberts again, looking like he did in the photographs in the exhibition.

After consulting Justin, she dressed carefully in a pair of black leggings topped with a red sweater. She threw her black waterproof jacket into a small backpack along with a smart cap with the Bellbird Bay logo and a pair of sunglasses, before adding a layer of sunscreen and her brightest lipstick. She was ready.

Justin had already left, citing the need for him to arrive before the passengers, so Cass ensured Hector's bowls were filled before heading to the car.

At the wharf, Cass was surprised to see the number of people queuing up to board. She hadn't realised how popular Mick's whale-watching cruises were, despite Justin bragging about them since he started to work there. When it was her turn to board, and Mick offered a hand to help her onto the deck, a warm feeling unfurled in the pit of her stomach. Cass swallowed hard, hoping she'd be able to hide her feelings and behave as if this was a normal occurrence, and Mick was just her best friend's ex and her nephew's boss. He could never be anything else.

'Welcome aboard.' Mick smiled, and her heart lurched.

'Thanks for this,' she said, her feet slipping slightly on the damp boards. Mick put a hand on her elbow to steady her. 'Thanks,' she said again with a smile, wishing he'd keep it there.

But he headed off to greet other passengers, leaving Cass to find a spot out of the breeze which had blown up since she left the car.

Soon they were off, and Mick was providing a commentary about whales and their habits. To Cass's disappointment, the shirt he was wearing covered more than the singlet she remembered from Martin's photographs. But her disappointment didn't detract from the excitement of seeing a pod of whales, including a couple of mothers and babies, swimming alongside the boat, followed by a pair of dolphins leaping out of the water.

Suddenly, one of the passengers called out, 'Look at that whale. There seems to be something wrong with it.'

Cass joined the others in peering over the edge of the boat to see a humpback whale clearly in trouble. 'What's the matter with it?' she asked Mick who was standing close by. 'There seems to be something on its tail.'

'It's a damned float with a rope on it.' Mick's lips tightened. 'Whales are a protected species but sadly this happens all too often. Can be deadly for them. The poor creatures become entangled.' He shook his head. 'We humans have a lot to answer for.'

'Can we help it?' one of the passengers asked.

Mick shook his head again. 'We're not able to do anything. I'll contact Parks and Wildlife and they'll send out a team of first responders to try to disentangle it.'

The trip continued, but the mood had changed, everyone concerned for the distressed creature. It was a silent cruise boat that returned to the wharf.

'Sorry you had to experience that,' Mick said. All of the other passengers had disembarked, leaving Cass alone with Mick and Justin.

'Does it happen often?'

'Too often.'

'But these people – the first responders – they'll manage to free it?' Justin asked.

'Hopefully. They don't always succeed. *Their* safety is paramount, too. But they'll keep searching for the whale,' Mick added, seeing Justin's downcast expression.

Cass was about to say goodbye and leave, when Mick's next words stopped her. 'I think we all need something to take our minds off what we've just seen. We have a couple of hours before the next cruise. Why don't I treat us to lunch at the surf club?'

Cass hesitated, unsure if she was included.

'Cass, too?' Justin asked.

'Of course, unless you have something else organised?' Mick looked at her, his eyes seeming to bore through her and sending shivers down her spine.

'No, nothing. That would be lovely, thanks.'

'Great,' Justin said.

*

There were only a few locals standing at the bar, and the deck was practically empty when the trio reached the top of the stairs.

'What'll you have? My treat,' Mick said. 'Why don't you two snag a table on the deck while I order?'

'Thanks, that's good of you,' Cass said. 'If you're sure, I'll have a glass of white.'

'And to eat? Do you want to see the menu?'

'No need.' Cass was familiar with the club's menu. She loved eating here and didn't come often enough. 'The burrito bowl, please.'

'And you, Justin?'

'Can I have a beer with a burger and chips?'

'A man after my own heart, though my heart won't take it these days,' Mick said with a grimace. 'I might try the burrito bowl, too, Cass. It's a new one on me.' He grinned, his eyes twinkling, and Cass felt her face burn.

It was a relief to head out to the deck, where Cass chose a table in the shade.

'I'll go and help Mick,' Justin said and loped off.

Left alone, Cass took a deep breath. Mick's invitation had been unexpected, though not unwelcome. But she was sure it was only because of the connection with Justin. They'd been the only ones left, and he probably thought it would have been rude to exclude her. Mick was like that. She remembered various things Greta had told her about her ex, how despite his womanising, he had a kind heart and had been a good father. It was such a pity they could never be…

'Here we are.' Mick and Justin returned, and Mick handed Cass a glass filled with white wine and beaded with moisture.

Cass took a welcome sip, in an attempt to stifle the thoughts whirling around in her head. 'Thanks, Mick. This is perfect. And thanks again for this morning.'

'Glad you enjoyed it. Sorry it had to end on such a sad note. When Dad and I were fishing these waters, we took care not to pollute the ocean, to keep the whales safe. But these days…' He shook his head.

Their meals arrived, and Justin began to quiz Mick about what it had been like to work with his dad, leaving Cass to her thoughts as she watched the two, thinking how much Justin had gained from just the short time he'd been working with Mick. But he couldn't do it for ever. Sooner or later, Vi and Roger would want him home, and he'd be forced to make a decision about his future.

Her phone buzzed. Checking it, Cass's heart sank. It was the nursing home. Most Mondays she visited in the morning, but today, having agreed to go on the whale watching tour, she planned an afternoon visit. Since her mother rarely recognised her, she didn't think it would matter.

She excused herself, rose and walked away from the table, conscious of Mick's eyes following her. 'Hello? It's Cass here.'

'Cass, we were expecting you this morning.' The nursing assistant's voice sounded tired. Cass was sure hers would, too, if she worked there. The staff at Rosebank had earned her respect with their tireless devotion to the residents.

'I'm sorry. I plan to visit this afternoon. Is there a problem?'

'Not really, but Jean's been a bit agitated all morning. I know she doesn't know one day from the next, but it's as if she was expecting you.'

'Oh!' Cass bit her lip, the customary wave of guilt flooding her. 'I'm sorry. I'll be there shortly.' *So much for enjoying Mick's company for a bit longer*, she thought, as she walked back to the table.

Mick and Justin were laughing about something, and Cass wished she'd been part of their conversation. Mick raised one eyebrow.

'It was the nursing home… where your grandmother is,' she said to Justin. 'I'm sorry, I need to go. Thanks for lunch,' she said to Mick.

'Sit down and finish your meal,' Mick said. 'I'm sure a few more minutes won't make any difference to your mum, and you need to eat.'

Cass sat down again, but her thoughts weren't there. They were in the nursing home with her mother.

'How *is* your mother?' Mick asked, drawing her back to the present.

'Much the same. It varies from day to day. It seems she somehow expected to see me this morning. It's when I usually visit.' She bit her lip again.

'Don't beat yourself up. You couldn't have known.' Mick's voice was gentle.

Cass felt the tension, triggered by the phone call, ease. He was right. She took a sip of wine. 'What did you decide… about your dad?'

Mick sighed. 'We've accepted a place for him for when he's discharged from hospital. We may meet there again. It should happen in a few days. He's not happy about it, but it's the best solution, and he finally agreed.'

'And afterwards?'

'That's going to present another problem. I doubt if he'll be capable of living where he has been. The house is too big for one person, especially if he has trouble getting around.'

'I'm sorry. I can understand your dilemma.' It was the one Cass had faced when her mother's health deteriorated. It was never easy making a decision about the person who had brought you up and cared for you.

'We're hoping he'll agree to moving to *Bay Village Lifestyle Resort*.'

'I hear good reports about it.' Cass wished it had been an option for her mother. 'You're lucky you have your brother here, too,' she said with a sigh. Her life would have been much easier if Vi had been willing to share the burden of their mother's care.

'I guess.'

'Now…' Cass drained her glass, and pushed her half-full bowl aside, '… I really should go. Thanks again.'

Mick half rose, and Justin said, 'See you, Cass,' as she picked up her bag, rose and left, her mind already on what she might find waiting for her at the nursing home.

But as she drove across town, she couldn't help a small frisson of pleasure at the memory of sitting opposite Mick with a glass of wine on the deck of the surf club, something she'd often dreamt about but never expected to really happen.

Twenty

It wasn't fair! Cass thumped the steering wheel with her fist as she sat in the nursing home car park. Why did she have to take sole responsibility for their mother while Vi remained in England? Sure, her sister paid her share of their mother's keep, but she left all the day-to-day matters to Cass.

Cass took a deep breath and swallowed hard. It had been difficult to see her mother today. The older woman had appeared to be so unhappy, lost in her own little world and seemingly unable to relate to anything or anyone around her. Cass had flinched when the matron suggested Jean be sedated to make it easier for everyone. She couldn't bear the thought. Sedation might make it easier for the staff, but what about her mother?

She'd spent the entire afternoon there and by the time she left, her mother had calmed down and was drinking a cup of tea. Cass was exhausted. She didn't know how long she sat there, but eventually she started the engine and drove home.

Justin was already there, his hair damp from the shower. 'They haven't managed to rescue the whale,' he said as soon as she walked in, 'but Mick says they'll keep trying to disentangle the rope or fix a satellite tag to the mammal before darkness. Do you think…? What's the matter? Is Grandma okay?' he asked, clearly seeing Cass's expression.

'Oh Justin, she'll never be okay again. Today was just difficult, that's all.' She dropped into a nearby chair and closed her eyes for a moment.

'Sorry, sometimes it just gets to me. It's easy for your mum. She gets away with sending her monthly contribution. She doesn't have to go there regularly, see…' Cass looked up to see a worried expression on Justin's face. 'Sorry, Justin. Your mum's lack of empathy isn't your fault. But I need to call her. She needs to realise what's happening.' She checked the time. It was still too early to call. She'd have a shower and a glass of wine. Then she might be in a better frame of mind to talk to her sister.

An hour later, Cass was ready to speak to Vi. Justin had gone out, muttering something about Zack and a group of friends, and she was alone with Hector. The cat, seeming to recognise her distress, had curled up beside her on the sofa and was purring loudly.

'What would I do without you, Hector?' she said to the creature who she had found in her backyard as a kitten and who had grown into a much larger cat than she anticipated. Until Justin's arrival, he had been her sole companion.

Cass picked up her phone and dialed her sister's number. She held her breath as she listened to the various dial tones patching her through to the English exchange, then heard her brother-in-law's voice giving their number.

'Hello, Roger. It's Cass. Can I speak to Vi?'

'Cass?' Roger sounded surprised.

She heard him call out, 'Vi, it's your sister calling from Australia,' then there was silence.

'Cass,' her sister said, 'is everything all right? Is it Justin? Has he got into trouble?'

'Justin's fine. He's a lovely young man and seems to be enjoying life in Bellbird Bay. It's mother. I need to talk to you about her.'

'Mother? Didn't our monthly payment arrive? Roger?' she called.

'It's not about the money.' Cass sighed. With Vi, it was always about the money. 'You need to know how she is. This disease… it's destroyed the woman we know, turned her into a stranger, a stranger who…' Cass's voice broke.

'What are you trying to say, Cass?' Vi's voice was stiff. 'I don't have time for this now. I need to get to work.'

Cass could picture her sister standing in her pristine kitchen tapping her foot impatiently, her husband looking pointedly at his watch.

'That's the trouble, isn't it, Vi? You never have time. You haven't had time for our mother since you swanned off overseas. Apart from a few short trips back over the years, you've tried to pretend we didn't exist… until you needed somewhere to send your problem son.' Cass paused, wondering if she'd said too much. It was certainly more than she'd intended to say and wasn't going to achieve what she wanted. She wanted Vi to understand what it was like for her, having all of the responsibility for their mother's care with no one to support her.

There was silence at the other end of the phone, then, 'I don't know what you expect me to say. It was your choice to return to Bellbird Bay. I never understood why you did. You had a perfectly good job in Sydney. You were going places. But you chose to bury yourself in the town where we grew up, while I managed to make a good life for myself here. Now, I really have to go.'

Cass stared at the silent phone. Vi had hung up on her.

She was still fuming at her sister when the phone rang. Forgetting to check the number, and hoping it was Vi calling back, Cass pressed accept. 'Hello,' she said aware of the barely suppressed anger in her tone.

But it wasn't Vi.

'Cass?' Mick said. 'I hope I'm not disturbing you.'

A familiar warm feeling unfurled in the pit of her stomach, much like the one when he had helped her board his boat. It seemed a long time ago now, but it had only been that morning. 'Not at all, Mick.'

'I…'he stammered, '…I wanted to check how your mum was. When you left the club, I could see how upset you were. Was everything okay?'

'Oh, Mick!' Mick would never know how welcome his call was. 'It's so kind of you to call… to be concerned. No, Mum was in a terrible state when I arrived. They were talking about sedating her.' She paused, the memory of that moment almost too difficult to bear. She heard his sharp intake of breath. 'I spent the afternoon there and by the time I left, she had calmed down. But I don't know what's going to happen next.'

'I'm so sorry. If there was anything I could do…'

'Thanks, but there's nothing any of us can do. I know she's getting the best care where she is. It's just that sometimes…' She paused again to wipe the moisture which was gathering in her eyes.

'My dad still has all his faculties, so I can't fully understand what you're going through, but if you ever need someone to talk to… I'm here.'

'Thanks, Mick. It's good of you. You're a good man.'

'I try to be,' he chuckled, 'though not everyone would agree with you.'

Cass suspected he was referring to Greta, but to give her friend credit, she had never badmouthed her ex to Cass… apart from complaining about his womanising. Cass remembered the blonde woman Mick had been with at the gallery opening. He wasn't interested in *her*. He was merely being kind.

'Thanks for your call, Mick.'

'No worries. Look…' he hesitated, '… you have my number. Feel free to call anytime.'

When the call ended, Cass was puzzled. It had been good of him to call, but… why did she feel there had been more to the call than his concern about her mother, that he had been about to say something else, then changed his mind?

'What do you think, Hector?' she asked the cat who had been lying at her side all through Mick's call. But Hector made no reply, merely stretching out his paws and yawning before settling down again.

Cass went to the kitchen to pour herself another glass of wine, wishing she knew what was going on in Mick's mind, the warm feeling she'd experienced when she received his call still flowing through her.

Twenty-one

Mick stared at his phone and cursed his cowardliness. Why hadn't he made arrangements to see Cass again? Lunch had been good, even with Justin there. It was a pity she'd been called away, but he understood the distress of worrying about a parent. It was why he'd called… or partly. He'd wanted to hear her voice, to let her know he cared. Over lunch he'd sensed her vulnerability, a vulnerability that made him want to protect her. And he'd blown it. He'd had the opportunity to ask her out, to invite her to dinner… and all he'd done was to remind her she had his phone number. What a fool!

Mick couldn't work out what it was about Cass that attracted him. She wasn't elegant like Greta, curvy like Brenda, nor flashy like most of the women he'd associated with over the years. But there was something about her… something that cried out to him, made him want to take care of her, to safeguard her from harm. He chuckled. Did he think he was some sort of knight in shining armour, set to ride in to save the fair lady from the evil monster? Only, in this instance, the fair lady had dark hair, hair which was a mass of curls he wanted to run his fingers through, and pale skin which looked soft to touch and… Mick grew hot thinking about her. This wouldn't do. He rose, poured himself a beer and took it out onto his deck.

Looking up at the stars, he reminded himself how much he valued his solitude, how he'd told Jo he was happy on his own. It was all true, but… somehow Cass Marshall had managed to slip under his radar, and he couldn't get her out of his mind. She'd been around most of his life. Why had he just noticed her?

He finished his beer and went back inside, determined to find something else to occupy him. Turning on his computer, he began to research boats for sale and to calculate how he could be able to afford to expand his business. The demand was there, if he could find a way to finance it.

*

After a restless night, Mick awoke, determined to make good his previous intention to invite Cass to dinner. He was aware she was in the habit of buying coffee for herself and Greta at *The Bay Café* each morning before spending several minutes in *Birds of a Feather*. Knowing it would be a mistake to attempt to speak with her in Greta's presence, he decided to arrange to meet her, as if by accident, at the café.

Dressed in his work outfit of shorts and a white tee-shirt bearing the logo *Bay Whale Cruises* and the image of a humpback whale, he sauntered across the esplanade. There was no sign of Cass and at first, he thought he'd missed her. Then, he spied her slim figure coming out of the café carrying two cardboard cups, a bag slung over one shoulder.

'Mick!' Her eyes widened. 'What are you doing here? Sorry, that sounds…' She blushed.

'I have a late start this morning and thought I'd grab myself a coffee before…' His voice trailed off as he realised she'd be perfectly aware he was lying. Justin would already be waiting for him at the wharf. 'I wanted to see you,' he said.

'Well, here I am.' She appeared puzzled.

'Last night when I called, there was something else I wanted to say.'

She didn't speak, but he saw a glimmer of amusement in her eyes.

Mick drew a hand through his hair. He wasn't accustomed to feeling tongue-tied with women. What was it about this one? 'I wanted to invite you to dinner. We didn't have much of a chance to talk during lunch with Justin… then you were called away. Do you like Italian food? I could book a table at *The Firenze* for Friday if you'd agree to join me.' Mick felt himself redden as he stammered out the worst invitation to dinner he'd ever made. He was sure even Justin could have done better.

He waited.

It was Cass's turn to blush. 'I like Italian food,' she said, so softly he could barely hear her.

Mick felt as if he wanted to yell with delight, but all he said was, 'How about I pick you up at seven?'

'Okay, now I must…' She held up the two coffees she was holding and gestured towards *Birds of a Feather*.

'Of course.' Mick moved away to let her pass. 'I'll see you then.' He watched with his heart racing as she made her way across the esplanade to push open the door to Greta's shop.

*

'Was that Mick I saw you talking with?' Greta asked before Cass could speak.

Cass flinched. How could she have imagined Greta hadn't seen them standing in the middle of the row of shops? They'd been the only two people there at that time in the morning, and Cass was still reeling from her encounter with Mick and his invitation to dinner when she walked into *Birds of a Feather*.

Greta would have been looking out for her, ready for her coffee.

'He wanted to ask me about Rosebank Nursing Home,' she said. It was the first thing that came into her head. 'Justin had mentioned seeing Mum there, and Mick's thinking of it for his dad.'

'Oh!' Greta didn't ask any more, but Cass saw the speculative look in her eyes.

She took a sip of coffee, hoping she'd managed to allay her friend's suspicions.

'How was the whale-watching cruise?' Greta asked, seemingly satisfied with Cass's explanation. 'I saw a news item about a whale in difficulty.'

'Yes.' Cass breathed a sigh of relief. The last thing she wanted was to be quizzed about Mick by Greta. 'We saw the poor creature. It was just at the end of the tour, but it put a dampener on the group. It's horrible how people feel free to discard their rubbish into the ocean with no thought for the sea creatures. Justin said they were hoping to disentangle the poor thing before darkness. I haven't heard anything this morning.' She should have asked Mick, she realised. He'd know. But she had been too surprised to see him, too stunned by his invitation, to think of anything else.

'They did. We heard it on the news this morning.'

'I'm glad.' Cass took another sip of coffee. She was finding it unusually awkward speaking to Greta this morning, knowing she was keeping a secret from her. But how could she tell her friend she'd had lunch with Mick and was having dinner with him on Friday? Though she'd find out soon enough, Bellbird Bay being what it was. Nothing in this town remained secret for long. She'd have to tell her before Friday. But not today.

Twenty-two

Early next morning, Mick received the phone call he'd been waiting for. The hospital deemed his dad well enough to be discharged on the condition he was able to be looked after. Aware he had two cruises booked that day, he immediately called Pete who agreed to oversee their dad's move into Rosebank Nursing Home. He would meet Pete there in the late afternoon when he had finished for the day.

Unlike the previous day, there were no dramas, the whales duly appeared, and both cruises ended with satisfied customers singing Mick's praises.

'I'm glad they managed to disentangle that whale yesterday,' Justin said as they were cleaning up after the afternoon's passengers had all left. 'I didn't realise the danger they were in. They're such magnificent creatures. I'd like to learn more about them.'

'Study them?'

'It'd be a lot more interesting than law.' Justin grimaced.

'That what you were doing in England?'

'I dropped out. Dad's a solicitor and wants me to follow him, but it bores me. I want to do something different.'

'Have you thought of marine biology?'

'No, what's involved?'

'I'm not sure exactly, but I do know a young woman who's a marine biologist. She'd be able to tell you.'

'In Bellbird Bay?'

'Sadly, not. But her mother, correction, her stepmother, lives here and could put you in touch with her.'

'Wow!' Justin's eyes lit up, then clouded again. 'But Dad would never agree. He'd never pay for something like that.'

Mick thought for a moment. 'Your mum was born here, wasn't she? That would entitle you to Australian citizenship. Then you'd be eligible for a student loan. I'd be happy to give you work here for a bit longer, too.'

Justin brightened. 'Really? Cool. I'll talk with Cass about it.'

'Right.' Mick frowned. He wondered if he'd overstepped the mark. Justin wasn't his kid, wasn't any relation to him. Maybe Cass would be annoyed, think he was giving the boy ideas, suggesting he defy his parents. 'I think we're done here,' he said, looking around the clean and tidy boat. Having Justin's help really made a difference. He checked his watch. There was just time for him to dash home, have a quick shower and change, before meeting Pete at the nursing home. He didn't want to turn up there smelling of oil and saltwater.

*

Mick was feeling anxious as he pulled into the driveway of the nursing home. Although his dad had finally agreed to spending time there to recuperate, the old man had grumbled that he'd prefer to be in his own home.

Pete was waiting for him at the entrance. He looked pointedly at his watch as Mick strode up to meet him. 'You took your time.'

'Sorry. I had to have a shower. I couldn't come straight from work. I'm not like you.'

'Hmm. Well, we'd better go in.'

'How's Dad been?'

'As you'd expect, grumbling all the way from the hospital. I don't envy the staff who have to deal with him here. But it seems like a nice place, and he has a room looking out onto the garden. It could be worse.'

Once inside, Pete led Mick to their dad's room. The older man was sitting up in bed chatting to a young nurse. He looked round when they walked in. 'So, you decided to visit the old man, Mick. Too busy to come by earlier like your brother?'

'I was out on the boat, Dad. You know how it is, I have a living to make. My time's not my own, not like…' He nudged his brother.

'Well, you're here now,' the old man grumbled.

'I'll leave you with your visitors, Mr Roberts,' the nurse said, then turning to Mick and Pete, 'Don't upset your dad. We've just got him settled in, and dinner will be served shortly. If you stop off at reception on your way out, you can pick up information about visiting hours.'

'That's telling you,' Fred chuckled when she had left. 'She's a sight for sore eyes, make no mistake.'

'Looks like you fell on your feet here, Dad. No pun intended,' Mick said with a grin.

'Less of your cheek. You're not too old for a clip around the ear.'

Glad his dad was sounding better, and more like his old self, Mick walked across to gaze out the window. 'Nice room.'

'Well, it's not home, but I suppose it'll do. Could be worse.'

Mick smiled as his dad repeated his brother's assessment of the place.

Mick and Pete took seats, one on either side of the bed, as their dad proceeded to quiz them on what they were doing to look after his house while he was *cooped up here*.

They must have answered to his satisfaction because, after a bit, he leant back against his pillow. 'You'd better be off now,' he said, 'or you'll have that lovely young nurse after you.'

'He'll be right,' Mick said as they made their way back to their cars. 'What are you doing now? Fancy dinner at the club?'

'Good idea.' Mick didn't have any idea what he was going to have for dinner, and the opportunity to spend time with Pete didn't come around very often. They lived different lives, mixed in different circles. Their dad was their only point of contact.

'Meet you there.'

Mick was walking to his car when he recognised a slim figure making her way towards the entrance to the nursing home. 'Cass?' he said. 'Isn't it late to be visiting?'

'Mick.' Cass stopped abruptly. She was looking frazzled, and Mick thought she'd been crying. 'Your dad's here, then?'

'Yes, we just got him settled in. But what's up with you? Your mum…?'

'She's taken a turn for the worse and they asked me to come in, though I don't know what...' A tear trickled down her cheek.

Mick wanted to take her in his arms and comfort her but wasn't sure if it would be welcome. 'I'm sorry. If there's anything...?' He realised he'd said that to her before but had the impression she was too independent to ask for help.

'Thanks, I'll be right. I must...' She gestured towards the entrance. While Mick and Pete had been with his dad, darkness had fallen, and the only light was the one streaming from the doorway.

'Of course. We still good for Friday?'

Cass smiled. 'Yes, all going well with Mum.'

*

The club was packed, probably due to the Tuesday special of a 250 gram Kilcoy rump steak, cooked on the barbecue and served with chips, salad and a choice of sauce. Mick's mouth watered at the prospect, but knew he had to stick to his doctor's orders. He ordered the grilled fish with salad and watched with envy as Pete ordered the Tuesday special. He did weaken to accept the beer Pete offered him.

'Who was that I saw you talking with when we left the nursing home?' Pete asked, when they had settled at the last vacant table on the deck with their beers.

Mick reddened. 'Cass Marshall, she's a friend of Greta's,' he said, hoping that would satisfy his brother.

It didn't. 'Cass Marshall,' Pete said, closing his eyes for a moment. 'I know who she is. Isn't she the woman who has that beachwear place, *Sassy's*, right next door to your ex's shop? These shops are worth a bomb these days.'

Trust Pete, always the realtor. But it surprised Mick he knew Cass. 'She is.' Mick decided to keep it brief.

'You could do worse,' Pete said using his favourite phrase again. 'It's time you found yourself a woman. You hankered after Greta for too long, and now she's off the market. Not my type,' he said referring to Cass again, 'but a bit of all right. May be just right for you, bro.' Pete laughed.

Mick felt a flash of anger. He wanted to punch his brother. But Pete was just being his usual self, and Mick was aware he'd once talked about women this way, too. No wonder Greta had given up on him.

Their meals arrived, preventing Mick's anger from erupting, and when Pete spoke again, it was to discuss how they were going to share looking after the family home while their dad was in the nursing home.

They came to an arrangement whereby Mick would call round every couple of days to check on the house and garden, and Pete would check their dad's mail and make sure any bills were paid promptly. Mick was tempted to say it seemed like an unequal distribution of labour but decided to stay silent.

Their meals finished, the brothers parted company. Back home, Mick thought about the evening, about Pete's comments regarding Cass, and wondered what she thought about him – if she even thought about him at all, given her challenges with her mother and her care of Justin. Perhaps he'd been right in the first place, and he should never have given in to the temptation to get to know her better, to invite her to dinner. He sighed as he looked around his house, the home he had been so proud of only a short time ago. Now it seemed only to emphasise how alone he was. But a woman wasn't the only answer to loneliness. Maybe he should get a dog.

Twenty-three

By the time Friday came around, Cass was a wreck. Her past three evenings had been spent at the nursing home, and she hadn't been able to sleep when she did reach home.

Justin didn't appear to notice when they met at breakfast. His social life seemed to be improving in leaps and bounds. 'Okay if I go to a party tonight, Cass? There's a crowd planning to go to this beach, and…'

'You don't need to ask my permission, Justin,' she said. 'But I do appreciate knowing where you are. Your mum expects me to keep tabs on you.'

Justin rolled his eyes. There was a restlessness about him this morning that she hadn't noticed before.

Cass wondered… 'Is there going to be someone special at this party?' she asked.

Justin shrugged, but the tips of his ears reddened. 'Just a few mates. Zack and his girlfriend and a couple of others.'

'Other girls?'

He shrugged again. 'Maybe. Probably Jenny and Megan. They're mates with Fliss. She's Zack's girlfriend. They're still at school but they're all right.'

Cass smiled to herself. She wondered what her sister would say to Justin dating a schoolgirl. But she wasn't going to find out, was she? She and Justin had made a pact to keep much of what he was doing in Bellbird Bay a secret from his parents on the basis that what they didn't know wouldn't harm them and would save Justin a lot of grief.

'Have fun. I'm going out tonight, too. I'll probably be home before you, so try to come in quietly and not disturb either Hector or me.'

At the sound of his name, the cat let out a loud meow. 'You wouldn't like to be disturbed, Hector, would you?' she said, much to Justin's amusement.

'Does he really understand you?' he asked.

'Every word. Don't you, Hector?'

The cat meowed again, causing Justin to chuckle.

'You going out with Mick?'

'How did you know?'

'I didn't. I guessed… I saw the way you two were when we had lunch at the club. He's one of the good guys.'

'Yeah. Now you'd better get on, or he won't be good with you for long.'

'See you.' Justin grabbed his bag and left.

Cass sighed. It was difficult to keep anything secret in this town. But Justin's words reminded her. She had still to tell Greta about her date with Mick and she was worried about her friend's reaction.

*

'Morning, Greta.' Cass placed the two cups of coffee on the counter in *Birds of a Feather*.

'How's your mum? I saw you rush off again after closing last night. That's three nights this week, isn't it?'

'Yeah,' Cass took a sip of the welcome coffee. She sighed.

'You're not getting much sleep either, I bet.' She peered at Cass.

'Do I look that bad?'

'No, but I can tell. You're not your usual bouncy self.'

Bouncy? Was that how Greta saw her? She did always try to put a positive spin on things, to look for the best in everything and everyone. Maybe that's why… 'Mum's not good,' she said.

'I'm sorry. If there's anything…'

Her words reminded Cass of the last person who'd said that to her. 'I have something to tell you,' she said before she could stop herself.

Greta's expression changed. She put down the coffee she'd been holding. 'What's the matter? Has something happened?'

Cass squirmed. 'Not really, but I wanted to tell you before someone else did.' She gazed at her friend. 'Mick has invited me to dinner.'

'Oh!' There was a moment's silence. 'But you refused, didn't you?'

'I said "yes". He's been so good to Justin, giving him a job and…' Cass's voice trailed off seeing Greta's shocked expression. This was exactly what she'd been afraid of.

'I'm surprised, after how he treated me. I know you told me his womanising had stopped, but…'

'I was trying to help. I thought the two of you were going to get back together.'

'Or were you setting things up for yourself?'

'Greta! How could you think that of me?' Cass was shocked that her friend might imagine she had an ulterior motive. 'I wanted you to be happy and I thought…'

'You know what thought did?'

Cass stifled a smile, remembering her grandmother's saying. Then she looked at her friend's face again and knew it had been a mistake to accept Mick's invitation. 'I'm sorry, Greta. I didn't think… now you have Leo…' But she had thought. She'd decided Mick was off limits… because of Greta, because of his womanising. It was only a couple of weeks since she'd seen him with the curvy, blonde woman at the gallery. She'd been surprised and flattered by the invitation to dinner and her resolution had weakened. How dumb was that?

'Tonight's a one-off, Greta. You don't imagine it's anything else, do you?' She bit the inside of her cheek at the outright lie. Then she remembered something Justin had mentioned the previous evening. 'He's been talking with Justin about the possibility of his staying in Australia and studying marine biology.'

'Well, that's all right then, isn't it? You and my ex can have a nice little tête-à-tête about your nephew over dinner.'

Cass had never heard her friend sound so bitter, not even when she thought Leo was going back to his ex-wife. 'Don't be like that, Greta. You know I'd never do anything to hurt you.'

Greta smiled. 'Of course I do. It was a shock, that's all. But be careful. I don't want you to end up with a broken heart like I did. What's this about Justin staying in Australia? In Bellbird Bay?'

'Probably not. I don't think the course is offered at the local uni, and James Cook is the place to study marine biology, isn't it?' She was on safer ground now, talking about Justin.

'I think you're right. What about a visa?'

'Mick seemed to think because Vi is Australian, he'd be right.'

'I don't know about that, but Leo would. I can ask him.'

'Thanks.'

'Isn't the daughter of Cleo's first husband working there, the one who helped us out with the information about dugongs to save Dolphin Beach from the developers?'

'I think you're right. I can check with Cleo, too. But I dread to think what Vi and Roger will say if he does decide to stay.'

'He's over eighteen.'

'Even so. Roger is a control freak and wants Justin to follow him into law. The poor kid hates the idea. It's why he dropped out of uni.'

'Not so much of a kid, but I can understand. We all want the best for our children. Lucky for Jo, Mick and I were happy to let her follow her inclinations, even when it took her to the other side of the world.'

'But she's back now.'

'Thank goodness, and has found herself a nice man. You need to find one, too, Cass. Not someone like Mick.' She jabbed Cass with her finger.

Cass knew it was time to leave. 'I have to go, Greta. See you for lunch?'

'If I'm not too busy.'

Cass knew it was the best she would get, but it was a sign Greta had forgiven her for accepting Mick's invitation. And, although it would hurt, she'd keep her word to Greta and make it a one-off. She didn't want another broken heart either.

By lunchtime, Greta seemed to have recovered her good humour and was chatting about Leo's latest plans for the hotel. 'You're still coming to dinner on Saturday?' she asked as she was leaving.

'If you still want me to.'

'Of course.' Greta gave Cass a hug. 'Sorry I was such a pain earlier. It was a shock. I know you'd never deliberately do anything to hurt me. Have a nice evening with Mick. Just remember…'

'I will,' Cass replied. How could she forget? But as she drove home that evening, she made a decision. If this was going to be her one and only date with Mick, she was determined to make the most of it.

Twenty-four

Cass was conflicted as she prepared for her date with Mick, the date she'd dreamt about for years, had imagined over and over again, was finally about to happen. But her anticipation was soured by Greta's reaction. She'd expected her friend to be upset, but she hadn't imagined the bitterness Greta still harboured. And the loyalty she felt for her friend outweighed any feelings Cass might have for Mick Roberts. After all, she'd lived without him until now, and she'd have been lost without Greta's support over the years and her help in setting up *Sassy's*. She owed Greta for helping her get back on her feet again when she returned to Bellbird Bay, stung by Ray Morgan's betrayal. Though she'd never revealed her reason for leaving the city, Greta had immediately recognised her pain.

Putting the morning's conversation behind her, Cass pulled on the flared black pants and the blue top patterned with tropical flowers she'd purchased from *Birds of a Feather*, and which always made her feel good. As she styled her hair and applied her makeup, she knew she was looking her best.

'What do you think, Hector, will I blow his socks off?' she asked her pet. But, as usual, the cat merely put his head in the air and stalked off, sensing he was going to be left alone for the evening.

Justin had already left, barely taking time to say goodbye when Zack drew up in the old car he'd managed to buy with his savings from working part time in *Bay Bikes*. Cass knew Justin would love to do the same and was saving his earnings from Mick. She hadn't been lying when she told Greta he had plans to stay in Australia. She just hoped she didn't have to break the news to her sister.

There was a knock on the door at exactly seven o'clock, and the butterflies in Cass's stomach began to do cartwheels. Taking a deep breath and with one last glance in the mirror, she went to answer it.

'You're looking lovely,' Mick said.

Cass's heart leapt. Mick was looking pretty good, too. It was almost the first time she'd seen him look this smart. He was wearing a pair of black pants and a black cord jacket over a pale blue shirt. A smidgeon of hair peeked out of the open neck of the shirt reminding Cass of the photos of him in the gallery. Unaware she'd been staring, she started when he asked, 'Ready?'

'Of course. You're looking very smart tonight, too.'

Mick reddened.

'Justin out?'

Cass nodded. 'Zack picked him up earlier. Some party on the beach. I think girls are involved.'

Mick chuckled. 'Remember when you were his age? I know you were quite a bit younger than me, but things don't change much in Bellbird Bay.'

'No.' Even then, she'd had a crush on Mick, but knew she was too young for him to notice, and he was way out of her league. Then he married Greta… and she finished school and left town.

As soon as they walked into *The Firenze*, Cass felt herself enveloped by the atmosphere of the restaurant. She loved coming here, loved the way it felt like being in Italy… even though she'd never been there.

With a questioning glance at Cass, who nodded her agreement, Mick ordered a serving of bruschetta to share and a bottle of Borgofiero Chianti. Then, after perusing the menu, Cass decided on the Spaghetti Alla Carbonara. while Mick chose the Cannelloni di Ricotta Spinici.

'How is Justin going?' Cass asked while they waited for their meals, thinking she night as well at least make an attempt to do what she'd told Greta.

'He's good. I don't know how I'm going to manage when he leaves.'

'He said you've suggested he could stay here and study?'

Mick squirmed. 'I did. I realise it's beyond my brief to make a suggestion like that, but I can see how much he likes it here, and his interest in the whales is impressive. It would be a pity for him not to capitalise on it.'

'Mmm.' Cass agreed with him on both counts.

'He tells me his dad wants him to study law.'

'His dad's a control freak, and my sister's not much better. I can imagine their reaction if Justin decides to study here.' *And the fallout for me.*

'He's old enough to make up his own mind. I rebelled against my dad, too, when I was his age.'

Cass had the vague recollection of Mick being gone for a year or more.

'They called it a gap year, but I just wanted to get away. I didn't see my future working on Dad's fishing boat. I went overseas, crewed on boats for some wealthy guys on the Mediterranean.'

'But you came back?'

He nodded. 'I decided Dad wasn't so bad… and I missed Bellbird Bay. I came back and married Greta.'

Mention of her friend reminded Cass.

'I think it's better…'

'I think maybe…'

Both spoke at once, then laughed.

'Ladies first,' Mick said.

'I think it may be better if we don't meet again like this,' Cass said. 'I feel… I'm too close to Greta… What were you going to say?'

'Much the same,' Mick chuckled. 'While I'd really like to get to know you better, it's awkward… you and Greta.'

Cass wasn't sure whether her primary feeling was one of relief or disappointment, but she was glad to have it out of the way.

Their meals arrived and they began to share memories of growing up in Bellbird Bay discovering that, despite the years separating them, their experiences had been similar. *It was a pity their connections with Greta stood in the way of their developing a closer relationship.*

Cass was sorry when the evening ended. She was filled with regret for what might have been. Then she steeled herself, knowing in her heart there could never be a happy ever after for her and Mick. There were too many obstacles. It was better to end it now, before it even started.

But there was a tear in the corner of her eye when they reached her house. Mick turned to her.

'Thanks for coming tonight. I'm sorry… I wish…'

'I'm sorry, too, Mick. Thanks for tonight. It was lovely.' She leant over to give him a brief kiss on the cheek, before opening the door and rushing into the house to prevent him seeing her tears.

Twenty-five

Although she knew she'd done the right thing with Mick, Cass felt dejected when she awoke next morning. The fact it was raining did nothing to improve her mood as she forced herself out of bed and into the kitchen to feed Hector.

'Hector!' she said, seeing the dead possum on the doormat, just inside the cat flap she'd forgotten to lock last night. She'd been tired and not thinking straight. She shovelled up the poor creature, determined to give it a proper burial later and vowed never to make that mistake again.

'Hi, Cass!' Justin, his hair standing on end, wandered into the kitchen. He stared out the window at the rain streaming down. 'Do you think Mick's cruise will be cancelled this morning?' He yawned. It was clear he'd prefer to go back to bed.

'I doubt it. Why don't you call him? Breakfast?'

'Uh. The phone's busy.' He looked up.

'Did you check your texts?'

'Oh, yeah.' There was a moment's silence, then, 'The weather's too bad so he's cancelled today's cruises. I'm going back to bed.'

'He's probably calling his passengers to reschedule. Good party?'

'Uh.' Justin disappeared.

Cass grinned. She tried to remember what it was like to party on the beach till the early hours. They'd probably stayed till the rain started. She peered out the window at the rain gauge – forty millimetres overnight and it was still pouring down. There wouldn't be many customers today, a good opportunity to catch up on her accounts.

'What a morning,' Greta greeted Cass when she walked in carrying the two coffees. 'But the garden needs the rain. Guess we won't be busy today. There won't be anyone on the beach or out on the bay.'

Cass made a sound signifying agreement. She didn't want to talk about Mick this morning. But to her relief, Greta made no reference to Cass's date.

'I saw Cleo and Will at the club last night,' Greta said. 'She mentioned that Kerri-Ann was coming for a visit – the girl she calls her other daughter. It's the perfect opportunity for Justin to ask her about the marine biology course.'

'Really?'

'Seems it's some sort of uni break, and she and Grace's son are travelling down together.' She tapped the side of her nose. 'I wouldn't be surprised if we have another wedding there. I don't usually gossip, but Cleo was excited at the two coming down together. I bet Grace is, too.'

'That would be nice,' Cass said. She couldn't summon up the energy to be excited about the news of another wedding in Bellbird Bay. They seemed to come around so often. But Greta was right. It would be a good opportunity for Justin to have his questions answered. He'd already done his research and confirmed his mother's Australian citizenship meant he was automatically entitled to it, too.

The day passed slowly for Cass. As she expected, there was only a small dribble of customers, and she was glad to put up the *Closed* sign a few minutes earlier than usual and go home.

Hector was waiting for her, jumping down from the sofa and winding himself round her ankles as soon as she walked inside. Justin was seated at the kitchen table spooning up a bowl of cereal.

'You haven't just got up?' she asked.

'No. Mick called, and I went over to the wharf to help him on the boat. I was hungry when I got back but didn't fancy cooking. Are you making dinner?' he asked hopefully.

'I'm afraid not. I'm having dinner with Greta and Leo at his hotel, *The Leonard Family Resort*.' She gazed at Justin and took pity on him. 'There are a couple of frozen meals in the freezer. I keep them for nights when I can't be bothered cooking. Feel free to choose one.'

'Thanks. I may go out later. I'll check what's happening.' He took out his phone. 'By the way, I found the remains of some sort of animal Hector must have brought in. I buried it in the garden. Hope that was okay.'

'Thanks, Justin.' One less thing to do. 'I'm going to soak in a hot bath till it's time to get ready to go out. Let me know what you decide to do. Oh, and I heard Kerri-Ann, the woman who's involved in the marine biology course at Townsville, is coming home for a visit. I can contact Cleo and set up for you to meet her, if you want.'

'Yes, please. Thanks. I've checked out the course and it looks awesome.'

Cass made her way upstairs, hoping the hot bath would re-energise her sufficiently to be reasonable company at dinner. It was good of Greta and Leo to invite her, and at any other time, she'd be excited to see the latest renovations to the hotel Leo was rightly proud of. But the way she was feeling, she'd prefer to spend the evening curled up on the sofa with Hector and one of the frozen meals she'd recommended to Justin, watching a soppy movie.

She filled the bath, poured in a generous amount of the bath oil her sister had sent on her last birthday and let herself sink into the hot, aromatic water. It was only then that she allowed herself to think of what she'd forced to the back of her mind all day, to think back to the previous evening, to her dinner with Mick.

*

When Cass arrived at the hotel, Greta was waiting to meet her in the foyer, looking as glamourous as ever, every bit the wife of the hotel's owner. 'Wow!' she said, looking around. 'Leo's done a lot since the opening.'

'Hasn't he?' Greta's eyes followed Cass's to take in the tiled foyer with sofas and soft chairs in nooks where people could relax, and the area at the far side which held a playroom for children.

'Checking out the improvements?' Leo appeared at Greta's side and wrapped an arm around her waist. 'Welcome to *The Leonard Family Resort*, Cass. You'll notice a difference from when you were last here.'

'I certainly do.' The spa had a separate entrance, so the last time Cass had stood here, the foyer had been thronged with people celebrating the opening of the hotel under new management. Tonight, she could see how Leo had fashioned it into the family hotel he'd promised the town. 'Well done, Leo.'

'Thanks.' He dipped his head. For such a successful man, he was surprisingly modest.

Cass guessed it was what had attracted Greta to him, won her away from Mick. She swallowed. Seeing Greta and Leo together like this emphasised her own single status. Seeing happy couples always made her feel envious, made her wonder when her turn would come. *She'd dated a few men over the years, but had she allowed her fixation with Mick to prevent her from forming an attachment to anyone else, persuading herself she was waiting for that special person who would come along and sweep her off her feet like the hero in a romance novel? Was it too late? Had she left it too long? As she'd watched all these other women in Bellbird Bay find their prince, had she been hoping for the impossible?*

'Shall we go in?' Leo led the way into the hotel restaurant which was filled with a mixture of locals and tourists. He made his way to a table set apart from the rest, looking out onto what would have been a beautiful view in daylight. Through the darkness, Cass could barely make out the outline of what she knew must be the tennis court and walled garden.

Although Cass had met Leo a few times, she didn't know him very well. But he went to great pains to make her feel comfortable, relating amusing stories of his early days in the hotel business and asking her about her decision to establish *Sassy's*.

The meal was delightful, the wagyu steak cooked to perfection, served with baby roast potatoes and spinach, and followed by a crème brûlée that melted in her mouth, all accompanied by glasses of prosecco.

Greta smiled when Cass complimented Leo on it. 'Ask him where he found the chef,' she said.

Cass turned to Leo who gave Greta an affectionate smile.

'He was working in a restaurant where I took Greta to lunch. The meal was so good I threatened to steal the chef... and I did.' He chuckled.

'Isn't he amazing?' Greta asked, gazing at Leo, her eyes filled with so much love, Cass had to look away.

The evening was almost over, when Leo casually said, 'You'll never guess who booked into the resort today… Ray Morgan.'

There was a moment's silence, then Greta gave a whoop of delight. 'I used to love watching him on his breakfast show. It was so sad to hear of his wife's death last month. I wonder what he's doing in Bellbird Bay.'

Cass felt a chill run down her spine. Ray was here… in Bellbird Bay, in this hotel. She was afraid to look around in case he was here in the restaurant. She was glad she hadn't accepted Justin's suggestion to expand into beachwear for men. He'd have no reason to come into *Sassy's*. With a bit of luck, he wouldn't be here for long, and she'd be able to avoid him. She'd managed to put her relationship with Ray Morgan to the back of her mind and intended it to stay there. The last thing she wanted was to be reminded of that shameful episode.

Twenty-six

Mick was glad it was raining on Saturday. The weather matched his mood perfectly, even though the heavy rain and wind meant there would be no whale-watching that day. He sent a text to Justin then, a cup of black coffee at his side, set about cancelling those passengers booked on cruises and rescheduling them where possible.

Although regretting the loss of business, he was glad to be spared having to pretend to be cheerful when all he wanted to do was to curse himself for being so weak as to tell Cass they couldn't meet again. *Had it been a mistake? Could they have formed a relationship?* There was something about Cass which spoke to him, something so different from other women he'd known, different even from Greta, though it was her vulnerability which had drawn him to her when he returned from his gap year to find her lost and alone. He'd seen his chance and taken it, and Jo was the result, his lovely daughter.

That reminded him. He was to have dinner with Jo and Bryan that evening, along with Bryan's daughter, Mia. Mick's face softened at the thought of the little girl who now called him Grandpa. She'd been through a lot, losing her mother, being uprooted from her home, but she'd come through relatively unscathed, and was now devoted to Jo, who loved her as if she was her own daughter, the daughter she'd lost.

Mick spent the morning calling passengers and catching up with the paperwork he'd let slide, then contacted Justin to join him on the boat to help with some maintenance. He wanted to ask the boy about Cass, how she'd been this morning, but decided it would be unwise, so kept his silence.

By the time the day was over, he was ready for a hot shower and looking forward to the evening ahead.

*

'Grandpa Mick!' Mia ran to greet him at the door, and he swept her up into his arms, pretending to groan under her weight. 'Did you see any whales today?'

'Not today sweetheart. It was too wet and windy for my boat, today.'

'Dad, are you sure you should be doing that?' Jo joined them as Mia slid out of his grasp. 'Remember what the doctor said about over-exerting yourself.'

'It would be pretty sad if I couldn't pick this little charmer up and give her a cuddle,' Mick said, but he knew Jo was right. He needed to take care if he was to avoid another heart attack. He'd had two already and a third could be fatal.

'Can I tempt you to a non-alcoholic beer?' Bryan asked, as they entered the kitchen. 'Jo bought some specially.'

Mick grimaced and threw his daughter a look. She was smiling. 'Okay,' he said, willing to go along with Jo for now, but sure the odd glass of beer wasn't going to kill him.

While Bryan was pouring the beer, Mick walked over to the glass door which opened out onto the deck facing the boardwalk. On the other side was the ocean which tonight was roaring in fury, just as it had been all day.

'I'm guessing you weren't out in it today,' Bryan said, joining him and handing him a glass.

'Thanks.' Mick took a tentative sip. It wasn't bad. Almost like the real thing. 'No, not today, Bryan. Only a fool would risk going out when it's like this. This is a great place you have here. Jo's mother and I would have given our eye teeth to have been able to afford one of these houses on the boardwalk.'

'It's thanks to Dad, Mick. I couldn't have afforded it, either. But when he moved in with Bev, he didn't want to sell, so it was a win for me… and Jo.' He put an arm around Jo and pulled her into him.

Mick smiled, glad Jo had found Bryan and was happy with him. He remembered the sad young woman who'd returned from London and marvelled at the difference in her. It was amazing what the love of a good man could do.

'We're eating in here, Dad. I thought it would be cosier,' Jo said, gesturing to the scrubbed wooden table set with cutlery and an array of colourful pottery plates. The aroma of cooking was making Mick hungry. He realised he hadn't eaten all day, apart from a sandwich at lunchtime.

After a delicious meal of spaghetti Bolognese, during which Bryan asked knowledgeable questions about Mick's whale-watching business, interrupted by Mia wanting to know more about the whales – she'd been fascinated by them on a tour the previous year – Jo said, 'Time for bed, sweetie,' to Mia.

'Can Grandpa read me a story?' She looked so pleadingly at Mick, he couldn't refuse.

'Are you sure, Dad?' Jo asked.

'I'm sure. It's a long time since I read a bedtime story, but I haven't forgotten how.' He grinned and followed Jo and Mia to the little girl's bedroom.

The book Mia presented him with was one which he remembered reading to Jo when she was Mia's age. *The Lion, the Witch and the Wardrobe* was an old favourite, and he was soon reunited with the adventures of the four children as they entered the kingdom of Narnia. He was reading along, enjoying the story, when he noticed Mia's eyes had closed. Closing the book, he placed it on the bedside table, kissed her forehead and left the bedroom, closing the door quietly behind him.

Downstairs, he found Jo and Bryan enjoying coffee in front of a wood fire.

'Coffee, Dad?' Jo asked, rising. 'It's been so cold today we lit the fire. Come and sit down. Did Mia tire you out?'

'Thanks to coffee, and, no, she didn't tire me. It took me back to when you were her age and I read the same book to you.'

'You did? I don't remember.' Jo wandered out.

'That's the sad part,' Mick said to Bryan, his eyes following Jo. 'They don't remember the way you do.' He sighed. 'Enjoy Mia while you can. All too soon she'll be grown up and have forgotten these special times you had together.'

'My dad says the same.' Bryan chuckled. 'It's amazing how Mia has changed in the short time we've been here. Jo's been a big help to her… first as her teacher, and then when we got together. She's been good for both of us.'

'Now, Dad,' Jo said when she'd returned with not only coffee, but a plate of brownies which Mick recognised as coming from *The Pandanus Café*. 'What's happening with you and Brenda? You were wrong when you said she wasn't interested in you. She's been asking me about you. You're not being fair to her, Dad.'

Mick took a sip of coffee and picked up a brownie, wondering how he could stall Jo. It was a reminder he hadn't called Brenda, hoping she'd forget about him. He should have known. He should call.

Jo was gazing at him expectantly.

'Nothing's happening. We had dinner a couple of times. She's a nice woman, but not for me, Jo. As I've told you I'm happy as I am, and quite capable of finding my own woman if I want one.' The image of Cass Marshall swam behind his eyes.

'But, Dad, don't you…'

'Leave your dad.' Bryan put his hand on her arm. 'I'm sure if and when he wants another partner, he'll find one. Look what happened to my dad. He and Bev are happy together and they didn't need you or anyone else to matchmake.'

'No, but…

'Leave it, Jo.' Mick knew she only had good intentions at heart, but it was a sad reflection on his love life – or lack of it – that his daughter wanted to fix him up.

The rest of the evening passed pleasantly, but when Jo was hugging Mick goodnight, she whispered, 'I haven't finished with you, Dad. I'll find someone for you yet. Just wait.'

Twenty-seven

Cass spent another restless night. She couldn't believe Ray Morgan had turned up in Bellbird Bay. It was the last place she'd have expected him to be. If he wanted a holiday he'd be swanning off to Bali, or the Maldives, even Florida. Certainly not a sleepy town on Queensland's Sunshine Coast.

Wakening unrefreshed, Cass spent longer under the shower than usual, trying to become fully awake. Today the sun was shining, as it often did after a day like yesterday. It made it difficult to believe it had really been such a dreadful day.

Justin was already finishing breakfast, and Hector had been fed, when Cass entered the kitchen. She had taken time with her makeup in an attempt to hide the ravages of her sleepless night and it seemed she'd succeeded. 'Looking good, Cass,' he said. 'Mick wants me to get going early, so although it's Sunday, I'll need to be off.'

After Justin left, Cass made herself a slice of toast and sat down at the table with a cup of coffee. This wasn't her typical morning routine. Preferring peppermint tea first thing, but this morning she was in need of a caffeine hit. But it didn't prevent her from buying her usual two cups from *The Bay Café* on the way past, one for her and one for Greta. It was a habit she'd developed soon after opening *Sassy's*, and she'd never questioned why she was always the one who bought their early morning coffees.

Those few minutes drinking coffee and chatting with Greta used to be the highlight of her day. But in the past few weeks, she'd come to dread them, fearful Greta might guess her feelings for Mick. Sometimes she wondered if it would really matter, if she was making a mountain out of a molehill. But Mick's refusal to continue to see her made her think she wasn't imagining it.

'Morning, Greta,' Cass said, placing the two coffees on the counter like every other morning and trying to pretend all was well.

But Greta didn't notice anything amiss. She was bursting to share her news with Cass. 'You should have stayed a little longer last night, Cass. After you left, Leo and I were having a glass of port at the bar, when Ray Morgan walked in. He's still a handsome man, but he looked saddened by the death of his wife. It must have been an awful shock, and…'

'You spoke to him?' Cass stared at her friend in disbelief.

'Of course. He recognised Leo and wanted to compliment him on the hotel. It seems he'd heard about it and when he wanted to get away from the press to recover from his loss, he chose to come here. Imagine?'

Cass couldn't… imagine. The Ray Morgan she knew had never been keen to avoid the press, quite the opposite. It had been over twenty years. Could he have changed so much? She didn't know what to say. Fortunately, she could see someone heading towards *Sassy's*. 'Customer. I'd better go. Catch you later,' she said, picking up her coffee and making her way out to greet her first customer of the day.

Fortunately for Cass, the good weather had brought out the customers and she didn't have time to worry about Mick or Ray until she closed up. But as soon as the last group of women left and she put the *Closed* sign on the door, it all flooded back – her misgivings about Mick and her worry about Ray.

*

Justin was his usual cheerful self over dinner, recounting various amusing episodes from his day, before saying he was going out again. *In the short time he'd been here, Justin had developed a better social life than Cass.* 'And I have tomorrow off,' he said. 'Could we maybe talk to that woman whose daughter is a marine biologist, find out when she'll be in Bellbird Bay?'

'Cleo? We can. We can have coffee there at the café.' It was some time since Cass had visited the *Pandanus Garden Centre and Café* and the cakes in the café were delicious.

'Awesome!'

Several minutes later, when Cass was filling Hector's bowls, Justin popped his head in again. 'There's a man at the door,' he said.

'What?' But Justin had already left. Curious, Cass made her way to the front door, Hector padding behind her. She stopped, her heart beating madly. 'What are you doing here?' she asked the man standing there.

'I came to see you,' Ray Morgan replied with the smarmy smile she remembered.

How could she ever have thought it charming? 'How did you find me?'

'It wasn't difficult. Are you going to invite me in?'

Cass hesitated, the unworthy thought flitting through her head that she wished she was wearing something smarter than the leggings and oversized sweater she'd changed into when she came home. Then she said, 'You'd better come in.'

She didn't want him here, in her house. But if they stood on the doorstep for long, it would be all round Bellbird Bay that Cass Marshall of *Sassy's* had been standing at her door talking to the famous Ray Morgan.

'I don't know why you're here,' Cass said, standing in the middle of the kitchen into which Ray had followed her. Her arms were folded. 'I don't have anything to say to you.'

'Don't be like that, Cassie, after I've come all this way to see you.'

'You what?' Cass swallowed, trying not to show her irritation. She was annoyed with herself for letting him into her house and just wanted him to leave again. 'I read about your wife. I'm sorry for your loss.'

'Come on, Cassie. This doesn't sound like you. You know how I've always felt about you. You never married? The young man I met at the door?' He looked around the room as if to see signs of a husband and family, but there was only Hector staring fixedly at him.

'My nephew. Ray, it's been over twenty years.'

'That long? But you know I'd have been with you if I could, but while Toni was alive… the television station…' He spread his hands.

Cass stared in amazement at the man she'd once loved to distraction. *Did he really think she'd fall for his lies again?* 'Your son – it was a boy, wasn't it? – he'll be grown now.'

'Archie. He has his own life.' He dismissed the son whose birth had forced her to see Ray for what he really was.

'As I have mine, and there is no place in it for you. I'd like you to leave now.' *Before I throw something at you.*

'You're not going to offer me a drink for old times' sake?'

'I don't keep alcohol in the house,' she lied. 'And even if I did, I wouldn't be offering it to you.'

Sensing her tone, Hector gave a yowl and extended his claws, ready to pounce.

Cass smiled at the cat's protective gesture. 'Even my cat wants you to leave,' she said.

'Okay, okay.' Ray put his hands up defensively. 'But I'm going to be in town for a bit, so I'm sure we'll see each other again. Maybe by next time, you'll have changed your mind.'

Cass closed the door behind him and stood with her back against it, breathing heavily, Hector winding himself protectively around her ankles. Thank goodness Ray had gone. She'd been afraid he wasn't going to leave. What would she have done if he'd sat down and refused to move?

Shaking from delayed shock, Cass made her way back to the kitchen and poured herself a glass of the brandy she kept for emergencies. Sitting there, the glass clasped in both hands, she reflected on how Ray seemed to think that after over twenty years he could turn up in her life and she'd be glad to see him, to pick up where they left off. Didn't the fool remember it was she who had left him? She had turned her life around and made a new life for herself. And, although she often felt there was a man-sized space in it, Ray Morgan was the last person she wanted to fill it.

Twenty-eight

Sunday had been busy, both morning and afternoon cruises fully booked, many of those from Saturday's cancelled cruises choosing to rebook as soon as they could. Mick sent Justin off early, sensing the young man had something planned for the evening and was eager to get away. He'd been pleased, too, when Mick told him to take Monday off.

There weren't any tours booked for the next day. Although he could have his bookings filled every day at this time of year, Mick was aware of his need to take things easy and of his promise to Jo. As a result, he made sure to keep some sort of balance in his life, and having the odd day off was his way of doing it.

In anticipation of the break, he decided a meal at the club was in order with maybe a beer to wash away the day. He'd be sure to find someone to talk to and while away a few hours.

A quick trip home to shower and change, and he was back in his car and on his way.

As he anticipated, as soon as he reached the top of the stairs, he saw Will Rankin and Martin Cooper standing at the bar. He joined them.

'Just the man we were talking about,' Will said, as Mick was placing his order.

'Oh, yeah?'

The young barman, who Mick knew was Martin's stepson, served his drink, and Mick took a gulp. It went down well. He wiped his lips with the back of his hand.

'What were you saying about me?'

'Coop was telling me how the women were swooning over the shots he took of you on your boat.'

'What?' Mick felt himself redden.

'Yeah, seems even an old guy like you can still attract the women.' Will chuckled.

'Mmm.' Mick took another gulp of beer.

'No, seriously, mate,' Martin said. 'The ones with you have sold out, even before those of the whales.'

'Still got it,' Will said with another chuckle. 'Maybe…'

'I'm done with women,' Mick said. 'All I want is a peaceful life but try telling that to Jo.'

'Your daughter trying to set you up?' Martin asked.

'Tell me about it. First with a woman she teaches with. I even took her to dinner. Nice woman, but…' He shook his head. 'I'm too old for all that stuff,' he lied, Cass's image flitting behind his eyes again. 'I thought Greta and I… but I was too late. I guess it was a sign.'

'A sign? You sound like Ruby Sullivan,' Will laughed.

Mick remembered bumping into the old woman at the gallery opening. He'd forgotten till now. What was it she'd said to him, something about the past and his fate being in that room? Well, half the town was there that night, plus a few tourists.

'Now she's more mobile than on that old bike of hers, she's everywhere,' Martin said. 'I caught sight of her at the garden centre the other day when I was talking with Bev. There's no stopping her.'

'And I suppose she's offering her nuggets of wisdom to all and sundry,' Mick said with a note of bitterness.

'Oh-oh, what has she been saying to you?' Martin asked with a grin.

'Nothing.' Mick shifted uncomfortably.

'She's not as foolish as you might think. It pays to listen to her,' Will said seriously. 'If she did tell you something, Mick, it's wise to keep it in mind. Don't dismiss her as a stupid old woman. She may be old but she's as wise as the hills.'

'Hmm.' Mick looked around the club, as Will and Martin prepared to leave. Seeing Jo and Bryan with Aaron and Mel Crawford at a table on the far side of the club, he decided to steer clear of them. He had enough ear bashing from his daughter last night to last him for some time.

He ordered his meal, one of the burrito bowls he'd had with Cass and, to his surprise discovered he enjoyed it, and headed out to the deck with the remains of his beer. He immediately found himself hailed by Ted Crawford.

'Mick, why don't you join us? Grace and I decided to eat out here and leave the young ones to chat inside. I see your daughter and her young man are with them this evening.'

'Thanks, Ted. Don't mind if I do.' He liked Ted, another local like Martin, who had left Bellbird Bay, only to return and find happiness. Grace wasn't a local, having only moved here a few years earlier. It was her son, Ben, who was involved with Kerri-Ann, the marine biologist he'd mentioned to Justin.

'How's life treating you, Mick?' Grace asked in her gentle voice. Ted had done well to find someone like her, someone without the baggage every other woman seemed to have. Though, he remembered, she did have three children, and not everything had gone well for her when she first arrived. But all was good now, with her daughter, Mel, married to Ted's son, Aaron, and another baby on the way, he'd heard.

'Not so bad, Grace. Can't complain,' he lied. But it was what you did in polite company. Where would they be if everyone unloaded their problems onto everyone else? What would they say if instead, he said, 'My daughter is trying to set me up with what she thinks are suitable women, while I'm falling in love with my ex-wife's best friend and...' He stopped himself. *Falling in love with Cass?* He realised Grace was speaking to him.

'Sorry, Grace. You were saying?'

'Have you heard that Sydney breakfast television host is staying at *The Leonard Family Resort?*'

'Who?'

'Grace,' Ted put a restraining hand on Grace's arm, 'Mick's probably not interested. He may not even know who you're talking about.'

'Sorry, Mick, and I don't usually repeat gossip. But when I lived in Granite Springs, before I came here and met Ted...' She sent her partner an affectionate glance which filled Mick with an unexpected envy. What he'd give to have Cass look at him like that. 'Ray Morgan was the face that filled our screens every morning. I think he's still on the air. I read his wife died recently. They'd been married a long time. Both Ted and I know how that feels.'

Ted squeezed her hand.

'What's someone like him doing in Bellbird Bay?' Mick asked, perplexed as to why they were even talking about some television personality he'd never heard of. But it was better than sitting with Jo and having her start listing possible women for him to date.

'Probably trying to avoid the media… and the gossips,' Ted said with a meaningful glance at Grace, who only smiled.

Their meals arrived, and Mick looked enviously at the club's special burger and chips on Ted's plate, wishing he didn't have to watch his diet. Grace had ordered the salmon with a salad.

'Another beer?' Ted asked, pointing to Mick's empty glass.

'No thanks, Ted. One's my limit these days. Doctor's orders.'

'But you're okay now?' Grace asked in concern.

'I'm fine, as long as I'm careful and keep up with my medication. Jo makes sure I stick to the plan,' he said with a rueful grin. *If only that was all Jo was concerned about.*

The conversation moved on from the Sydney television star and Mick's health to the cricket currently being played in England, and the prospects for the Australian team. Mick wasn't a rabid cricket fan, but could talk the talk and understand Ted, who was a keen follower and had played in his younger days.

Grace tuned out when they were talking sport, only joining in again when Ted said, 'I hear you have a young offsider with you these days, Cass Marshall's nephew.'

'Yes.' *How did Ted know?* 'He's been a big help.'

'Isn't he from England? Won't he be going home soon?' Grace asked.

Mick rubbed his chin. 'Maybe not. I may have put the cat among the pigeons there. He's developed a real interest in the ocean and sea creatures, whales in particular, and I might have suggested he stay on in Australia and study marine biology.'

Ted nodded. 'He'd be best going to James Cook University.'

'That's what I told him.'

'What does Cass think about it?'

Mick looked down at the table. 'I don't know.'

'Ben and Kerri-Ann are planning to come down for a few days. Maybe he could arrange to meet her. It's what she does up there in Townsville – marine biology.'

'I thought of her,' Mick said. 'So your son's still up that way too?' he asked Grace.

'Still working on the archeological dig. He and Kerri-Ann have been seeing a lot of each other. We're hoping…' She sent a glance in Ted's direction.

'Nothing to do with me,' Ted said, 'but Grace and Cleo have their hopes up. Another wedding!' He pretended to sigh in annoyance, but the twinkle in his eyes belied it.

'I'll let Justin know,' Mick said. He wondered if Cass knew, and whether she thought he'd overstepped the mark with his suggestion to Justin. He wished he could talk to her about it, that they could at least be friends. But her statement that it would be better not to see each other again had sounded very final.

Twenty-nine

Cass loved Monday mornings. Much as she enjoyed *Sassy's*, the prospect of having the whole day to herself, the chance to sleep for as long as she liked, was something she relished. This morning the sun was shining through the plantation shutters when she woke up later than usual and wandered through to the kitchen. To her surprise, she'd slept well, though it had taken her a long time to fall asleep, the memory of Ray's visit refusing to leave her.

But today was a new day and she had promised to take Justin to *The Pandanus Café*. There would be little chance of meeting Ray there. The Ray she remembered wouldn't be seen dead in a garden centre, and the attached café wouldn't be to his taste.

Had he really come to Bellbird Bay to see her? Cass shuddered at the thought. Who in their right mind would try to rekindle a twenty-year-old love affair – if that's what it had been? She'd imagined herself in love at the time, and thought he was, too. But she'd soon changed her mind, disillusioned when he'd announced his wife's pregnancy on air. And, having seen so many couples here in Bellbird Bay who obviously loved each other, she now knew what she had thought was love had been something else entirely.

'Who was he?'

'Who?' Cass looked up from her peppermint tea. She'd been lost in thought, holding her mug in both hands.

'The man at the door last night… when I was going out.'

'Oh, him. Someone I used to know. No one important.' Cass wished she could dismiss the memory of Ray as easily.

'Oh.' Justin lost interest. 'When are we going to this café?'

'As soon as I get myself organised. Okay with you if we stop at the nursing home first? Mum seems to expect me on a Monday morning, even though she hasn't been well.'

'Okay. I promised to see someone this afternoon for a game of beach volleyball.' He blushed.

Cass smiled to herself. She'd been right. There was a girl involved. She knew the girls he'd mentioned seeing with Zack. Zack's girlfriend was Fliss, who'd arrived in Bellbird Bay with her mother and was staying at Headland House with Ruby Sullivan. Her mother now ran the successful catering business, *Celebrations*. She provided cakes for *The Pandanus Café*, baked the most spectacular creations for special occasions, and had catered for Greta's wedding. Fliss's friends were Jenny and Megan and all three girls often shopped at *Sassy's*. Cass wondered which of them had caught Justin's eye.

Cass gave a sigh. She remembered what it had been like to suffer the pangs of first love. She'd been several years younger than Justin – girls did mature earlier – and her teenage passion for Mick had been unrequited. She sighed again. *Why did almost everything make her think of Mick?*

Cass drained her cup and swallowed the last bite of toast. Then she checked on Hector, before heading to the shower.

Half an hour later, dressed in a pair of jeans, a sweater in her favourite shade of hot pink, and a pair of white sneakers, Cass popped her head into Justin's room. 'Ready?'

Justin hastily closed his phone, but not before Cass caught sight of a string of messages. 'Okay, Cass.'

Cass hid a smile. Both Jenny and Megan would be in school right now. She could understand why some schools were banning mobile phones. In her day, it had been notes on slips of paper passed around the classroom. 'All done?' she asked.

Justin shrugged and stuffed his phone into his pocket. The tips of his ears turned red.

*

'Should I come in to see Grandma with you?' Justin asked when they were on their way.

'Not if you don't want to. If she's lucid, I'm sure she'd love to see you.' She glanced at her nephew out of the corner of her eye. 'I know your last experience with her wasn't a good one. Let's decide when we get there.'

'Okay.'

When they reached the nursing home, Cass could tell Justin wasn't keen to go inside. 'You wait here,' she said. 'I probably won't be long. Mum hasn't really been up to visitors lately.'

'Thanks, Cass.' Justin took out his phone.

Once inside, Cass made her way to her mother's room and pushed open the door. Today, as on her last visit, the older woman was in bed, her eyes wide open but unfocussed. 'Hello, Mum. It's me. Cass,' she said, going towards the bed and taking her mother's hand.

Jean pulled it away and made no sign of recognition.

The door opened and one of the nursing assistants walked in. 'Your mother's been like this since you last visited. I'm afraid she might be coming towards the end. I'm sorry.'

A tear formed in the corner of Cass's eye and trickled down her cheek. She wiped it away, and looked at her mother's face, pale against the white pillow. She appeared peaceful, neither happy nor sad, and the agitation and anger she'd previously shown during Cass's visits was nowhere to be seen. *This was almost worse.* Cass sat there for another fifteen minutes before deciding to leave. 'Can I come back later?' she asked at reception.

'Of course. At this stage, you're able to visit any time.'

'Thanks.' Cass hurried out. She knew she'd need to call Vi again. Maybe the news their mother was dying would strike a chord with her. Cass could only try. It was too late to call now. She'd do it this evening, when it would be morning there.

She was so engrossed in her thoughts, saddened by the realisation her mother was at the end of her life, despite the fact she hadn't been the woman Cass remembered for some time, that she didn't notice the man chatting to Justin, until she was almost at the car.

'Morning, Cass.' Mick smiled.

Cass's heart began to race. Of course, he would be here to visit his dad. 'Mick.'

'How is your mother – bad news?' he asked.

Cass became aware her eyes must be puffy from crying. 'Yes. She's on her last legs. I knew it would be soon but…'

'You're never prepared for something like that.' He made a tentative movement towards her, then stopped, as if frozen. 'I'm sorry,' he said.

'Thanks,' she said, part of her wishing he would pull her into a hug. It was what she needed right now, to feel his arms around her, to feel some sort of affection. But she had no right to expect that from Mick.

'Is Grandma going to die?' Justin asked, when Cass got into the car.

Cass could only nod. It wasn't till they had almost reached the garden centre that she managed to find her voice. 'I'm going to call your mum tonight,' she said, 'tell her if she wants to see our mother again, she needs to book a flight.'

'Mum? Here?' Justin sounded appalled.

'She's her mother, too, Justin. I think… hope… she'd want to be here.' *And I shouldn't have to deal with this on my own.*

'But…' Justin fell silent.

Cass couldn't stop thinking about her mother passing. She'd known it was only a matter of time, but had hoped… What had she hoped – for a miracle?

'We're here.' Cass tried to inject a more positive note into her voice when she drew up in the garden centre car park. She owed it to Justin to be more cheerful. He'd only met his grandmother once and couldn't be expected to feel sad about her passing. But Cass remembered the kind, loving woman who had brought her and Vi up, who had encouraged them both to follow their dreams. It was difficult to associate her with the sad figure lying in Rosebank Nursing Home.

But they were here to help Justin follow *his* dream. Life went on. She took a deep breath and stepped out of the car.

When they walked through the hedge into the café, Cass could see Cleo talking to some customers. She and Justin chose a table close to the kitchen and ordered camomile tea for her and coffee for Justin, along with a plate of Ruby Sullivan's delicious brownies. Cass knew that although Sandy of *Celebrations* had taken over most of the baking for the café, Ruby still provided many of the items for which she was famous.

They had almost finished their drinks and the plate of brownies was reduced to crumbs by the time Cass managed to attract Cleo's attention. Justin had shown a surprising degree of sympathy for his age and had asked Cass about what his grandmother had been like when she and his mother were growing up. The recounting of happy memories had gone some way to helping Cass recover from the sad news.

'You wanted to speak to me?' Cleo took a seat at their table. 'Can I get you something more to drink?' she nodded to their empty cups.

'Justin?' Cass asked.

He shook his head. 'But maybe another brownie?'

'Thanks, Cleo. And I'd love another cup of camomile tea.' Cass found the tea was helping soothe her.

Cleo called on a waitress to place the order. 'Now, what's up?' she asked. She peered at Cass. 'You look as if you've had bad news.'

'It's my mother...' Cass felt close to tears again. 'Sorry, I just visited her in the nursing home, and they told me she doesn't have long left.'

'Oh, Cass. I'm so sorry.'

'Thanks. But it's not why we're here.' She closed her eyes for a moment, then glanced at Justin. 'Justin's working with Mick Roberts. *Bay Whale Cruises*,' she added.

'Really? I thought Mick liked to work alone.'

Cass ploughed on, 'Mick has suggested that given Justin's interest in sea creatures, he might enjoy studying marine biology. I know your... Kerri-Ann is a marine biologist and thought, maybe...'

The waitress returned with Cass's tea and Justin's brownie, which he tucked into eagerly.

'Thanks,' Cass sipped at her tea.

'I'm sure Kerri-Ann would be delighted to talk with him about it. She'll be here in a few days' time, her and Ben, Grace Winter's son. Why don't you both come to dinner while she's here?'

'Oh, we couldn't...' Cass felt awkward, almost as if she'd asked for the invitation. She'd only wanted to fix up a time for Justin to talk with the girl. Although she'd known Cleo for years, and they belonged to the same book club, they weren't close friends and she'd never visited her and Will's home.

'Of course you can. It's time we got to know each other better, anyway. I always seem too busy for any sort of social life. It's amazing

Will and I ever managed to get together, and now he's mayor…' She chuckled.

Cass felt even worse. 'That's very kind of you.' She stole a glance at Justin who was beaming with delight. 'We'd love to.'

'Good, that's settled. Give me your number and I'll get a date to you when I know what we're doing. It's always a challenge trying to arrange things with the young people.'

'Thanks,' Cass said again, quickly sending a message to the café's number.

'Now, I really should get back to the kitchen. It's been lovely talking to you, and meeting you, Justin. Always good to meet a young person who knows what they want to do.'

'She's nice,' Justin said, when they were back in the car. 'Thanks, Cass.' He hesitated. 'When you talk to Mum, will you need to tell her…?'

'Not yet, Justin. But she'll find out what you're doing and your plans when… if… she comes to Bellbird Bay.'

Justin sighed. He didn't speak for the remainder of the trip home.

*

Cass had been on edge ever since they returned from the garden centre to find an enormous bunch of flowers waiting for her on the doorstep. She didn't have to check the card to know who they were from. They had Ray Morgan written all over them. It reminded her of how impressed she'd been when he sent her flowers all those years ago. Not anymore. To Justin's obvious surprise, she tossed them in the bin, glad when he didn't comment. She'd been anxious enough knowing she needed to talk with her sister, without the reminder of Ray's presence in town.

Now, Justin was in his room and, if she didn't phone Vi now, she wouldn't catch her before she went to work. That was the trouble with trying to communicate with her sister. The time was never right. She picked up her phone.

This time, to her relief, it was her sister who answered, her voice irritated. 'Hello?'

'Vi, it's Cass.'

'Cass, what is it now? I don't have much time.'

'It's Mum.'

Vi must have sensed something in Cass's voice, because hers immediately softened. 'She's not…?'

'Not yet, but they say it won't be long. If you want to see her again, you should arrange to come… as soon as possible.'

'Oh! Oh, Cass, I know you said she was poorly, but… I didn't realise…' There was a pause, during which Cass heard her sister talking to her husband, the words indistinct, then, 'I'll check out the flights, see if I can get time off work. Roger won't be able to come, of course.'

'Of course not.' *As one of the most successful barristers in England, Cass's brother-in-law was too important to travel to Australia because his mother-in-law was dying.* 'I'll let you know when I have a flight booked. Tell Justin we…' The remainder of her conversation was lost as the line crackled, and the call ended.

Thirty

Mick watched Cass and Justin drive away, wishing he'd given in to the temptation to pull her into his arms and give her a warm hug. She had looked so sad and vulnerable, but he had no right to give her the sort of comfort he knew she needed. If only… He shook his head and continued on his way. It had been serendipity that his visit to his dad coincided with Cass's to her mum. His heart had given a leap when he saw her car, then Justin. Then, when he saw her diminutive figure walking towards them, her head bowed, he had known her mother had taken a turn for the worse.

But there was no sense in worrying about what might have been. They'd made their decision. Now, he needed to focus on his own family challenges, visit his dad and attempt to have the difficult conversation about what was going to happen when Fred was able to leave the nursing home.

He found his dad sitting by the window staring out at the garden. 'Nice view, Dad.'

'Hmph.'

Not a good start. 'How are you feeling today?'

'I'll be feeling a lot better when I get home again.'

'And that won't be till the doc says you can. Are they taking good care of you?'

'I suppose. But it's not home.'

'About that, Dad. Pete and I have been talking…'

'I'm sure you have. It's all you two do… talk. I suppose you're going to go on about moving me into a retirement home, are you?' He folded his arms.

'*Bay Village Lifestyle Resort* isn't a retirement home. It's for over-fifties. Hell, Pete and I could move in.'

'Then why don't you?' he chuckled. 'Then I could visit *you* there.'

'Dad! We're only trying to help. The house is too big for you on your own. It has been since Mum died. It's too much work. In a smaller place…'

'It's where your mother and I spent all our married life. It's filled with memories. You wouldn't know about that, you or Pete. Neither of you could sustain a relationship. Moving from there would be like losing her all over again.' Tears formed in the corner of his dad's eyes.

Mick felt bad. He only had his dad's best interests at heart. He hadn't considered how much the house meant to him, the memories. It had memories for him, too, memories of Pete and him growing up there, playing in the backyard, doing their homework at the kitchen table while their mother was cooking in the big family kitchen, their dad pottering in the garden. 'I remember Mum there, too, Dad, but you'd take your memories with you.'

By the time he left, Mick wasn't any further forward. His dad was still adamant he wasn't going anywhere, that he'd only leave his house in a wooden box. He sighed. He'd tried. He'd promised Pete he would. Now it was up to his brother to see if he could persuade the old man.

Driving home, his thoughts were filled with the memories the conversation with his dad had evoked, memories of his happy childhood. What would happen to the family home if Dad did move, if it was sold? It would be the end of an era. Neither he nor Pete wanted to live there. It was a family home, not one for a single man, and he already had a house he loved.

He respected the sense of history his dad had, the connection of the house to his past. Mick didn't have that. The house Jo had grown up in had been sold at the divorce, Greta going to live in her old family home, which he guessed held memories for her. He wondered if Jo missed it. It hadn't occurred to him until now. He had been too distressed by the entire process, by the ending of his marriage. Even though he knew he was to blame, it had been a wrench. And now he and Pete were trying to drag their dad away from the only home he'd known in Mick's lifetime.

The house he currently lived in, the one he had bought after he and Greta separated and divorced, held no memories. His thoughts turned again to Cass, visualising her there. He could see her there, on the deck, drinking a glass of wine with him, enjoying the view. They could be making memories of their own, if only…

*

'You're looking very cheerful this morning,' Mick said next morning, when Justin arrived with a big grin on his face.

'That marine biologist you told me about. Cass took me to meet her mother. She's coming to Bellbird Bay and I'm going to meet her.'

'That's great.' Cass had pre-empted Mick's own news about Kerri-Ann coming to town. 'Any more news about your grandmother?'

Justin shook his head. 'Cass called this morning and there was no change. She called my mother, too.' He grimaced.

'Not good?'

'She asked her to come here.'

'You won't be pleased to see her?'

'She's going to find out I'm working with you and… about me staying in Australia to study.'

'She was going to find out sometime.'

'Yeah.' Justin looked down at the deck as if he could read the future on the worn boards. 'I suppose. Anyway,' he looked up, 'she may not come.'

'And your dad?'

'He's too busy, too important…' Justin sneered. 'He's always considered Australia to be the end of the earth, tried to pretend Mum didn't come from here.'

'And your aunt?' Mick couldn't stop himself enquiring about Cass. She'd been on his mind since seeing her in the nursing home car park.

'She's sad about Grandma, and I think she wants Mum to come to share her burden of grief.'

'Right.' *What a perceptive attitude from one so young.* This young man was a constant surprise to him. He sometimes seemed old beyond his years.

'Okay, the passengers for the morning tour will be arriving shortly, so we'd better get to work.'

Justin didn't reply but set to doing the tasks Mick had allocated him, and by the time they were ready to cast off, everything was organised.

The day went swiftly. The whales appeared on schedule. And Mick once again considered his options. Buying another boat would stretch him financially, and he'd have to take on more staff. Justin would be gone at the end of the season – or maybe the end of the year. But the extra income would more than compensate for the additional outlay. He'd do the numbers, talk with his accountant and his bank manager, and see what he could come up with. He was already turning away customers due to lack of places.

If only his personal life could be solved with a chat to the accountant and bank manager. If Cass wasn't Greta's best friend. Or if he could develop an interest in one of Jo's matches – he was sure she'd come up with more, now he had dismissed Brenda as a possibility. She'd been graceful, when he called to say he'd prefer to stay friends, but he didn't think they had a future together. It had almost made him change his mind – almost.

He thought of the conversation with Martin about growing old alone. Was that what he wanted to do? Was he too old already? At fifty-eight, he didn't feel old, but what did old feel like? His dad said he still felt like he was twenty inside. It was only his body that had aged.

He conjured up the image of Cass as he'd last seen her. Maybe he'd bump into her again next time he visited his dad. Meantime, he'd concentrate on his business, check out his options, and talk more with Pete about how they could convince their dad to move.

Thirty-one

It was two days since Cass had called Vi, and there was still no news from her. Cass was visiting the nursing home each day now after closing *Sassy's*, but there was no change, her mother still confined to bed and failing to recognise her. Each time she visited, Cass harboured the faint hope she'd see Mick there again, but what was the point? Their last meeting had proved awkward. It would be best to forget him, forget the feelings he'd aroused in her, and become accustomed to spending the rest of her life alone.

Cass was hurrying from *Sassy's* to the car park, her mind on what she was going to find at the nursing home, when she got the strange feeling she was being followed. She turned and stared around, but there was no one in sight. She continued on her way, but the feeling persisted. She was glad when she reached her car and was safely locked inside.

Her mother looked exactly the same as she had yesterday… and the day before, and the day before that. She was beginning to wonder if there was any point in visiting day after day but knew if she stopped and something happened, she'd never forgive herself. Damn Vi! She should be here, too.

Back home, Justin had fed Hector and had taken a chicken casserole from the fridge and put it into the oven. 'I thought it would save you the hassle,' he replied in response to Cass's fervent thanks.

He was a good kid. Cass couldn't imagine why Roger and Vi had thought it necessary to send him away. But their loss was her gain.

After dinner, when Justin had gone to his room, where he seemed to spend most of his time when he was home, Cass curled up on the sofa with Hector on her lap. 'You're my best buddy, Hector,' she said to the recumbent cat, 'the only male I need in my life.' But she couldn't help thinking about Mick, remembering their one date and the frisson she'd experienced at his touch.

Then she remembered the strange feeling she'd had on her way to the car park. Had she been imagining it? Who would be following her in Bellbird Bay? It must have been someone else taking a similar route. She put it out of her mind. But later, when she was closing her bedroom curtains, she thought she caught sight of a figure standing across the road in the darkness. It sent a shiver down her spine.

*

'What's up with you this morning?' Greta asked, when Cass entered with their coffees next morning. 'You look as if you haven't slept.'

'Thanks a lot.' Cass had tried to conceal the dark shadows under her eyes with makeup, but clearly hadn't succeeded. 'I had the strangest experience last night. I felt I was being followed to the car park, but there was no one there. Then I thought I saw someone watching the house.' As she spoke, Cass realised how stupid it sounded. 'Oh, I'm probably imagining things. Forget it.'

Greta stared at her. 'Who could be following you?'

'I don't know.' But Cass had a sneaking suspicion. It was just the sort of thing Ray would do in an attempt to intimidate her. But surely even he wouldn't dare risk something like that in Bellbird Bay?

It was two hours later, and Cass was helping a young woman decide between a daring bikini and a less revealing one-piece swimsuit when she glanced out the window and there, standing on the other side of the esplanade was Ray Morgan, leaning against the sea wall. She gulped and lost track of what she was saying.

'What do you think?' the customer asked, seemingly unable to make up her own mind.

'You look great in the bikini,' Cass said, anxious to get her out of the shop, lest Ray take it into his head to walk in.

'Thanks, I think you're right. My boyfriend will love it,' she said.

Cass glanced out again. Maybe Ray was the boyfriend the customer was referring to. Maybe he hadn't been serious when he came to her house. When the customer left, she peered out the window again, but he had gone. *Had she imagined him? Was she seeing things?*

The rest of the day passed uneventfully, ending again with her visit to the nursing home. Tonight, her mother seemed fractionally more alert than before, leading her to hope the nursing staff might have been wrong. There was still no word from Vi and, tempted though she was to call her sister again, she refrained. She'd told her their mother was dying. It was up to Vi to decide whether to visit or not. But it wasn't fair of her to leave everything to Cass.

Back home, Cass was almost afraid to look out of the window, but when she did, the street was empty. There was no sign of the figure she'd seen the night before.

Cass was dropping off to sleep when her phone pinged with a text. Suddenly awake, alert to the fact the nursing home could contact her anytime, though they normally didn't text but called, she picked up the phone.

Booked on a flight tomorrow. Arriving Sunshine Coast 10am Monday. Can you pick me up?

Cass heaved a sigh of relief. Vi was finally coming. And Monday was perfect. Cass would be free to pick her up at the airport. She only hoped their mother would survive till then.

She quickly typed a reply.

No problem. See you then. Safe trip.

Then she closed her eyes again and fell asleep.

When she awoke next morning after the best sleep she'd had all week, the first thing Cass remembered was her sister's text.

'Your mum will be here on Monday,' she said to Justin at breakfast.

'Dad?'

Cass shook her head. 'Just your mum.'

'I suppose Dad's too busy.' Justin continued eating his Weet-Bix. 'I guess it'll be good to see her, though…' He grimaced. 'Have you heard from Cleo about her daughter?' he asked, his mind moving to what was more important to him than his mother's arrival.

'Not yet.' Cass bit her lip. Cleo had mentioned Kerri-Ann would be arriving in a few days. That had been on Monday. 'Maybe I'll hear today.' She had barely finished speaking when her phone rang.

'Hello?'

'Cass? This is Cleo.'

'Cleo. We were just talking about you.' Cass smiled across at Justin who gave her a thumbs up.

'Kerri-Ann arrived last night. She's only here for a week, but we thought we'd have a bit of a get together on Saturday evening. Just a few friends and neighbours. It would be lovely if you and Justin could join us.'

'Saturday evening.' Cass mouthed to Justin, to receive a wide grin and another thumbs up.

'That would be lovely thanks, Cleo.'

'You know where to come? I'll text you the address. Around seven?'

'Perfect, thanks. Can I bring something?'

'Just yourselves. You'll know most of the people who'll be here. Look forward to seeing you then.'

'Awesome,' Justin said when the call ended.

Justin left, and Cass cleared up the breakfast dishes and made sure Hector's bowls were filled before leaving for work. She was feeling more cheerful this morning, the news of Vi's arrival, plus Cleo's invitation putting a spring in her step and she made her way across the esplanade carrying two coffees and a bag containing two blueberry Danish pastries.

'Yum,' Greta said when she opened the bag. 'Feeling better this morning?'

'Mmm. I heard from Vi. She'll be here on Monday.'

'Oh, Cass, I'm pleased for you. It must have been hard. Your mum will be pleased to see her, too.'

'If she recognises her. But, yes, it's good news. And... Cleo rang this morning to invite Justin and me over on Saturday. It'll give him the chance to talk to her daughter, find out more about this marine biology course he's interested in and maybe provide him with information to give his mum. She's not going to be pleased, but...' Cass shrugged. She'd given up worrying about what her sister might think. It was her own fault for sending Justin to Australia.

They had finished their coffee and Cass was about to go to open Sassy's, when Greta said, 'The strangest thing...'

Cass stopped in her tracks, her stomach churning. 'What?'

'I saw Ray Morgan on the esplanade when I was coming to work this morning. He looked as if he was searching for someone or something. It was odd.'

Cass felt a shiver run down her spine. She hadn't been imagining it.

*

Cass couldn't put Greta's words out of her mind. She worried all day, finding herself staring out of the window each time the shop was empty, afraid of seeing Ray standing there watching her. But, to her relief, there was no sign of him.

She had relaxed too soon.

She had barely reached home, when there was a knock at the door. Assuming it was Justin who had forgotten his key, she opened the door, prepared to give him a roasting then laugh it off, when she saw Ray standing there, looking more penitent than last time.

Before Cass could speak, he put up one hand.

'I know what you said, Cassie, but hear me out. Please?' His pleading expression reminded Cass of how charming he could be, how he had managed to charm her in the past.

She hardened her heart. 'Say what you have to say, then you can leave.' She felt Hector appear and rub himself against her ankles. The cat wanted to protect her.

'I never forgot you, Cass. It was always you. You have to believe me. Won't you give me another chance, have dinner with me?' He smiled. 'The place I'm staying has a good restaurant, surprising in a town of this size. We could...'

'No!' Suddenly Cass, who had been lulled into a false sense of calm, came to her senses. This was the man who had promised her the world, then torn that world apart. 'I'm not the gullible young woman you knew, the one who believed your lies. I don't know how you could ever imagine I'd be interested in rekindling a relationship which died, which you managed to kill. It was a long time ago, another lifetime. I've moved on, Ray. If, as you say, you came here to see me, you're wasting your time.'

Cass was shaking when she finally closed the door behind him, hoping she'd managed to make him believe there was nothing for him here. She had enough to worry about without this reminder of her past folly appearing to torment her.

Thirty-two

Mick didn't normally follow the entertainment news, but on Saturday morning, an item caught his eye.

Sydney television breakfast host holidays in Bellbird Bay.

Reading on, he learned that the Sydney personality who he'd vaguely heard about, had been seen in their small town, presumed to be recovering from the sudden death of his wife. The article continued to list his many achievements, chief of which had been the award of the Gold Logie, the epitome of Australian television awards, awarded each year to the most popular Australian television personality. There was a photo of a man in his fifties, his dark hair sprinkled with silver, smiling at the camera.

Mick tossed the paper aside. Nothing to do with him, unless the publicity brought more tourists to Bellbird Bay and to his whale-watching cruises. He hoped the news item didn't trigger a media frenzy. The beauty of Bellbird Bay was its peaceful ambiance, and a mob of reporters and photographers arriving in the town wasn't conducive to that.

Everything went like clockwork on the morning cruise. A mother and baby humpback appeared and frolicked within sight of the boat, much to the delight of Mick's passengers, and another couple followed the boat for some distance before disappearing.

'Any word about your mum?' Mick asked Justin, when they were eating their lunch on the deck of the surf club.

Justin grimaced. 'She contacted Cass. She's arriving on Monday.'

'Do you want time off?'

'No way! I want to keep out of her way, but I don't suppose I can. Cass is pleased, though.'

Mick was glad for Cass's sake. He knew how much he relied on Pete to help out with his dad. It must have been hard for Cass to shoulder the burden of her mother's illness on her own. 'And your grandma?'

'Much the same.' Justin shrugged.

Mick checked the time. 'Better eat up. It's almost time to go, and we're fully booked again this afternoon.'

Back aboard, Mick busied himself in the cabin, leaving Justin to check the passengers on board. He'd found they responded well to the young man's cheerful manner, and his English accent prompted discussion. So, it wasn't until they were out of the bay, and he picked up the microphone and let his eyes roam over the group, that he recognised the man whose photo he'd seen in the paper that morning. Dressed in a blue blazer, a scarf loosely knotted inside the collar of a white shirt, he was lounging against the railing, wearing a supercilious smile, as if he hadn't a care in the world. He didn't give the impression of someone grieving for his wife. But what did Mick know? Maybe he was just good at hiding his emotions.

Mick glanced around, relieved there was no sign of the feared media frenzy. He began his commentary.

The tour was over, the boat tied up at the wharf, the passengers disembarking, when, 'You do that very well.' The voice was patronising, but Mick was used to all sorts.

Mick glanced up. It was the man who'd been featured in the paper, the television personality. 'Thanks'

'Ever think of filming your spiel?'

Mick felt his hackles rise. 'Not my style.'

'Hmm.' The man walked off.

Who did he think he was, coming here and suggesting…? Mick shook his head.

'Who was that?' Justin stared at the man who was heading towards the main part of the esplanade.

'Some television personality. I read about him in the paper this morning.'

'I think I've seen him somewhere before. Looks like a bit of a wanker.'

Mick stifled a grin. 'Party tonight?'

'Yes and no. Cass has arranged for us to meet this Kerri-Ann person at Will Rankin's place tonight. Should be cool. I'm hoping she can give me more information than I've been able to find on the website.'

'Good plan.'

'Mmm. It'll be good to have all the facts before I tell Mum.'

'Good luck with that.' From what Mick had heard, Justin would need all the luck he could get when he told his mother his plans.

*

Mick was home. He had just showered and changed into a pair of track pants and an old sweater and was contemplating what to have for dinner when his phone rang. A glance at the screen showed it was Jo calling.

'Jo, honey.' He hoped she wasn't about to try to introduce him to another of her teaching colleagues, or someone from her yoga class, or…

'Hey, Dad. What are you up to?'

'About to make dinner and settle down to a night in front of the television. It's been a busy day.'

'On a Saturday night? You need a better social life.'

Mick mentally shrugged. The evening he'd planned sounded all right to him.

'I know! We've been invited to welcome Kerri-Ann and Ben back for a visit. It's being held at Cleo and Will's. I'm sure you'd be welcome.'

'How…?'

'Oh, you know Bellbird Bay. Cleo and Bev are close, and now Bryan's dad and Bev are a couple… we've been invited, too. Anyway, I know Cleo's daughter, Hannah, from school. You will come, won't you?'

Mick looked down at his comfortable outfit, thought of the frozen meal he'd planned to reheat. Then he remembered what Justin had said about him and Cass being invited to Cleo's. 'Maybe I will,' he said.

Thirty-three

Cass and Justin could hear voices and music as soon as they got out of the car. It sounded like more than a few friends and family. Cass could see Mel Crawford's little girl, Isla, running around the yard and Justin let out a yell as he saw Zack chasing her.

'I didn't know Zack was going to be here,' he said with a grin. 'How does he know Cleo?'

'Bellbird Bay is a small community,' Cass said. 'Zack's stepmother's brother is Kerri-Ann's partner. They travelled down together. I expect Grace and Ted will be here, too, along with Will's son, Owen. Then there's Nate, who's the boyfriend of Cleo's daughter, Hannah, and his parents Martin and Ailsa – you've met Martin Cooper. I expect Bev and Iain will be here, too,' she said, now thinking aloud, 'and Iain's son, Bryan, and…' Her voice faltered as she remembered Bryan was now living with Mick's daughter, Jo. Greta hadn't said anything about coming tonight, in fact she'd said she and Leo were eating at the hotel, but what if Mick was here?

'Wow! You know all these people?'

'I've lived here a long time, Justin. I don't know all of them well, especially not the younger ones, but I guess I do.' There was something comforting about being part of a community like this, it gave one a sense of continuity, something that had been missing when she lived in Sydney. The thought of Sydney sent a shaft of fear through her at the memory of Ray, and his invitation, and what she'd read in the paper that morning. If it was widely known Ray Morgan was in town, it wouldn't be long before the media pack followed. Another reason to keep out of his way.

'Cass, I'm so glad to see you. Let me get you something to drink. I think you know everyone here, except perhaps Kerri-Ann and Ben. I'll...' Cleo looked around. 'Well, I'll introduce you later. Wine? White?'

'That would be lovely, thanks.' Cass followed Cleo through the house into a large family kitchen which seemed filled with people. Justin had disappeared to catch up with Zack, leaving Cass by herself for a moment till Cleo returned with a glass of wine. 'Thanks,' she said, taking a sip and glancing around. Sure enough, she did know almost everyone. The group comprised exactly the people she'd listed to Justin. They were all familiar to her, apart from a tall dark-haired young man standing with Grace and Ted and the tall girl with thick blonde hair he had his arm around. She didn't live in Bellbird Bay, but Cass recognised her from the time she'd helped the community save Dolphin Beach from the developers. It was Kerri-Ann, the girl Justin was eager to speak with.

'Hello, Cass.'

Cass turned to see Mick standing behind her. Her heart leapt. 'Mick,' she said, her stomach churning, 'What are you doing here?'

'Jo dragged me along. She's trying to improve my social life,' he chuckled. 'And...'

Cass detected a wicked gleam in his eyes.

'...Justin may have mentioned you'd be here.'

Justin! But how could he have known her secret yearnings? 'Oh!'

'He's still set on studying marine biology. I may have created a monster.'

Cass laughed as she felt her tension slip away. This was Mick. They may not be able to have the sort of relationship she yearned for, but they could be friends.

'He tells me his mother is arriving soon.'

'Monday. It's about time. My sister seems only to remember she has family here when it suits her. But at least she'll see Mum before...' She surreptitiously crossed her fingers. Surely their mother would live to see Vi again, Vi, who had always been her favourite. It was a bitter pill to swallow that she, Cass, the daughter who had always been overlooked, was the one who was left to care for their mother in her old age.

'Sorry to interrupt.'

Cass turned to see Cleo with Kerri-Ann, the girl's thick, blonde hair falling around her shoulders.

'You remember Kerri-Ann, don't you?'

'Of course. I hear you're now lecturing at James Cook. Enjoying it up there?'

'I love it. Cleo tells me your nephew is thinking of enrolling in our marine biology course. He's here?'

'Somewhere. He dashed off with Zack almost as soon as we arrived. I'll… Oh, here he is,' she said as both boys appeared. 'Justin, come and meet Kerri-Ann.'

'Hello.' Suddenly shy, Justin held out his hand. 'You're the marine biologist? Awesome!'

Kerri-Ann laughed. 'Let's find a quiet corner and I'll try to answer all your questions. I hear you're interested in whales?'

The pair disappeared.

'Thanks, Cleo. It's good of Kerri-Ann to take time to talk with him. He's been really looking forward to meeting her.'

'No worries. She's always happy to talk about her pet subject. It was a blessing when she discovered us, though we may not have thought so at the time, especially Han.' She looked across to where her daughter was laughing in a group comprising Nate, Owen and Bronte.

Cass had forgotten about Bronte when she listed the people she expected to be here. Owen's girlfriend was part of the group of young people, the next generation of Bellbird Bay. She had moved to Bellbird Bay with her father who had grown up here. Neil now managed *Bay Books* which *his* father had owned for as long as Cass could remember. She wondered if Neil was here, too, with his new partner, Ali, who was now director at the local women's centre and was the sister of the famous author, Adam Holland. She felt a warm glow at the realisation she was a part of this tight community of friends.

'Thanks again for inviting me, Cleo,' she said.

'Not at all. We must get together more often. I haven't seen you at the book club recently.'

'No… Mum…' Since her mother had gone into the nursing home,

Cass had let several things slide. The book club had been one of them. 'Maybe…'

Cleo patted her arm. 'I understand. We all know your mum is your first priority. But we've missed you.'

'Thanks.' Cass had missed the group, too. She had always enjoyed their monthly get-togethers when they discussed the book chosen by one of their members, followed by tea and cakes, and catching up with local news. She wondered what they'd have to say about the news of Ray Morgan's arrival in town, glad she wouldn't be there to hear it.

When Cleo left her, Cass decided to mingle, moving around the groups. To her surprise she discovered one of the main topics of conversation was the newspaper article about Ray Morgan. Grace was particularly interested.

'I used to watch him every morning when I lived in Granite Springs,' she said. 'He was quite the heartthrob in those days.' She chuckled. 'Nothing for you to worry about, sweetheart.' She gave Ted's arm a squeeze and everyone in the group laughed.

Everyone except Cass. She wondered what their reaction would be if they knew about her past, about her affair with Ray… and what they would say if they knew he was stalking her, trying to renew their relationship. She hated the way he was watching her, following her, confronting her with his reminders of what had been between them, making her feel uncomfortable.

She moved on and found herself standing with Mick again. But, even he, it seemed, was affected by the news.

'Did Justin tell you we had a television personality on board today?' he asked.

Cass flinched. Surely Ray couldn't know Justin was her nephew, couldn't have booked on Mick's cruise to…? No, even Ray wasn't as devious as that, was he? She was tempted to tell him just what she thought of the television personality. She opened her mouth to speak, then thought better of it. Best no one here knew about her past mistakes. And surely Ray would be gone soon?

Thirty-four

Mick was lost in thought as he fixed his morning coffee and dropped a couple of slices of bread into the toaster. He was glad he'd gone to Will's last night. It had been good to see the old crowd and to connect with Cass again. But there was something bothering him. He had the distinct impression Cass had been going to tell him something. Then the moment passed. He sighed. Now he'd never know. Maybe she was just worried about her mother, about her sister arriving from England.

His phone rang. Who was calling this early on a Sunday morning?

'Dad. I thought I'd catch you before you left for work.'

'Hi, sweetheart. You're up early, too.'

'Not really. I didn't get much of a chance to talk with you last night. Bryan's taking Mia to enroll in Nippers this morning, then they're going to visit Grace and Ted. Why don't we meet for lunch?'

'I have to work, honey.'

'But you have to eat. Twelve-thirty? You should be between cruises.'

As always, it was difficult to refuse. 'Okay, sweetie. The club?'

'Where else?'

'I may have Justin with me. That okay?'

'I guess.' But Jo didn't sound pleased.

'See you then.'

The call ended, Mick sat looking at the phone. These days, Jo always had an agenda. He wondered what it was this time.

*

As it turned out, Mick was on his own when he walked along to meet Jo at the club. Justin had made arrangements to meet Zack and a couple of girls for a pizza. Mick smiled to himself at the boy's embarrassment when he revealed his lunch plans. 'They're just a couple of mates, Mick,' he said, blushing.

Jo was already seated out on the deck at the surf club with a glass of wine, and a beer waiting for Mick, the glass beaded with condensation.

'Just what the doctor ordered,' Mick said, taking a long gulp, after giving his daughter a hug and kiss.

'It's non-alcoholic, Dad,' she said reprovingly.

'Lovely to see you, Jo. It was a good bash last night. Thanks for persuading me to go.'

'No problem.' She had a suspicious gleam in her eyes.

They ordered, both choosing chicken salad, then Jo put her elbows on the table and cupped her chin. 'I saw you last night, talking to the woman who has the shop next door to Mum's.'

'I talked to a lot of people.' Mick took another slug of beer. He was getting used to this non-alcoholic stuff. It wasn't bad.

'But I saw how you looked at her. It's Cass, isn't it?'

'Cass Marshall,' he said, hoping his voice didn't give him away.

'You've known her for a while?'

'We all grew up together, though Cass was younger.'

'She seems nice.'

'You spoke with her, too?'

'No, but I've been in her shop, *Sassy's*. Her beachwear is fantastic. I don't remember seeing it before I left.'

'So?' Mick thought he could see where Jo was going with this.

'Have you...' she twisted the stem of her wine glass, '... have you thought of inviting her out?'

'Jo! I told you...' Mick felt a surge of anger. Jo was still trying to organise his life. It didn't matter that this time, she was trying to match him up with the one woman in Bellbird Bay who interested him. 'I can make my own decisions.'

'But, Dad. I'm just trying to help. I asked Bev, and she says Cass is single, so...' She stared at Mick, her brown eyes so like his own.

He was the first to look away.

Their meals arrived, and their conversation stalled as they began to eat. But Jo hadn't finished. As soon their plates were empty, she put her hand on Mick's. 'I'm only trying to help, Dad. It seems to me you just need a little nudge in the right direction. Okay, maybe I was wrong about Brenda, but Cass…?'

Mick felt himself redden. 'She's your mum's friend, Jo, and she's having a difficult time. Her mother's dying.' He hated to be so blunt, but he had to say something to stop Jo matchmaking again.

'Oh, I didn't know.' She paused. 'But neither of those things matter. Surely Mum would be pleased to think…' Her voice trailed off. 'Well, maybe not. Have you spoken to her about it?'

'Jo, listen to yourself for a moment. Can you really imagine your mum and I having a conversation about me dating her best friend when it was only just over a year ago I was hoping we…'

'Hmm. You might be right. Leave it with me.'

'Leave what with you?'

'Trust me. Hadn't you better be getting back?' she asked sweetly.

Mick glared at her. Trusting his daughter with his love life was the last thing he intended to do. But it was time he got back to work. 'I'll pay on my way out,' he said. 'And, for pity's sake, don't mention any of this to your mother.'

Thirty-five

At breakfast on Monday morning, Justin wasn't his usual self, slumped in his chair, his eyes dull, instead of filled with their usual eagerness for the day ahead.

'Not looking forward to seeing your mum?' Cass asked. She was glad Vi was finally coming to Bellbird Bay. Their mother was failing fast, and Cass had been on tenterhooks ever since she first called her sister. When she'd visited the nursing home the previous evening, the nursing staff said there had been no change, but Cass thought she'd seen a flicker of movement in her mother's eyes when she told her Vi was on her way.

Justin shrugged. 'She won't be pleased when I tell her I plan to stay in Australia. But…' his eyes brightened, '… it was great to talk with Kerri-Ann on Saturday. What she does… It's amazing.'

'I thought she lectured at the university.'

'Yeah, she gave me a brochure about the course. But she does a lot of other things to help protect the environment on the Barrier Reef… and she's a qualified divemaster. I'd really like to learn to scuba dive.'

Cass gave him an affectionate smile. It was good to see him so excited about his future, this young man who'd arrived in her life out of the blue. She just hoped Vi didn't do or say anything to dent his enthusiasm.

Once Justin had left, Cass pottered around for a bit, then, ensuring Hector had enough food and water, she set off for the airport. As she left, she was aware of a black car sitting on the opposite side of the road. It was one she'd noticed there several times recently but didn't know who it belonged to. None of the neighbours she knew owned a black car. There seemed to be someone sitting in the driver's seat, but she drove past so quickly, she couldn't tell if it was a man or a woman. She hoped it wasn't Ray, then she gave herself a shake. She was allowing herself to be spooked by shadows, ever since he'd come to town.

As soon as she left the neighbourhood, she forgot about the car, her mind focused on the meeting with Vi and what she was going to say to her. It was several years since the sisters had met, and Vi had never been the easiest to get along with. She'd become even more difficult since she and Roger married. But this wasn't about them. It was about their mother, and they'd need to put on a united front for her sake, regardless of their feelings for each other.

The plane was late.

Cass bought herself a coffee and rang the nursing home to explain the delay. Even though it seemed her mother was unaware of her surroundings, Cass liked to keep her and the staff informed of her movements.

Finally, the Jetstar plane touched down and Cass moved forward with all the others awaiting friends and family. She peered at the figures exiting the plane and making their way across the tarmac, giving a sigh of relief when she recognised her sister.

The two greeted each other with a hug, Cass surprised how Vi had aged since she had last seen her. She was still as elegant as ever, still as expensively dressed, but there was an air of exhaustion about her which Cass didn't remember. Perhaps it was only the aftereffect of the long flight, though she had been able to spend a night in a hotel in Sydney.

'How is she?' Vi asked when they pulled apart.

'No change. We should go there now.'

'Okay. It's why I'm here.'

'Where's Justin?' Vi asked in the car. 'I thought he'd be here to greet me.'

Cass bit her lip. She should have been prepared for this question. Now wasn't the time to tell Vi her son was working on a whale-watching boat. 'He had to go out,' she said. 'He came to visit Mum with me once and found it disturbing.'

To Cass's relief, the explanation seemed to satisfy Vi. 'You'll see him this evening,' she said.

'Hmm.' But Vi's mind was on her mother. 'Tell me about this nursing home,' she said.

'It's the only one in Bellbird Bay,' Cass replied. 'Mum has a room overlooking the garden, and she enjoyed looking at it. She hasn't been able to do that for some time, and now she's bedridden. She hasn't recognised me for days, Vi. Don't expect too much.'

Vi didn't reply.

Cass shot a glance at her sister, but Vi appeared to be lost in thought.

They travelled the rest of the way in silence.

'Here we are,' Cass said, as she pulled into the nursing home car park.

'It looks okay.' Vi stared at the large red brick building which had once been the family home of a wealthy, retired, member of the British Government Colonial service. It had been built in the nineteen thirties and gone through several incarnations – rumour was it had been a casino and a brothel – before its present status as a nursing home.

They entered the building, and Cass led Vi to their mother's room.

Cass had tried warning Vi but was afraid her sister didn't understand how much their mother had deteriorated. She heard Vi's indrawn breath as they walked into the room where their mother was lying in bed, her paper-thin skin almost indistinguishable against the pillow.

'Mum.' Vi took the old woman's hand and their mother, who had been staring blankly into space and hadn't uttered a word for days, suddenly focused on the new arrival. 'Vi? Is it you?' she croaked. A bitter taste filled Cass's mouth. After all she'd done for her mother, it was Vi who she chose to recognise.

Cass swallowed hard. This was no time to feel jealous of her sister. She took a seat on the opposite side of the bed from Vi and patted her mother's other hand, noticing how claw like the older woman's hands had become. She'd lost a lot of weight as her illness progressed and was now a shadow of her former self. She saw a tear begin to trickle down her sister's face.

'I didn't realise…' Vi said, her voice breaking. 'I'm sorry, Mum. I should have come sooner. You did try to tell me,' she said, looking across the bed at Cass.

Cass didn't reply. She tried to suppress the tiny hint of satisfaction she felt at her sister's words. Now wasn't the time for that, either. It was enough that Vi was here to share the burden of grief.

The two sisters sat there without speaking, the sound of their mother's breathing growing fainter and fainter until…

'Has she…?' Vi whispered.

'I think so,' Cass whispered back. It was as if, having seen Vi, their mother had finally given in and let go of life. 'She's been waiting for you.'

Vi burst into a flood of tears. 'Oh, Cass! What if I hadn't come? I almost didn't. Roger said…'

But Cass never heard what her brother-in-law had said, though she could imagine. A staff member arrived, alerted by the alarm on the machine which had been monitoring their mother's vital signs.

Cass and Vi were asked to leave.

'You can come back later,' the nurse said. 'Why don't you get yourselves a cup of tea?'

They walked out in a state of disbelief, following the sign to a café Cass hadn't known existed, and which seemed to cater more to ambulatory patients than visitors. Cass ordered tea, while Vi claimed a free table.

'Thanks,' Vi said, when Cass handed her the surprisingly dainty cup and saucer. 'I can't believe it. One minute she was holding my hand, the next…' Her voice caught.

'It was her time,' Cass said. Her eyes were wet with tears, too. 'I'm glad she held out… that you were able to…'

'Thanks, Cass. It must have been hard… I didn't… Roger… Well, he'll be glad he won't have to pay our share of the fee now,' she said bitterly, giving Cass some indication of what Vi might have been about to say earlier. She sipped her tea. 'Justin should have been here. His grandmother…'

'Justin saw her soon after he arrived. She recognised him, then became agitated. I think it scared him. It's better he didn't see her like this.'

'You're probably right.' Vi sighed. 'What happens now?'

Cass tried to remember the process when their dad died. Vi hadn't made it home until the funeral. At least there were two of them this time. 'I'll contact the funeral directors. I know what Mum wanted. She put it all in place after Dad died, almost as if she knew she was going to... Oh, hell, Vi... She's gone! She's really gone!'

Cass felt as if a part of her had been torn away. Her mother had always been there, first as a support, then someone who needed *her* support. Now there was only emptiness. She looked at the plate of sandwiches she'd bought along with the tea. But they lay untouched, neither feeling any desire to eat.

Thirty-six

It was almost five by the time Cass and Vi arrived back at Cass's house. Justin was already there, sitting at the kitchen table with his iPad, Hector curled up on his lap.

'Mum,' he said warily, as Hector leapt down and scurried off. Cass noticed Justin had changed from the shorts and *Bay Whale Cruises* tee-shirt he wore for work. He peered at them, clearly noting their glazed expressions. 'How's Grandma?'

Cass and Vi looked at each other. Vi seemed lost for words. 'She died, Justin,' Cass said gently.

'Oh! I'm sorry,' he said awkwardly. Then he got up and hugged his mother.

'Oh, Justin!' Vi held her son tightly, their tears mingling.

Cass stood apart, feeling envious of her sister. She had no one to comfort her. 'Tea?' she asked, her mother's failsafe remedy for all ills.

'Please.' Vi pulled herself out of her son's embrace.

'I'll make it.' Justin seemed glad to have something to do.

While he was making the tea, Cass led Vi through to the living room. They sat together on the sofa.

Vi looked around the room, as if hoping to see some remnant of their mother.

'I put Mum's things in storage, when she went into the nursing home, when we sold the house,' she said.

'I remember. Roger said you'd taken care of everything.' She was silent, then, 'I wish I'd come sooner, been able to say goodbye properly. Now she's gone…' She began to weep again.

'Vi, the mum we knew and loved has been gone for some time. I've visited regularly ever since she moved into Rosebank. Some days she recognised me, but more often she had no idea who I was. She demanded to come home, wanted to see me, you…' Cass had no tears left. She'd shed all of them over the past weeks and months her mother had been in the nursing home.

'But…' Vi bit her lip. 'I'm sorry, Cass,' she said again.

'Tea!' Justin walked in, balancing a tray containing two mugs of tea, a bowl of sugar and a milk jug. He must have searched the pantry for those.

Cass gave a watery smile. 'Thanks, Justin.'

'Sit down here.' Vi patted the sofa beside her.

'But I…' Justin glanced at Cass, then did as his mother asked.

'We should eat something,' Cass said.

'I couldn't…' Vi objected. 'How can you even think of food? Mum's dead.'

'And we're still alive and need to keep going. There will be a lot to do in the next few days. We can get a takeaway.'

'I'll go,' Justin offered, apparently eager to leave the strained atmosphere. 'I can go on my bike.'

*

It was late. Vi had gone off to bed, jetlag seemingly having finally caught up with her. Cass knew she wouldn't sleep a wink. She looked out the instructions her mother had written down before she lost the ability to think straight, smiling at the familiar handwriting. She'd contact Greta first thing in the morning and ask her to put a sign on *Sassy's* door. *Closed due to a family bereavement.* Wasn't that what people did?

Hector, who had disappeared earlier, had reappeared to take up his favourite position on the sofa, his purrs drowning out all other sounds in the house. Justin had gone to bed, too.

When her phone rang, Cass was startled. She stared at Mick's name on the screen before accepting the call. 'Mick?'

'Cass. I heard about your mum. I'm so sorry. I can't imagine how you are feeling.'

At the sound of his voice, Cass felt a warm glow. At last, someone was offering her some comfort. 'How…?'

'I was visiting Dad, and one of the staff had seen us together. She thought I'd want to know.'

'Oh!' People were so kind.

'I know you have your sister with you – Justin told me – but if you need… if there's anything I can do, you only have to ask.'

'Thanks, Mick. It's kind of you. Mum set out what she wanted done, so it's only a matter of fulfilling her wishes, but if we need any help… Thanks.'

'Any time… and, Cass…'

'Yes?'

'No, it's nothing. You take care.' He ended the call.

Cass wondered what he had been going to say. She was glad he'd called. They might not be able to form a relationship, but he was a good friend to have. She rose and stretched her arms above her head. Maybe, now, she would be able to sleep, she thought. Imagining Mick's arms around her, she shivered.

Peeking out of the window as she closed the curtains, she saw the black car parked opposite again. It couldn't be Ray. Perhaps it did belong to one of the neighbours; perhaps one of them had bought a new car.

Thirty-seven

When Mick heard about Cass's mother's death, his immediate reaction was to go round to comfort her. Then he remembered Justin telling him his mother, Cass's sister, was arriving that morning. Cass wasn't alone. She had her sister with her. He'd only be in the way. But he wanted to do something.

It was late by the time he decided to make the call, and he was afraid Cass would be asleep. It was a relief when she answered straight away. He could tell she'd been crying, and every instinct made him want to rush round, throw his arms around her and pull her into a warm hug. Instead, all he could do was offer his sympathy and help if it was needed. When he ended the call, he felt useless.

After a restless night, when he dreamt of holding Cass in his arms, it was a shock to awaken to find himself alone in his king-sized bed. Remembering his call the previous evening, he cursed his awkwardness, his inability to say what he was thinking. And it should have occurred to him to say Justin didn't need to come to work until he was ready. He didn't know how close the boy was to his grandmother, but a death in the family was always difficult for everyone.

Mick remembered when his own mother had died. But at least his dad had still been alive. For Cass and her sister, it was the end of a generation. It would happen to him and Pete too, one day. Hopefully not for some time. Despite his fall, Fred Roberts was still reasonably hale and hearty. Thinking of his dad, reminded Mick they still had to have the conversation about *Bay Village Lifestyle Resort*. He'd enquired and discovered two of the villas were on the market. It would be ideal for his dad, if only the old man would agree.

He made his first coffee of the day and slid a couple of slices of toast into the toaster before taking out his phone and pressing Justin's number.

'Mick? Is everything all right?'

'Justin, I heard about your grandmother. I'm sorry. I know it must be difficult for you. You'll want to spend time with your mum and Cass. Take as much time off as you need.'

'But you need me to help out, Mick. I'd much rather be with you. It's a bit…' he mumbled something Mick couldn't hear, '… in the house. There's nothing for me to do here.'

'If you're sure… and if it's okay with your mum and Cass.'

'It will be.'

'Give them a hug from me.'

There was no reply and Mick regretted the words as soon as he'd spoken. 'Give them my sympathy,' he said.

'I will.'

*

The mood was sombre at breakfast in Cass's house. She and Vi were drinking peppermint tea and trying to choke down toast spread with ginger, lime and lemon marmalade, when Justin joined them. He was wearing his work shorts and tee-shirt.

'I don't think that's an appropriate outfit, Justin. Your grandmother has just died,' Vi said.

Justin looked at Cass. 'I… it's what I wear to work.'

'Work?' Vi's eyes swivelled in Cass's direction. 'What's he talking about?'

'I'm here, Mum. You can ask me. I'm helping out on *Bay Whale Watching Cruises* for the season. I need to leave soon.'

Vi's mouth fell open. 'Whale-watching cruises? You mean you're working on a boat, doing manual work?' Then her lips tightened. 'I don't know what your father's going to say about this. But you can't go to work today. I'm sure your employer will understand.'

'Mick said I could take time off, but I'd rather be there. There's nothing I can do here. It's too depressing.' He fixed himself a coffee and helped himself to a bowl of Weet-Bix, before joining Cass and his mother at the table.

'Who's this Mick and how did Justin get mixed up with him?' Vi turned her attention to Cass again. 'We didn't send him here to become a deckhand on a tourist boat.'

Cass stifled a smile, the first smile which had crossed her face since her mother died. 'Mick's a local businessman. He's well respected in the community and runs a successful business. Justin is enjoying working with him. He's doing well. I thought you and Roger would be pleased to know he's doing something worthwhile,' she said, tongue in cheek. She was well aware her sister and brother-in-law wouldn't approve of Justin working with Mick. He certainly would never fit in with their snooty friends.

'Hmm.' But Vi made no more objections, and Justin was able to finish his breakfast in peace.

After he'd left, Vi said, 'And what about you? I hope you don't intend to open that shop of yours today, too.'

Cass counted to ten before replying, resenting the reference to *Sassy's* as *that shop*. 'Of course not. I've asked a friend to stick a notice on the door. But it's my livelihood, Vi. I can't remain closed indefinitely. Just till after the funeral.'

'About that. We need to…'

'It's all arranged. Mum did it before…'

'Oh! I didn't know.'

'You weren't here, Vi. She wrote it all down. All we need to do is contact the appropriate people. She didn't want a fuss – a simple service, then to be buried next to Dad. She's with him, now.'

They sat in silence, contemplating the enormity of the change in their lives.

'I guess we can call ourselves orphans, now,' Vi said at last.

'Yes, it's strange. I imagined she'd always be there, even when…' Cass took a deep breath. 'Here are Mum's notes.' She handed her sister the written instructions she'd read the night before.

Vi read them silently then folded the sheets of paper. 'Just like Dad's,' she said. '*Amazing Grace* and *Abide With Me*. I don't know if I can bear it.'

'We'll be together.' Cass stretched out her hand to clasp her sister's, their grief uniting them in a way nothing else had for years.

Vi nodded. 'I feel I just want to tell her what happened. It's so silly. As if I could.' She sniffed. 'I should call Roger.'

'You didn't call last night?'

'I was too upset. And he's never at his best in the morning. He'll be home from work by now.' Vi disappeared to make the call.

When she had gone, Cass made a half-hearted effort to clear up, then decided she should follow her mother's instructions. The sooner she called the funeral director and the church, the sooner it would all start to happen. She picked up her phone.

*

It was a week before the funeral was held, a week of inactivity during which Cass and her sister reminisced about their happy childhood, growing up in Bellbird Bay, and the reasons they had left, both eager to explore the world outside this small, coastal town. Cass knew Vi despised her for choosing to return, but if she hadn't, what would have happened to their mother? As they sat in Cass's living room, sharing memories and looking at old photographs, it was as if the years disappeared, and they were once again the two young girls who had thought the world their oyster.

When the day of the funeral dawned, even Hector seemed to sense the pall of grief which pervaded the house, enveloping its occupants. As soon as he'd been fed, he scurried away to hide in a corner where he wouldn't be disturbed.

This morning, Justin had made his apologies to Mick and, like his mother and aunt, was dressed soberly. His dark pants and white shirt had been bought especially for the occasion. Cass still had the black outfit she'd worn to her father's funeral, and which had hung in the wardrobe ever since, waiting for this occasion. True to form, Vi had come prepared with a smart black suit no doubt purchased from an expensive London boutique. As expected, Roger had been unable to travel to attend the funeral.

The funeral service passed in a blur, Cass and Vi clutching each other's hands in a way they hadn't since they were small. It was a relief to get out into the open air, though the sight of their mother's coffin being lowered into the grave was one Cass knew would keep her awake for nights. It was when she turned to leave that Cass noticed a tall figure in the distance which looked vaguely familiar. It couldn't be... surely not even Ray would stoop so low as to stalk her at her mother's graveside? But who else could it be? She'd been so caught up in grieving for her mother, she'd almost forgotten about him, hoped he'd left town.

'Something wrong?' Vi asked, when Cass stopped suddenly.

'No, I thought I saw someone who... I must have been mistaken,' she said as, when she turned around, there was no one to be seen. But she couldn't forget how creepy it was to even imagine seeing him here.

As Cass and Vi were making their way back to the car, Cass saw Justin speaking to Mick. She was surprised to see him here, but pleased he'd taken the time to attend. He must have cancelled his afternoon cruise, she thought, in the part of her brain that wasn't filled with what she had just seen.

'Mum, this is Mick Roberts, the man who...' Justin brought Mick forward.

'I'm so sorry for your loss.' Mick was speaking to Vi, but looking at Cass.

She blushed.

'So, you're the man with the tourist boat,' Vi said, glaring at him.

'That's me. Justin has been a big help as my assistant.'

'Hmm. Cass?' She started to move towards the car again.

'Thanks, Mick. It was good of you to come,' Cass said, shuddering as he put an arm around her shoulders and gave them a squeeze.

'Of course I came... as a mark of respect... and friendship.'

'Thanks,' she said again. 'I'm sorry, we need to go,' she added as she saw Vi wave to her from the car.

'See you soon,' Mick said, before she walked off.

Comforted by Mick's words and the way his arm had snaked around her shoulders just when she needed the contact, Cass joined her sister and Justin in the car. In line with her mother's wishes, there was to be no get-together of mourners, so they drove straight home.

It was a sad trio who entered Cass's house to be greeted by Hector.

The cat seemed to sense something was wrong, as he wound himself around Cass's ankles before sauntering off.

'Tea?' Cass asked.

'How can you think of tea at a time like this?'

'Someone has to, Vi. And it's what Mum would have suggested if she was here. You've been gone so long, you've forgotten. It's been me who's had to take care of her all those years, while you lived your posh life in London.' Cass knew she sounded bitter. She *was* bitter. After ignoring her and their mother for years, Vi had suddenly floated back like the prodigal daughter, pretending to have a monopoly on grief.

'I'm off.' Justin appeared, having changed out of his funeral outfit into a pair of jeans and sweatshirt.

'Where are you going? We should stay together,' Vi said.

'Out. It's too morbid here. I need some fresh air.' He left, Hector following him through the door.

Cass made tea and a plate of sandwiches which both she and Vi managed to eat. Then she said, 'I have a copy of Mum's will. She told me what was in it. She left everything equally between you and me. She didn't have much, but there was Dad's life insurance, what was left from the sale of the house, and what she saved from her pension. She scrimped and saved all her life, and for what?'

Vi's face fell.

'What? You expected more?'

Vi pleated the edge of her blouse. 'No… maybe… I thought… The thing is, Roger and I… things haven't been so good.'

'Oh!' So, the scales had fallen from her sister's eyes? But if she'd been hoping for a windfall from their mother to enable her to leave her husband, she was going to be disappointed. 'How long were you intending to stay?'

'Only till everything's sorted out. My life's in London now, regardless of…' Her voice trailed off.

Cass felt an unexpected wave of sympathy for her sister, immediately dispelled when, with a shudder, Vi added, 'I won't be staying here any longer than I have to. I don't know how you can bear it.'

They sat in silence for several minutes, the only sound the ticking of their mother's grandmother clock which Cass had fallen heir to, and the hum of the refrigerator from the kitchen. Then Vi said, 'I can't believe you allowed Justin to start working on a tourist boat.' She uttered the words as if Mick's boat was a den of iniquity.

'He's happy, Vi,' Cass said gently, 'and he's not getting into any trouble. Isn't that what you wanted? He's been surfing and swimming, has made friends, and…' She bit her tongue. It wasn't up to her to reveal Justin's plans.

'It was Roger's idea,' she said. 'To teach him a lesson. We… he thought he'd miss us, his friends, would be begging to come home, would realise…. Instead…'

'He's made a life for himself here.'

'So it seems.' There was a pause, then she said, 'I think I'll go and lie down.'

Left alone, Cass took the dirty dishes through to the kitchen where she found Hector lying in his favourite corner. He'd returned, but chosen to steer clear of her and Vi. Cass didn't blame him, she wished she could steer clear of her sister, too. As she made her way to bed, Cass remembered the warm glow she'd experienced at Mick's touch and wished for what must be the hundredth time, that they could be more than friends.

Thirty-eight

Mick couldn't get Cass out of his mind. Seeing her at her mother's funeral had brought out all his protective instincts. He'd been unable to check the urge to put his arm around her shoulders and incapable of stifling the thrill it gave him to be able to comfort her.

But the moment hadn't lasted. She'd left with Justin and her sister, the sister who'd looked daggers at him. It seemed Justin might have been right when he said his mother wouldn't approve of him working for Mick. The woman had stared at him as if, to quote one of his mother's favourite sayings, he was something the dog had brought in. They'd never had a dog, but both Pete and he knew what she meant. How had Cass come to have a sister like her?

But two days had passed, and he had to forget about Cass. Tonight, he and Pete planned to talk to their dad, try to make him realise the foolishness of maintaining the large family home, how it would be much better for him to downsize. They had visited the villas at *Bay Village Lifestyle Resort* and taken photographs to show him, hoping the sight of the tidy kitchens and established gardens would do the trick. Dad often complained about the old stove in his existing kitchen, and he loved pottering around in the garden. If that didn't succeed, Mick didn't know what they'd do. They couldn't force the old man to move, but if he didn't, Mick could foresee a day when one of them would have to move in with him… and it wouldn't be Pete.

He was about to leave, when his phone rang. It was Pete.

'All set, Mick?'

'As much as I can be. Dad'll be expecting us.'

'I heard from the resort today. They want a decision. These places don't last. One's been sold already. It's vital we get him to agree. The old place is worth a bomb. There'll be enough left for him to live in comfort for however many years he has left.'

'I hear you, but it's his decision.'

'Hmm.'

'See you there.' Mick ended the call. With Pete, it was always about the money. No doubt he was already counting on the commission he'd make for selling the old place, while Mick just wanted to see their dad settled and happy. He knew it would be a wrench for him to leave the home he and Mick's mother had bought together, lived in all of their married life. But it was really the best solution, to avoid him having another fall, one which might leave him unable to look after himself.

*

The darkening sky, signalling an approaching storm, gave the nursing home an eerie appearance, like something out of an Alfred Hitchcock movie. The building so elegant in daylight, set among its manicured gardens, looked different this evening. Mick shivered as he hurried to the entrance to meet Pete.

'Ready?' Pete asked.

'As much as I'll ever be.' Mick gave a wry grin.

'What have you two been up to?' their dad asked as soon as they walked in. Tonight, he was out of bed and seated in a comfortable armchair. He looked well.

His dad's words took Mick back to his childhood when their dad took him and Pete to task for some misdemeanor, real or imagined. He flinched. 'You're looking well, Dad,' he said.

'The doc says I can go home in a couple of days if I have someone to look after me. Fat chance,' he said, glaring at his sons.

Mick and Pete looked at each other. It was Pete who spoke first. 'About that, Dad.' He cleared his throat. 'Mick and I…' he glanced at Mick, '… we've been considering your options and…'

'My options? I just want to get out of this damned place, get back home. I'll be fine when I'm in familiar surroundings.'

'That's just it, Dad. The house is too big for you to look after on your own. It has been for years, since Mum died. I… we've been looking around and…'

Mick took over. 'Dad, we know the house is dear to you. It is, to us, too. It's where we grew up. It has so many memories… of Mum… We understand how difficult it would be for you to leave it. But the memories will go with you. We… Pete and I… have been to visit *Bay Village Leisure Resort*. There's a villa available. It would be a good solution.'

'Solution? To what? You might as well put me in a box and be done with it.' Their dad's voice was as strong as ever, but it held a hint of fear.

Mick decided to capitalise on what might be a moment of weakness. 'We have some photos, Dad.' He took out his iPad and scrolled to the photos they'd taken of the villa which was still available.

Fred took the iPad and stared at it for a few moments, before scrolling through the shots showing each room of the modern home, the garden and the community facilities. 'Hmm,' he said at last, 'you've done your homework, and this place… you say it's available? What does that mean?'

'It's for sale, Dad,' Pete said eagerly. 'You could buy it with a fraction of what you'd get for the old house and…'

'And I suppose you'd get the commission? Is that what this is about? What's in it for you?' he asked Mick.

'I have no financial interest in the transaction, Dad. I just want what's best for you,' Mick said.

'And you think this is best… this…' He pointed at the photo showing the outside of a neat white villa set behind a well-maintained garden.

'We do.'

'Hmm,' their dad said again. 'And I suppose you'll expect me to like it?'

But Mick could see he was weakening. 'How about Pete takes you to have a look?' he said.

'I can take you tomorrow,' Pete said, 'if the doc agrees.'

'I suppose it can't do any harm.'

Mick could see his dad was reluctant, but it was the first step. He gave a sigh of relief and glanced at Pete again.

'Good man,' Pete said. 'I'll check with the staff on duty before we leave and hopefully see you tomorrow.'

Both men were ebullient as they walked towards their cars.

'I think we've done it,' Pete said. 'Thanks, bro. It was your words that swayed him.'

'Maybe, but don't get excited too soon. You know Dad. This may just be a ploy to get us off his back. Let's wait and see what happens when you get there.'

'It'll be fine. Just wait. I'll give you a call when we're done.'

'Thanks.' Mick was almost at his car when he saw a familiar figure hurrying across the car park. What was Cass doing here?

'Cass?' he said, tapping her on the arm.

'Oh Mick. I didn't see you. Sorry, I wanted to get inside before the rain started.'

Looking up, Mick saw the sky, which had been darkening earlier, was now looking ominous. It was definitely going to storm.

'I'm here to collect Mum's belongings,' Cass said. 'There's not much, and I didn't have the heart to do it before now.' She looked up at the sky. 'I could have chosen a better time.'

'How are you coping? It can't be easy.'

'No. My sister's still here. It's not easy, either, having to see her and Justin at odds. Your dad?'

'Hoping to go home. Pete and I have just been trying to persuade him to downsize. There's a villa vacant at *Bay Village Lifestyle Resort*.'

'He's agreed to move?'

'To look at it. We can only hope.'

'I hope for your sake, he agrees. I hear good things about it. I know a woman who lives there and loves it… but it's not for everyone.'

'No,' he sighed. 'That's the trouble.'

'I'd better go before the storm hits.'

'Right.' Mick didn't want her to leave. He hesitated then, 'What are you doing after this? How about a drink somewhere?' As soon as the words left his mouth, he knew it was a mad idea. Nothing had changed since his earlier decision, and it was about to storm. The forecast had been for strong winds, rain and possibly hail.

For a moment Cass seemed undecided, then she smiled. 'Why not?' she said. 'I'll feel like one after picking up Mum's things.'

'Great. How about…' he thought for a moment, discarding his usual haunts. '*The Leonard Family Resort* isn't far away. We could meet in the foyer?' He didn't normally frequent the hotel owned by his ex's new partner but was sure neither of them would be there at this time in the evening, and it did have a comfortable bar.

After only a moment's hesitation, Cass said, 'Okay. I'm not sure how long it'll take me here, but if you don't mind waiting…'

'I'll see you there.'

*

There was a spring in Cass's step as she made her way into the nursing home. She hadn't expected to see Mick here tonight. Collecting her mother's belongings was a task she'd been putting off. It was as if, as long as she didn't pick them up, her mother was still here waiting for her. Foolish, she knew, but the mind did foolish things when a loved one passed away. She'd hoped Vi might come with her, but her sister, despite her prostrations of grief, had no desire to help when it came to taking any action. She preferred to sit at home and mourn. A drink with Mick after completing this, the last thing she could do for her mother, would be a welcome relief from the atmosphere currently permeating her home.

The bundle of her mother's belongings seemed so small; Cass wondered why she had delayed picking them up. Her mother wasn't here. She brushed away a tear as she thanked the nursing staff member who she remembered from her many visits, glad this would be her last contact with her and the nursing home and hoping she never ended up there herself. No matter how pleasant it might be, it was still an institution and not a good place to spend one's final days.

When she walked into the hotel, Cass looked around warily, remembering what Greta had told her. But there was no reason to imagine she'd bump into Ray here. It was a hotel. There were lots of guests. And she and Mick would have one drink and leave. But she couldn't stifle her apprehension. Why had she agreed to meet him, to meet here? She'd been so surprised to see him, by the unexpected invitation, a means of delaying returning home where Vi was still mourning their mother with no sign of wanting to return home.

'Hi!' Mick came forward to give her a friendly kiss on the cheek. He led her into the bar, its welcoming atmosphere putting her fears to rest. Only a few tables were occupied and there was the low sound of music. There was no sign of Ray. 'What would you like?'

'Wine, please, red. Thanks for inviting me, Mick. It's all a bit fraught at home. It's good to have a break.' Cass took a seat at a corner table from where she had a good view of the entrance which led from the hotel foyer and, for what seemed like the first time in days, began to relax.

They were chatting pleasantly about Mick's dad, his plans for the business, Cass's sister and Justin's plans for the future, when Cass stiffened.

'Something wrong?' Mick asked, looking around to see what had upset her.

'No,' she said in a strangled voice, hoping the man who had just entered the bar hadn't noticed her. She tried to slide down in her seat.

'He's the television personality everyone's talking about,' Mick said, nodding towards the newcomer. 'Was on one of the cruises. Bit of a wanker according to Justin.' He chuckled. 'Heard the media pack is on the way, too. That's all we need.' He grimaced, then he peered at Cass. 'Are you sure you're all right? You've gone pale.'

Cass swallowed. She'd felt the blood drain from her face, a chill run down her spine. Ray hadn't seen her yet, but what if he did, came over…? How would she explain it to Mick?

'I'm not feeling too well,' she said. 'It's just come on suddenly. I think I should go home. Sorry. Thanks for the drink and the company. I appreciate it, but I need…' She rose quickly and, before Mick could speak, slid out of her seat and out of the bar, holding her breath till she was outside the hotel.

Damn Ray Morgan. She'd been enjoying having a drink with Mick, pretending they might be more than friends. Ray's arrival had ruined her evening. As she drove home, she just wished he'd leave Bellbird Bay, knowing she'd never have a minute of peace until he did and was out of her life again for ever.

Thirty-nine

By the time she arrived home, Cass had regained her equilibrium somewhat, but was still shaken by how close she'd come to meeting Ray again. While it had occurred to her that the black car which kept appearing outside her home might be his, she hadn't wanted to believe it. Surely even he wouldn't be so crass as to sit outside her house waiting for… what? Nevertheless, she was careful to take precautions.

'You took a long time,' Vi greeted her when she walked in, to be met by Hector. Vi wasn't fond of cats and, recognising this, the creature tended to keep out of her way, only appearing when he knew Cass was around to pet him.

'I bumped into a friend and went for a drink.' Cass didn't know why she felt the need to explain herself to Vi. They weren't fifteen anymore.

'Did you get Mum's things?'

Cass looked at her empty hands. She'd forgotten all about them. 'They're still in the car. I'll fetch them.' It gave her an excuse to go out to the car again and rail silently against her sister.

'Here they are,' she said, dropping the small collection of personal items on the coffee table.

'Is that it?' Vi appeared shocked.

'Mum didn't have a lot there, and much of what she did have became lost. It happens. I told them to do what they wanted with her clothes. I didn't think…'

'No.'

At least Vi agreed with her about that. Cass collapsed into a chair. It had been a long day and a strange evening.

'Tea?'

'If you're making it.' A cup of tea was exactly what Cass needed, her mother's answer to all life's problems. She wished she and Vi had a better relationship, that she could share her worry about Ray. But she knew her sister, and to share her previous relationship with Ray and her fears would open up a can of worms she wasn't prepared to deal with. She knew very well what Vi's attitude to her involvement with a married man would be. Cass would be painted as the scarlet woman and would arouse no sympathy from her sister.

'I need to talk to you. Look what I found in Justin's room.' Vi held up the brochure from James Cook University which Cass knew Kerri-Ann had given him.

Cass's expression must have given her away,

'You knew? You knew and you didn't tell me! When were you both going to tell me?'

'I know Justin was intending to tell you, but with Mum…' Her voice trailed off at the rage in her sister's eyes.

'So this is what you've been getting up to with my son, you and that… that…' Vi ran out of words.

'It's not what you think,' Cass said weakly. She had no idea what Vi was thinking, but it seemed to be some plot between her and Mick to keep Justin in Australia. She was glad her sister didn't know Mick was the friend she'd had a drink with.

'Wait till I tell Roger… and talk to that young man,' she fumed.

'Calm down, Vi. It's not the end of world.' Cass almost grinned at the pun. It was exactly how her brother-in-law described Australia. 'Don't confront Justin when he comes home tonight.' As usual, Justin was out with his friends. 'Sleep on it. You can talk to Justin in the morning, when you've had time to calm down, and he's rested.'

'Maybe.' She took a sip of tea and grimaced. 'I need something stronger than tea. Do you have any brandy?'

Sighing, Cass fetched two small glasses of brandy. It had been quite a day. She'd be glad of it, too.

Vi seemed to have calmed slightly by the time she rose to go to bed. Cass could only hope her rage would have died down before she spoke to Justin in the morning.

When Cass entered her own bedroom and peered out the window, there was no sign of the black car. Was it because Ray was in the hotel bar, she wondered, or had he nothing to do with the car. Was it all in her imagination?

*

Next morning Cass and Justin were already eating breakfast when Vi walked into the kitchen. A quick glance at her sister's tight lips indicated to Cass the night's sleep had done little to stem her wrath. She sighed inwardly.

'Morning, Mum.' Justin was as cheerful as usual.

'Justin, we need to talk,' Vi said, sending a glare in Cass's direction, but Cass didn't intend to leave. It was her kitchen, and she was in the middle of her breakfast.

'Yeah?' Justin continued to shovel up his Weet-Bix.

'What's this?' Vi flourished the brochure she'd shown Cass the previous evening.

Justin turned red. 'I was going to tell you,' he began.

'When exactly?'

'I… after… Gran died, and I didn't think…'

'You never do. It was why you got in with a bad crowd, why we sent you here, which was clearly a mistake.' She glared at Cass again. 'You realise when I tell your dad what you've been up to, he's going to insist you come home?'

'He can't do that.' Justin continued calmly eating his breakfast.

Cass admired his self-control. She'd never been able to handle her sister that way when she was his age.

'Of course he can. He's your father. You're dependent on him for your allowance.'

'Not anymore.' Justin finished his cereal and took a gulp of coffee. 'I'm over eighteen, Mum, officially an adult. I'll soon be twenty. I can make my own decisions, choose where I live. I like Australia. And I don't need your permission to enroll in university. I plan to study the marine biology in that brochure you're waving around. I met a woman who lectures in it, and it sounds awesome.'

'But what'll you do for money? The university fees alone…'

'That's all sorted. I'm earning my own money. I have the job with Mick. He says I can stay there till the end of the year, and Kerri-Ann says I should be able to pick up part-time work in Townsville if I'm accepted into the course. And I won't need to pay the uni fees up front. I can repay it when I start working.'

'Who's Kerri-Ann?'

'She's the woman who lectures at the uni.'

'How did you meet her?' Vi turned to look at Cass.

'She's the daughter of a friend of mine. She was back for a weekend and…'

'So it's *your* fault!'

'Mum, don't blame Cass. I'm responsible for my own decisions. Working with Mick, I got to see how we need to protect the marine environment and the native species, particularly the whales. It made me realise what I want to do. Meeting Kerri-Ann was just the icing on the cake. I know Dad wants me to follow him into law, but I hated it. It's why I dropped out. I needed direction. Now I've found it. You should be pleased. It was you who decided to send me here, after all… and I'm grateful you did.'

Cass felt like applauding. Justin sounded so reasonable, so grown-up. She looked at her sister who seemed deflated.

'Now I've got to go.' Justin carried his mug and bowl to the dishwasher and was gone before Vi had time to respond.

'Well!' She turned to Cass. 'See what you've done? You've turned our son against us. This would never have happened if…'

'If you hadn't decided to punish him by sending him to Australia. But it didn't turn out to be a punishment, did it? You should be proud of him, Vi. He's grown up, worked out what he wants to do with his life. Just because it's not what you and Roger had in mind for him doesn't mean it's not a valid choice. He can have a good career as a marine biologist.'

'In Australia!'

'What's wrong with that? You grew up in Australia. It's a wonderful country.'

'I don't know what Roger's going to say.'

Cass realised that was the problem. Vi was under her husband's thumb. If it had been her idea to send Justin to Australia, he might well blame her for their son's decision. She remembered her earlier thoughts concerning the state of her sister's marriage. 'Is everything all right, Vi… with you and Roger?'

'Of course,' her sister snapped. 'Just because you can't get a man, you needn't think my marriage is in trouble.' She checked the time. 'He should still be awake.' She took her phone outside leaving Cass alone in the kitchen with Hector.

'What a fuss about nothing, Hector,' Cass said. Though Justin's decision about his future was hardly nothing, and Cass knew that although it would take some time for his parents to accept it, they'd eventually be proud of him and brag to their friends about their son, the marine biologist.

Then her sister's accusation hit her. She knew it was Vi's own unhappiness talking, but it hurt all the same. Vi had no idea about Cass's love life or lack of it, and assumed she wasn't married because she hadn't had the opportunity. The truth was that, although there had been men over the years, none had measured up to Mick, not even Ray, she'd realised when she returned to Bellbird Bay. But her sister was right about one thing. She would like to have her own special someone, someone to come home to, to cuddle up with at night, someone for whom she was special, too.

Forty

Last night had been weird, Mick thought, as he sat out on his deck with his coffee. First there had been the visit to their dad and the surprise of his agreement, albeit reluctant, to look at the villa in *Bay Village Lifestyle Resort* with Pete. He was glad it was Pete, not him, who'd face their dad's objections. Then there had been the unexpected meeting with Cass and the invitation to join him for a drink, the words seemingly flying out of his mouth of their own accord. All had been going well – the hotel Greta's new man set up boasted a pretty nice bar – when Cass had suddenly decided to leave. He thought back, trying to figure out what had caused her sudden departure. Had she really been suddenly taken ill? It had been just after he mentioned the arrival of that celebrity guy, the wanker, but it couldn't have been anything to do with him, could it?

He shook his head and drained his coffee, just as the resident kookaburras began their morning ritual. They were lovely birds, but boy did they create a racket. He was glad to go back inside.

The morning cruise was fully booked, so he was pleased Justin arrived early.

'Morning, Mick.'

'You're early this morning, Justin.'

'Glad to get out of the house.'

'Trouble?'

'My mother! She found the brochure Kerri-Ann gave me and went ballistic. Thinks she and Dad can still tell me what to do. As if…'

'You hadn't told her?'

'I was going to. I just hadn't got around to it. With Gran dying and all. I would have. She had no business going into my room and looking through my things.'

Mick stifled a grin, remembering doing exactly that with Jo. 'It's what parents do,' he said. 'You knew she'd be upset. Maybe that's why you put off telling her. Hmm?'

'Maybe.' Justin grinned. 'Anyway, she knows now. I guess she'll call Dad and he'll get on to me. But I'm not going to change my mind. I'm not going to spend my life stuck in a stuffy office to please them. I like it here. I feel free, able to… I don't know.' He shrugged.

'You'll still have to study hard. It's not an easy course.'

'I know. Kerri-Ann said. But she also said how I could learn to dive and visit the reef and…'

'Okay, it's not me you have to convince. I'd probably have made the same decision in your shoes. Instead, I took off overseas.'

'How did *your* dad react?'

'Not too well. I'd been crewing on his fishing boat when I decided to take off. I was Dad's big hope. My brother had never been interested. I started working with my dad before I left school. Then, when I did leave, I wanted something different. I thought I could find it by leaving home, crewed for some wealthy guys for almost a year, before I saw the light.'

'You came back to work for your dad?'

'I did, decided it wasn't all bad, and I missed Bellbird Bay. Then I met Greta, and we had Jo.'

'But you stopped working with your dad.'

'Yeah, when Greta and I divorced, I felt I needed a change. That's when I set up this, and I've never looked back. Dad's sold the boat now.' And Pete would be picking him up soon to take him to inspect the villa. Please God the old man liked it. It would set their minds at rest to have him living in a secure community, in a house of a manageable size, with support when the time came that he needed it.

The sight of some early passengers straggling along the walkway put paid to their conversation, and Mick busied himself in preparing the boat for the trip, while Justin made ready to welcome them on board. This was no time to worry about his dad… or Cass, he thought, his mind instinctively moving back to her and her odd behaviour the previous evening.

*

Cass waved to Vi before she left for work, glad her sister was still on the phone, presumably having managed to reach Roger. She wasn't sure she'd manage to be polite to Vi after her last comment. How dare she! She was still fuming when she pushed open the door to *Birds of a Feather*, and almost slammed the two coffees down.

'Oh-oh. Get out of the wrong side of the bed this morning?'

'Sorry, Greta.' At least the coffee hadn't spilled. 'I don't know what's got into me this morning. Well, actually, I do. My blasted sister!'

'What's she done now?' Greta chuckled.

Cass had been bending her ear with stories about Vi since she arrived in Bellbird Bay, and even before that.

'It's Justin,' she said, and began to recount the altercation at breakfast. 'I feel for him,' she finished. 'He's doing well. Mick's happy with his work. He's saving his wages. He even offered to pay me rent. But all Vi can think about is what Roger will say. I'm glad Justin got out from under their feet. I know if he was my son…'

'But he's not,' Greta said gently. 'I'm a mother. I understand where she's coming from. Try to put yourself in Vi's position. You send your only child off to visit your sister, only to find he prefers living there and is making plans to stay, plans you knew nothing about and which she did, which she might even have encouraged.'

'But I didn't.'

Greta raised an eyebrow.

'Well, maybe a little.' Cass remembered how she had made a pact with Justin to keep his work with Mick secret from his parents, and it had been her who had arranged for him to meet with Kerri-Ann. '*Your daughter spent years overseas,*' she remembered.

'She did. Unlike your sister, I encouraged it, encouraged her to do what I hadn't been able to. But it didn't mean I enjoyed the fact she was living on the other side of the world. I missed her every day and I love that she's back home now and intends to stay here.'

'I hadn't thought of it like that.' Cass took a sip of coffee. 'Vi and I left our parents, too, when we weren't much older than Justin. Maybe I should remind her.'

'No, probably better not. We never like to be reminded of our own choices.'

'No, you're right. And maybe she'll come to accept Justin's right to make *his* own choices too.'

'Let's hope so. But give her a bit of leeway. Remember he's her only child. She may see you as a threat.'

'Me... a threat?' But Cass remembered some of what Vi had said and realised her friend could be right. She was becoming attached to Justin, wishing he were her son. She needed to be more careful, especially when Vi was around.

The conversation stayed with Cass all day while she was dealing with customers and doing her accounts. She was still thinking about it and how she could mend fences with Vi when she closed up. Her mind was so taken up with her thoughts, she didn't see the man standing across from the shop until she heard her name called.

Cass looked up, her stomach dropping as she saw Ray walking towards her. She glanced around quickly, but there was nowhere to hide. She took a deep breath.

'What are you doing here?' she asked, staring up into the face she remembered so well. He was older now, more lined, his dark hair shot with strands of silver, but he was still a good-looking man. It would be easy to become involved with him again, but the chemistry which had held them together had gone. All that remained were some pleasant memories and the sense of betrayal that had sent her back to Bellbird Bay. 'Why have you been stalking me?'

'Stalking? Don't you think that's a bit of an exaggeration? I've been trying to find another opportunity to speak with you.'

'But I told you... when you came to my home... both times. I don't want anything to do with you. What we had together is over, has been for years. I have a new life now, one I'm happy with. Now if you'd please let me go. I need to get home. And I'd appreciate it if...'

'Everything all right?' Greta poked her head out of her door and gazed at Cass's companion in surprise.

'Fine, Greta. This gentleman's just leaving.' Cass turned back to face Ray, but he was already walking briskly away. 'You must have frightened him off,' she said.

'Was that…?'

'Ray Morgan? Yes.' Cass sighed.

'You didn't say you knew him.'

'It was a long time ago. It's a long story.'

'I have time, and you look as if you could do with a cuppa. Come in. I've finished for the day, and Leo is going to be tied up till later. You're not in a rush to get home, are you?'

'No,' Cass said, thinking of what was waiting for her at home. Vi was probably still annoyed with her, and she could bet Justin was keeping out of his mother's way. She joined Greta, following her into the small room at the back of the shop, and taking a seat while Greta fixed two cups of peppermint tea.

'Sorry I don't have any camomile here,' Greta said, handing her a cup. 'Now, tell me.'

'Well,' Cass began, 'it all started when, as a rookie reporter, I was sent to interview the new breakfast host on Channel Twelve…'

'Wow,' Greta said, when she had finished. 'What a story. And you hadn't seen or heard from him since?'

'Not till he showed up in Bellbird Bay.'

'And you wouldn't…? He's still pretty hot.'

'No way. There's nothing left, Greta. I'm not the same person, not that young girl, flattered by the attentions of the famous man. There's no going back.'

'I can see what you mean,' Greta said, after a pause, 'but you have to ask yourself, why is he making all this effort if he's not serious about the two of you getting back together.'

'Who knows? He's always been used to getting what he wants.'

'And now he's decided he wants you?'

'So it seems. But he can't stay here for ever. Bellbird Bay isn't his sort of place. Sooner or later, he's going to get bored, hopefully sooner.'

'Well, for your sake, I hope so.'

'Thanks. Thanks for the tea and thanks for listening.' Although she'd been determined to keep her past with Ray secret, it had been a relief to share it with Greta, who had listened and been sympathetic rather than judgmental. 'I should be getting home now. I can't avoid facing Vi for ever. With a bit of luck, she's had time to think about things and decided what Justin plans to do isn't all bad.'

'Don't be too hard on her.' Greta gave Cass a hug. 'Remember what I told you and remember I'm always here. You can tell me anything.'

'Thanks, Greta.' Cass sighed, wishing her life wasn't so complicated right now. Greta was a good friend, but there were some things she wouldn't dare share with her. What would she say if she discovered Cass's secret feelings for Mick?

Forty-one

Mick was feeling happy when he arrived on board next morning. The call from Pete the previous evening had been optimistic. His brother had reported their dad was impressed with the villa and not entirely averse to moving, the only obstacle seeming to be which items from the family home he was willing to part with.

'So,' Pete had said, 'Looks as if it's a goer. We can get the old place on the market, and Dad can move into *Bay Village*. I have a number of possible buyers lined up.'

Mick could picture his brother rubbing his hands at the prospect, but while it was good news, and what they'd been urging their dad to do for some time, Mick knew he'd be sad to see the old place go. It didn't just hold memories for their dad, his whole childhood was tied up in the red brick building, built in the nineteen sixties.

'Hey, Mick!' Justin swung on board, a wide grin on his face.

'Someone's happy this morning,' Mick said.

'Sent off my application to James Cook Uni. I don't care how much Mum rants about my lack of what she calls filial duty and family obligation, I know Cass supports me. I heard her reminding Mum how both of them left home when they weren't much older than me. It's odd, isn't it? Mum couldn't wait to leave here, and I want to stay. Even though I won't be staying in Bellbird Bay, Cass says I can use her place as my base. She's amazing.'

She certainly is. Mick was having trouble getting her out of his mind. 'Good for you,' he said, 'But try to mend fences with your parents.

They love you and want what's best for you. It's unfortunate you don't agree with them as to what that is, but it doesn't mean you should stay angry with them. They are your parents, Justin, and you're stuck with them. I know I'd hate to be at odds with Jo. She annoys the heck out of me sometimes…' he thought of her attempts at matchmaking, '… but I still love her to bits and would do anything for her. It's what parents do.'

'Yeah, yeah,' Justin muttered, but Mick could see his words had got through to the boy.

*

It was another typical day out on the bay, finishing up with a second lot of satisfied customers heading home.

'Okay if I go now?' Justin asked, when they had finished the cleanup.

'Sure. See you tomorrow.' Mick watched the young man leap onto the wharf, hop onto his bike and ride away, and wished his life was as uncomplicated as Justin's. He checked his watch. He had an appointment with his accountant in an hour's time, and Pete had called to say their dad wanted to talk with them both that evening. He hoped the old man hadn't changed his mind. Pete hadn't lost any time in putting the house on the market and was already planning an open house.

After a quick trip home for a shower and change of clothes into an outfit more appropriate for the meeting with his accountant, Mick pushed open the door to the firm he'd dealt with since starting his own business. Alec Harper had been at school with Mick and had followed his father into the accounting firm which handled many Bellbird Bay businesses. He'd helped Mick out on a few occasions, and Mick valued the other man's advice. It was the first step in looking at expanding the business. If Alec thought it possible, the bank would be Mick's next port of call.

The meeting didn't go as Mick had hoped.

After laying out his proposition, Mick sat back to listen to his old friend.

Alec leant forward on his desk and steepled his fingers. 'I see what you want to do, Mick, and I agree it's the next step for *Bay Whale Cruises* but…' he dropped his hands and scratched his chin, '… money's tight at the moment. I can't see a bank advancing you the amount you'd need to buy another boat of the sort you're talking about, plus the additional funds to get it all underway. They'd consider a business like yours, dependent on the tourist trade, too great a risk. I'm sorry to be the bearer of bad news, but better you hear it from me.'

Mick's heart dropped. He'd been counting on Alec's support with the bank, but if he thought there was no hope of a loan, there was no point in going through the time-consuming application process.

'Perhaps in a year or two…' Alec said. 'Sorry, mate.'

'Thanks.' Mick rose to go, his hopes of expansion dashed.

'Maybe we can get together for a beer one of these days. It's been a while,' Alec said, rising, too, and shaking Mick's hand.

'Yeah, maybe.' Mick didn't want to discuss it now. He knew it wasn't Alec's fault. He didn't control who or what the bank would sink money into. But it was a big disappointment.

There was no time to get anything to eat before he was to meet Pete at the nursing home, so Mick headed straight there. His mood was already bad, whatever his dad had to say couldn't make it any worse.

'Hey, bro. Good news.' Pete greeted him at the entrance of the nursing home with a grin. 'Got a good offer on the house – ten thousand above the asking price. Dad should be pleased.'

'If he hasn't changed his mind,' Mick said sourly. 'Why else would he be so anxious to see us?'

'Not like you to be pessimistic. What's up?'

'Had a meeting with my accountant.'

'Alec's not cooking the books, is he?' Pete knew Alec well, too.

'Hardly.' Mick managed a tight smile. 'No,' he sighed, 'I was hoping to add another boat, but he tells me money is tight.'

'I could have told you that.'

'So, I should have asked you… not my accountant?'

'Don't take it out on me. I'm not responsible.'

'No, sorry.'

By this time, they were at the door of their dad's room. Pete knocked gently, then pushed open the door.

'About time,' their dad said tetchily. 'I'd just about given you two up.'

'It's half-six, Dad. It's the time we agreed.'

'Hmm.'

'Good news, Dad,' Pete said in a breezy voice. 'We have an offer, a good one.'

'I think you mean *I* have an offer. It's what I wanted to talk with you about.'

Mick's heart sank for the second time that day. It was as he feared. The old man was going to renege on his agreement to sell and they'd be back where they started with him going home to rattle around in that big old house, probably have another fall and need care – his care.

He was wrong.

'I got a surprise when Pete here told me what the old place was worth. Your mum and I paid a lot less than that for it.'

'That was a long time ago, Dad,' Pete said, trying to humour the old man.

'I'm aware of that, son. I'm not stupid. As I say, it was a surprise. I knew house prices had risen, but not quite how much.' He paused. 'I looked at the documents on the villa… and I've been doing my sums. Oh, I'm not so old I can't calculate anymore.' He chuckled.

Mick began to sweat, wishing he'd get to the point, but he knew his dad. He'd get there eventually.

'What I've been thinking is this. Once everything's settled, there's going to be quite an amount left over. I have a bit put aside, enough to last me, to keep me comfortable for as long as I have left, so…' he smiled at them, '… I've decided not to make you wait till I pass away to get your inheritance.'

Mick and Pete looked at each other. Mick felt his stomach churn. *Did his dad mean what he thought he did?*

'Don't look so surprised,' Fred said. 'Did you think I was going to leave it in the bank to be at the mercy of the fluctuations of the economy? I know you want to buy another boat, Mick, and I have no doubt your brother has his eye on another investment property. My money's going to do more good in your hands than in some banker's.'

All of a sudden, it was as if Christmas had come early. 'You mean it, Dad? You'd do this for us?' Mick could scarcely believe it.

Forty-two

Mick couldn't believe his luck. He was still feeling in high spirits when they left the nursing home.

'The old devil,' Pete said. 'I wonder how long he's been thinking about this. It calls for a celebration.'

'Too right.'

'Surf club?'

'Good idea.' Mick was grinning as he drove the short distance to park close to the surf club, the thought of a full-strength beer and a burger and chips making his mouth water. For once, he was determined to ignore the doctor's advice, convinced Jo would never find out.

Pete was already at the bar when Mick reached it, two beers sitting there ready.

'Thanks, bro. To Dad,' he said, raising his glass.

'To Dad,' Pete agreed.

'I ordered two burgers with chips. Is that okay? I know you tend to be more careful with your diet since…' He cleared his throat.

'It's perfect. This is a celebration.' All the way to the surf club, Mick had been mentally itemizing what he needed to do to secure the boat he'd seen advertised. It was for sale up the coast in Pelican Crossing. The money wouldn't be available till the house settled, but he could contact the marina and pay a deposit. It would be his by Christmas, all ready for the holiday tourist trade. He already had his eye on a likely young fellow to crew it, a man who had worked with his dad, who had taken an office job and who, Mick knew, was keen to get back on the water.

Tonight, the surf club was thronged with people, most of them strangers.

'The barman said the media circus has hit town,' Pete said, as they settled down at a table on the deck to wait for their meals. 'Something to do with some television celebrity.'

'Ray Morgan. He's a television breakfast host. It was in *The Bugle*. He's staying at *The Leonard Family Resort*, and he came on one of my cruises.'

'Still keep in touch with Greta, then?' Pete raised an eyebrow and took a slug of his beer.

Mick reddened. 'Not really. I saw him there when I was having a drink with a friend.'

'Oh yeah?' Pete looked interested. 'Anyone I should know about?'

'Since when have you been interested in who I have drinks with?'

'Oh, I don't know. It hasn't always been easy, but I've always tried to keep up to date with your… what shall I call them… fancy women.' He grinned.

Mick grimaced. As someone who'd been married *and* divorced three times, Pete was the last person to cast aspersions at him. Okay, he might have been a bit of a womaniser in the past, he admitted it. It was what had come between him and Greta. But that *was* all in the past. All he wanted now was a quiet life with… He caught himself thinking of Cass. He was so lost in his musings, he thought he'd imagined the voice he heard.

'Hello, Mick.'

He looked up to see Cass standing by their table with the woman he remembered meeting at her mother's funeral. Pete was glancing at him with a grin on his face.

'Hello, Cass,' he said, rising to greet her. 'Hello,' he said to her companion. 'We met at your mother's funeral.'

'I remember you.' The woman's lips tightened. She sounded very English, though Mick knew she'd grown up here.

'Mick, Mick Roberts.' He held out his hand which she ignored. 'This is my brother, Pete.'

Pete rose, too. 'Cass Marshall,' he said. 'I remember you. You're the woman who owns *Sassy's*. Good location. If you ever want to sell…' He fished a business card out of his pocket and handed it to her.

'Never forgets he's in real estate,' Mick said, embarrassed by his brother's crassness. 'Are you two ladies here for dinner? Why don't you join us?'

'Oh, I don't know.' Cass looked at her sister whose eyes were darting around the deck in search of another table. But since Mick and Pete arrived, the deck had filled up. Suddenly, she seemed to decide. 'Thanks, it's kind of you to offer. We'd love to.'

*

Tired of the morbid atmosphere in the house, and too exhausted to think about what to cook for dinner, Cass had suggested they eat out at the surf club. Vi had given no indication of when she intended to return to England, and Cass was becoming irritated with her sister's company… and the disapproval which had been apparent ever since Vi learned of Justin's plans. An evening out might help them recover somewhat from the cloud of grief which had been hanging around them ever since their mother's death, and perhaps even bring about some kind of reconciliation.

It had taken an inordinate amount of persuasion to encourage Vi to leave the house, but they were finally here. They were searching for a free table on the deck when Cass saw Mick. Her heart leapt and she couldn't resist saying hello, despite her sister's obvious reluctance to become involved with the two men sitting with glasses of beer.

When Mick invited them to join them, she sensed the waves of antagonism emanating from Vi. Her sister knew he was the owner of the boat Justin was working on, the person she blamed – along with Cass – for her son's decision to stay in Australia. But there were no free tables, and every part of Cass relished the opportunity to spend another evening in Mick's company. 'Thanks, it's kind of you to offer. We'd love to,' she said, taking a seat, and forcing Vi to join them.

'Wine, ladies?' Mick's brother asked.

'Thanks.'

For some reason Pete seemed amused by their arrival.

'How's your dad?' Cass asked Mick, when Pete had disappeared to order wine.

Vi was staring straight ahead as if she could pretend he wasn't there.

'He's on the mend,' Mick said. 'Pete and I are actually celebrating. Dad's agreed to move into *Bay Village Lifestyle Resort*, the house is on the market and we've had a good offer for it.'

'Oh, congratulations. You must be pleased.' She turned to Vi in an attempt to include her in the conversation. 'Mick's dad has been recovering from surgery in the same nursing home Mum was in. He's been holding out on selling the family home and downsizing.'

'Oh!' Vi didn't evince any interest.

Cass reddened, embarrassed by her sister's rudeness.

'Here we are.' Pete returned with two glasses of wine and two menus which he placed on the table. 'We've already ordered. When you've decided what you want, I can order for you both, too. Our treat. Right, Mick?' He gave Mick a knowing look.

'Right.'

'Thanks. It's kind of you, isn't it, Vi?'

Vi shrugged.

'Sorry,' Cass mouthed to Mick, who only grinned.

After checking out the menu both Cass and Vi ordered chicken schnitzel with salad, and Cass began to relax, deciding that if Vi couldn't bring herself to make polite conversation, she'd ignore her.

Pete started asking Cass about her business, showing a surprising knowledge of the ups and downs of the fashion trade, while Mick listened.

By the time their meals arrived, the men had finished theirs, and Cass expected them to leave. Instead, Pete went inside to order more drinks, this time a non-alcoholic one for Mick who grimaced and, holding it up, said, 'Doctor's orders.'

Finally, Vi decided to speak. 'I suppose you think it's okay to encourage my son to leave his friends and family to study in this godforsaken place?'

'Vi!' Cass was horrified. 'Sorry,' she said to Mick, her face reddening again. 'We've been through this Vi,' she said to her sister in a low voice. 'It's Justin's decision.'

'Don't try to tell me this man…' she pointed at Mick, '… had nothing to do with it,' Vi said.

Cass saw a gleam of interest in Pete's eyes, but he didn't speak.

'Well,' Mick said, 'I may have had something to do with it, put the bug in his ear. But the decision was all his. And I think it's a good one. James Cook University is world famous for its degree in marine biology. The lad couldn't do better than study there.'

'But he's not going to become a marine biologist. He's destined to be a lawyer, like his dad. Roger has had plans for him to join the practice ever since he was born.'

'Maybe that's the problem, Vi. It's Roger's plan, not Justin's,' Cass said, to receive a glare from her sister.

'I don't need to stay here and hear this.' Vi rose. 'Coming, Cass?'

Cass looked at the uneaten food on her plate, her half-full glass of wine. 'I…' she began.

'It's okay, I can find my own way.' Vi started to leave.

Torn between wanting to stay, and loyalty to her sister, Cass frowned. She looked at Mick to see what appeared to be encouragement in his expression. 'You'll need a key,' she said, rifling in her bag before handing it over. 'I'll see you later.'

When Vi had left, Cass let out a sigh of relief. 'I'm sorry she was so rude,' she said. 'Sometimes…' She sighed again.

'We all have challenges with our siblings.' Mick nudged Pete, who grinned.

'Speaking of which,' Pete said, 'I need to go, too. Sorry, folks.' He rose and left.

Alone with Mick, Cass felt very exposed. What if she and Mick were seen together, if Greta heard? If she'd known Pete was about to leave, she'd have gone with Vi. Now…

'You should finish your meal,' Mick said, his eyes twinkling. 'It would be a pity to waste it.'

'I didn't expect your brother to leave, too,' she said, as she picked up her cutlery again.

'That's Pete,' Mick said, 'always unpredictable. Seems your sister is much the same. It's difficult for you?'

'You have no idea. But she's not normally quite this rude. I think there's something else going on with her… with her and Roger.'

'Her husband?'

'Mmm.' Cass took a sip of wine. 'She denies it but doesn't seem eager to go home. I thought she'd be off immediately after the funeral.'

'And she's really so upset about Justin's decision to study here?'

'You heard her. But I'm glad to say he's adamant.'

'Yeah, told me today he's sent in his application. He'll do well. He's a bright guy, a lot brighter than I ever was.'

'I'm sure that's not true.' It was strange to hear Mick downplaying himself. It made him even more attractive in Cass's eyes, so different to Ray who was always big-noting himself. She gave herself a shake. What was she doing, thinking about Ray now? The two men were nothing alike.

As if reading her mind, Mick said, 'You'll have noticed the media have arrived in town. it was only a matter of time, I guess.'

Cass peered around warily. If the media were here following Ray, was he in the club, too? She exhaled when there was no sign of him. She assumed the men and women in the noisy group at the far end of the deck were who Mick was talking about. 'I should go now,' she said, feeling the need to distance herself from Mick. Although she dreaded returning home, she knew she had to face Vi again sometime, and the sooner the better.

'Are you sure?' Mick sounded regretful.

'I am. Thanks for the meal. I'm sorry you had to suffer my sister's bad temper.'

'No worries. I hope for your sake, she goes back to England soon.'

'Thanks.' Cass picked up her bag and left, very conscious of Mick's eyes following her. She was determined to confront Vi as soon as she got home, berate her for her behaviour in the club, and ask her when she intended to leave.

But when she returned home, the house was silent, apart from Hector's purrs as he wound himself around her ankles. Vi was in bed and there was no sign of Justin. Cass picked up Hector and gave him a cuddle, rubbing her nose in his soft fur. Hector was the one creature in her life who loved her unconditionally and would never let her down.

Forty-three

To her surprise, Cass slept soundly, awaking at her usual time only to remember Vi's behaviour the previous evening. Grimacing, she slid out of bed and went into the shower, wondering, as the water cascaded over her, what she was going to say to her sister. While she couldn't allow her behaviour towards Mick and his brother to remain unchecked, she didn't want to have a full-scale argument with Vi.

She was saved from an immediate decision when she walked into the kitchen to see Justin eating breakfast and Hector standing over an overfilled bowl. 'Thanks for feeding Hector,' she said.

'What's up with Mum?' Justin paused, his spoon in the air, dripping milk onto the table.

'What do you mean?'

'She barely spoke to me when she came back last night, and I heard her on the phone to Dad.'

'Oh, dear!' No doubt Vi had been eager to call Roger to unburden herself about Cass and her unsuitable friends.

'What happened?'

'We went to the surf club for dinner and bumped into Mick and his brother. We shared a table, and they bought us dinner. Your mum… she was as grateful as…'

'I can imagine.' Justin laughed. 'I know what she can be like… and she's taken a dislike to Mick, probably because I'm working for him.'

'She was most unpleasant, then she left.'

'You stayed?'

'I hadn't finished eating.' But Cass knew that wasn't the only reason she'd stayed. She'd been enjoying Mick's company and wanted to delay taking Vi to task for her rude behaviour.

'Good morning.' Vi appeared in the kitchen wearing an outfit more suited to London than Bellbird Bay.

Both Cass and Justin gaped at her, while Hector disappeared out the cat flap.

Ignoring Cass, Vi spoke to Justin. 'I called your dad last night. He agrees with me you've been unduly influenced by your aunt and this boat owner. It's not too late for you to pick up your law studies. We're willing to permit you to stay for another month, but we expect you home before Christmas.'

She turned to face Cass. 'I'm not sure if I can forgive you for what transpired last night. To suggest Roger and I have anything in mind other than what's best for Justin's future is ridiculous. He's our son, and we know what's best for him.' She turned back to Justin. 'Your dad's willing to fund your flight home. He's being very generous, after how you've behaved.'

Stunned by Vi's outburst, the words Cass had been carefully planning to say to her sister flew out of her head. 'Why don't you take a seat, Vi, and have some breakfast and a cup of tea?'

Vi checked her watch. 'I just have time. I'm going home. My flight leaves in two hours' time. I have an airport shuttle booked,' she added, as Cass opened her mouth to offer her a ride, even though it would have meant delaying opening *Sassy's*.

'That was a sudden decision, Vi,' Cass said. 'What prompted it?'

'It was when I talked to Roger last night. I told him all about what's been happening here, about Justin… and Mick… and your inability to understand our ambitions for our son. He suggested it was time I came home. I have a husband who misses me, Cass.'

Cass blanched. Vi never did miss an opportunity to comment on her single status, on what she saw as Cass's inability to attract a husband. It appeared that despite all the hints all was not well between Vi and her husband, she considered it better to stay with him than to be in the same position as her sister.

Cass looked across at Justin, who had a face like thunder, and shook her head. There was no point in him arguing with Vi now. Roger and

Vi couldn't force him to return home. But it was a sad state of affairs they'd decided to take this attitude, rather than accept his decision and feel proud he'd discovered what he wanted to do with his life.

*

It was a busy morning in *Sassy's*, giving Cass little time to ponder on Vi's ultimatum to Justin. While she was glad her sister had left, she hated that they'd parted on such bad terms. It had never occurred to Cass that by helping her nephew move forward with his life, she'd be seen as undermining his parents. Well, she had to admit suggesting keeping his job with Mick secret from them, but surely that wasn't enough to make Vi so angry with her?

Close to lunchtime, the swarms of tourists all intent on purchasing new swimwear thinned, and Cass had time to draw breath. At the sight of Greta in the doorway holding up a bag from *The Bay Café*, and asking, 'Lunch?' she grinned, glad to have the opportunity to get off her feet for a short time at least.

Putting a *Closed for lunch* sign on the door and locking up, Cass joined Greta, and the two women made their way across the esplanade to a bench overlooking the beach. It was where they often lunched together on days like this, when business slowed down in the middle of the day.

'Busy morning?' Greta asked, opening one of the bags and taking out an avocado and ham baguette.

'You wouldn't believe it. I don't know where they all came from.'

Greta took a bite before answering, 'Leo says he's fully booked for the next week. A squillion journalists trying to get an interview with your friend.'

'Not my friend.' So, Mick was right. The noisy crowd at the club last night had been the media. Ray would be revelling in the attention.

'Anyway, they don't seem to be short of cash. I had a busy morning, too.'

'They can't all be from the media.'

'I guess not, but who cares if it brings in customers.'

'Vi has left,' Cass said, opening her own bag to reveal one of the tuna, tomato and olive baguettes she liked.

'What? You waited till now to tell me?'

Cass had been too annoyed with her sister to break the news over their morning coffee. 'It took me by surprise. It seems she had a heart-to-heart with her husband last night and decided it was time.'

'You'll be pleased. Justin, too, I bet.'

'Yes, but I wish…' Cass bit her lip.

'What?'

'I wish we'd been able to part on better terms. We've never been close, but this time, apart from sharing our grief over Mum's death, we seemed to be at odds more often than not.'

'That's families for you.'

'Mmm.' Cass bit into her baguette. Greta might be right. But now their mother was dead, Vi and Justin were the only family she had. She comforted herself with the knowledge that at least she had Justin's affection, but it came at the expense of her sister's.

They sat in silence while they finished eating, then Greta said, 'Are you doing anything tonight? You sound as if you need some company. Leo and I are having dinner at the hotel. Why don't you join us?'

'Thanks, but I have a few things to take care of at home.' It was kind of Greta to suggest it, but Cass's heart sank at the risk of bumping into Ray again at the hotel… along with the media circus which would now be following him around.

Forty-four

'Cass, look at this.'

Cass and Justin were eating breakfast together, enjoying the reprieve from Vi's presence. After her departure, vowing to tell Roger all about Cass's attempts to alienate Justin from his parents, Cass and Justin had celebrated with dinner at the club. To Cass's relief, there had been no sign of either Mick or Ray, though the media contingent were still making their presence felt. She supposed it was good for business, if nothing else, and surely they'd either soon tire of following Ray around or discover some other newsworthy celebrity.

Cass put down her cup of peppermint tea and glanced at the screen of the iPad Justin had angled towards her. She began to read the news item.

NOT SO GRIEVING WIDOWER

Sydney breakfast show host, Ray Morgan, who recently lost his wife of over thirty years, has been spotted with a new lady in the small Queensland coastal town of Bellbird Bay. A little bird tells us the lady in question is a former journalist who he was seen about town with some years ago before she disappeared from the Sydney scene. Is this the rekindling of an old love, or has she been Morgan's secret lover all this time? The woman has been seen accompanied by a young man, rumoured to be their love child.

Ray Morgan has fronted the Channel Twelve Breakfast Show for the past...

Cass stopped reading. Where had this come from? She and Ray had never gone anywhere together. The only times she'd spoken to him had been… She tried to remember if it had been before or after the journalists arrived. Surely the time he had confronted her outside *Sassy's* had been before the horde of journalists had descended on the town? She began to shiver.

'Is it true, Cass? Not about me, of course.' Justin laughed. 'But there's a photo.' He scrolled down to show Cass a blurred image of her and Ray standing outside her shop.

A curl of fear started in her stomach. The photo had been taken on the last day they'd spoken. Cass hadn't seen anyone with a camera, but it could have been someone with a mobile phone. She began to shake.

'Cass, are you okay?'

She was far from okay, and sensing her distress, Hector began to yowl. 'Shh, Hector,' she said. For Justin's sake, she tried to pull herself together. 'It's nothing, Justin. Only media hype.' She could see Justin wasn't convinced, but he didn't say anything more.

Cass looked at the half-eaten toast on her plate and pushed it away. She'd get something to eat later. 'Hadn't you better get going?' she asked.

'I have the day off. No cruises today. Mick had something he wanted to do. Zack's off, too. We're going to the beach. He promised to show me a few more moves on the board.'

'Right.'

Somehow, Cass managed to get herself ready and drove into town more slowly than usual. She parked and bought her usual two coffees at *The Bay Café*, but when she started to head across towards *Birds of a Feather*, she stopped in her tracks, stunned to see a crowd of journalists outside *Sassy's*. She dropped the coffees, heedless of the hot liquid splashing onto her pants, unsure what to do, her only thought how to avoid the reporters and the accompanying cameras waiting for her.

She was standing undecided whether to brave them or turn and flee when she heard a familiar voice.

*

'Cass, come with me.'

Mick had seen the article on the news and rushed to intercept Cass before she was mobbed by the reporters he knew would be waiting for her to arrive at work. It was lucky he had no cruises booked today. After his dad's surprising announcement, he'd decided to make the trip to Pelican Crossing to view the boat he'd had his eye on and make an offer. If it looked as good as it sounded, it would be a perfect addition to his business, and he didn't want to risk missing out.

When he reached the esplanade, he could see he'd been right. There was a mob outside *Sassy's* with cameras and microphones, but no sign of Cass. Then he saw her coming out of *The Bay Café* carrying two coffees. She stopped, and the coffees fell to the ground.

It was a no-brainer to yell her name.

Cass turned, her eyes widening when she caught sight of him.

'Come with me,' he said again, reaching for her hand and pulling her in the opposite direction from the one in which she had been headed.

'What are you doing?' she asked, when they were some distance from the shops. 'I have a shop to open.'

'Not today you haven't. That mob could tear you to pieces, metaphorically speaking. You saw what they wrote about you?'

Cass nodded, almost in tears.

By this time, they were close to Mick's car. He bundled her into the Toyota Landcruiser.

'Thanks for coming to my rescue,' she said. 'But there's no need to… What were you doing there?' she asked, as if suddenly realising how unusual his presence was.

'I suspected they'd be waiting for you.' He bit his lip. 'Cass, I have to know. Is there any truth in the article?'

Cass blushed, sending a flash of something akin to jealousy through Mick.

'You don't have to answer me right now,' he said. 'Let's go.'

'Where are we going?' She peered around as he started the car and began to drive off. 'I can't just disappear.'

'You can contact Greta, ask her to put a notice on your door. You've done that before, haven't you?'

'When Mum died. But Greta…'

'They won't bother her. It's you they're after.'

'You haven't said where we're going.'

'Pelican Crossing. There's a boat for sale I want to have a look at. I was planning to go there today. It's why I gave Justin the day off. We can spend the day there, have lunch...' Mick felt fate had suddenly given him and Cass another chance. It was as if it was meant, a sign they could be together.

'Oh, but I can't...'

'The reporters will eventually give up when you don't arrive. And you can have a nice day away from Bellbird Bay.'

Cass leant back in her seat as if accepting his decision, and Mick sensed the tension leaving her.

'Thanks,' she said.

*

It had all happened so suddenly. One moment she was standing on the esplanade staring at the people crowding around *Sassy's*, the next, she was in Mick's car heading north. She couldn't believe how he had appeared to rescue her like a knight in shining armour. She snuck a glance at him out of the corner of her eye. Mick was hardly a knight in shining armour in his usual work outfit of shorts and *Bay Whale Cruises* tee-shirt, but he had managed to extract her from a difficult situation. She had no idea how she'd have handled the media scrum which was waiting for her. To think she'd once wanted to be one of them.

Now they were to spend the day together. Cass began to relax, but at the back of her mind was Mick's question about the article, about her and Ray. How was she going to explain how she knew Ray Morgan? If she told him about her affair with him all those years ago, was he going to believe her when she denied it had continued? She'd already lied to him – and others – by omission, by hiding the fact she knew Ray. Regardless of his faults, Mick Roberts was an honest man. How would he react to her deceiving everyone about her former relationship with Ray?

To Cass's relief, Mick turned on the radio. It was tuned to a music channel, precluding the need for conversation, and leaving her alone with the thoughts which were swirling around in her head. She was still undecided how much to reveal to Mick when they drew up in the main street of Pelican Crossing.

The town was larger than Bellbird Bay, and older, some of the original buildings still standing. Many had been renovated in recent years, including the restaurant on the main street. *Crossings* had begun as a fish shop and was now touted as one of the best restaurants on the coast, having been featured in several foodie magazines as well as the popular television program, *Weekender*.

Today, Mick had parked outside a café not unlike the one where Cass bought her coffee every morning. 'Coffee?' he asked. 'I noticed you spilled yours earlier. And maybe something to eat?'

Suddenly Cass realised she was hungry. It was some time since the breakfast she hadn't eaten. 'Yes, please,' she said, unfastening her seat belt. A few minutes later, she was enjoying a cup of cappuccino and a croissant filled with ham and cheese.

'So,' Mick said, his arms folded on the table, 'are you going to tell me about how you know Ray Morgan?'

Cass's stomach churned. All the way up the coast, she'd been dreading this moment, and she still hadn't decided what to say. But, looking at Mick's eyes gazing into hers, she knew she couldn't lie any longer. 'It was all a long time ago,' she began.

By the time she'd finished, assuring Mick everything else in the article was a lie, manufactured by the news feed eager to sensationalise the story, he was holding her hands on the table to stop them shaking, and tears were streaming down her cheeks. She pulled one hand free to brush away her tears. 'I'm sorry I didn't tell you – or anyone – that I had history with Ray,' she said. 'I was too ashamed. I'd put it all behind me. It was a shock to see him in Bellbird Bay, and when he started to pursue me, I just wanted it all to go away.'

'I wish you'd told me he was bothering you. I could have…'

'No, there was nothing you could do. I had to handle it myself. I thought I had,' she muttered almost to herself.

'Well, I can do something now.'

'What?'

'We can be seen together.'

'As a couple?' Cass's heart leapt as she tried to stifle her excitement. To have her dream come true, even if it was a pretense, was so unexpected, she didn't know what to say.

'Of course.'

'But…' What about Greta, she wanted to say.

As if reading her mind, Mick said, 'There's no need for us to broadcast it, just let the media bods see us together a few times. I know where they hang out. It shouldn't be hard.'

'Okay, but there's really no need to… Thanks,' she said, looking up into his eyes. They were filled with such a warm expression, Cass wished they could be together for real, not only to fool journalists eager for a story.

'I think there is,' he said, with a smile. 'We're friends. It's what friends do.'

'Thanks,' she said again.

'Now, I have a man to see about a boat,' he said, gesturing across the road to where rows of boats and yachts were sitting in the large marina, gleaming in the sunlight. Pelican Crossing was a jumping off spot for people who wanted to explore this part of the coast and the islands offshore. From its humble beginnings as a fishing port, it had become a mecca for yachties from all over the world and was now on the tourist route for many international travellers, while still managing to retain its unique ambiance. 'Our conversation about boats might be boring for you, but you're welcome to join us.'

'Thanks, but I won't. It's a long time since I've visited this part of the coast. I'll just have a wander around till you're finished.'

'Right. I'll give you a call, and we can have lunch. I've heard the yacht club do a good seafood platter.' Mick kissed her gently on the cheek and strode off.

Cass watched him go, admiring his broad shoulders and confident gait as he made his way towards the entrance to the marina, before turning away to investigate the town.

The rest of the day passed pleasantly for Cass. She spent a couple of hours refamiliarising herself with the shops she remembered, and discovering new ones, and splashed out on a pottery giraffe she couldn't resist from a tiny shop called The Mousehole. It was manned by a couple of fascinating women who told her they were part of a collective of women whose art and craft was for sale. Then Mick called, and lunch in the yacht club proved to be even better than expected. Sitting at a table overlooking the ocean, they enjoyed sharing a large seafood platter, washed down with an excellent sauvignon blanc, while Mick described the boat he was buying. It was a delight to see him so excited about this addition to his business, and Cass was pleased for him.

She was sad when it was time to leave and drive back to Bellbird Bay. She wished this day could last for ever, just her and Mick together.

Forty-five

Cass and Mick had been meeting secretly for several weeks, aiming to be seen together in places frequented by the media hounds who were still in town, as was Ray Morgan. At first that was all it was, a subterfuge to distract them from any further stories about Cass and Ray. But the more time she and Mick spent together, the closer they became, until one evening, when they were walking back to Mick's car across an uneven stretch of the footpath, Cass stumbled.

Mick reached out to save her, and Cass ended up in his arms.

For a few moments, Cass clung to him, her heart beating madly, her breaths coming in gasps, a rush of desire engulfing her. Then she pulled away, embarrassed Mick might have sensed her feelings. 'Sorry,' she muttered, aware she'd gone red.

'I'm not.' Mick pulled her to him again. 'I've been wanting to do this for so long.'

Cass senses reeled as his lips travelled across her forehead, over her eyelids and down her cheeks to finally meet hers. It was as if all her dreams had come true, as Mick's mouth claimed hers, his warm body pressing against her.

When they finally parted, she looked up into his familiar face, afraid to see signs of disappointment. She had waited so long for this moment. What if…?

Mick was smiling down at her. 'Why did we wait so long,' he said, pulling her close again, his lips in her hair. 'We need to talk.'

Talk… he wanted to talk? They had just kissed for the first time, she had sensed his arousal, and he wanted to talk?

'My place?' he asked, his voice thick with desire.

Cass nodded.

It was a short drive to Mick's home behind the harbour, and the first time Cass had been there, all their previous meetings having taken place in public, in view of the media and, hopefully, out of sight of Greta or their other friends.

'This is lovely,' she said, walking across the living room to stand at the French windows leading out to the deck and a perfect view of the harbour. *Why was she here? What did Mick have to say that he couldn't have said in the car?* Cass shivered and wrapped her arms around herself.

'Come and sit down.' Mick took her arm and led her to the sofa which was strategically placed to take advantage of the view and to provide access to a wide-screen television on the far wall. 'Would you like tea, coffee, wine?'

'Wine, please.' If what he had to say was going to upset her, she needed alcohol to soften the blow.

Mick disappeared into the kitchen to fetch their drinks.

While he was gone, Cass tried to still the myriad thoughts swirling around in her head, trying to figure out why she was here. They'd kissed. They'd finally kissed, and Cass had thought… Then, Mick seemed to have had some sort of mental snap.

'Here we are.' Mick handed Cass a glass of wine and took a seat next to her on the sofa, reaching an arm around her shoulders.

Somewhat comforted by this show of affection, Cass took a sip of wine and began to relax. *Maybe this was going to be okay.*

'I wanted to bring you back here,' he said, his fingers playing with strands of her hair and making her nerve ends tingle, 'so we could talk about what happened. It's been hell spending so much time with you and having to keep control of my feelings. I didn't want to scare you away and… we had agreed it was only to fool the reporters. I've noticed in the past few days, they've begun to leave town. Only a few are still here, and I've heard on the grapevine Morgan is planning to leave too. The network wants him back. Seems his replacement doesn't have the same drawing power, and strangely, the rumours about you seem to have increased his popularity. So, it was only going to be a matter of time till there was no need for us to spend time together.'

'Oh!' Cass was stunned. To think that, while she had been wishing their time together would never end, Mick had been wishing the same. Then she remembered. 'But you said we couldn't…'

'I know.' Mick removed his arm and let both arms drop between his knees. 'I'm an idiot. I was worried Greta had poisoned you against me. I know what good friends you are, and she and I didn't part on good terms, though we've always tried to be amicable because of Jo. And last year…' He sighed.

'I know you wanted to get back together with her… before she and Leo…'

'Yeah, well it's water under the bridge. I realise now it could never have worked.'

Cass waited, wondering what was coming next.

'I feel I've known you for years, Cass, but until recently, I never really saw you. You were always just one of the younger crowd, then Greta's friend. It was when we met at the nursing home…' he dragged a hand through his hair, '… it hit me. I knew I wanted to get to know you better.'

'But…'

'I know. I messed up when we had dinner. I thought Greta had talked about me, warned you against me. I know I didn't treat her well when we were married, but I'm a different person now. I hope you can believe me.'

'Greta didn't need to tell me anything, Mick. I think all of Bellbird Bay knew about your women.' But she remembered Greta's warning.

'Ouch! But I deserved that. I hope you can accept that's no longer who I am.'

'I do, and I'd like to explore what I sense is growing between us. But Greta is still my best friend, Mick. I don't want to do anything to jeopardise our friendship.'

Mick looked surprised. 'You don't think…? Is that why you didn't want us to see each other again… when we had dinner?'

Cass nodded. Nothing had changed.

'Greta doesn't own me. She has Leo. She had her chance last year and blew it. Don't you think she'd be pleased to know…' His voice trailed off.

'I'm not so sure, Mick. Maybe, if we can find the right time to tell her.'

'Hmm. Well, I do know one person who'll be pleased. Jo's been trying to set me up with someone. She's been forever telling me I need to find a woman to take care of me in my old age.' He dodged as Cass pretended to throw a cushion at him. 'So, are we agreed? We stop the pretense and let everyone see us together?'

Cass hesitated. It was what she yearned for, what she'd thought about for so long, to spend more time with Mick, to receive more of his kisses, to… A wave of heat engulfed her making her forget about Greta. She'd worry about that later. 'It's what I want too, Mick,' she said.

Forty-six

'It's what I want too, Mick.'

Mick's heart leapt at the words he'd been waiting to hear. He drew Cass into his arms again, kissing her until they were both out of breath. What a lot of time they'd wasted, time when they could have been enjoying each other's company, not to mention the other delights which would follow. It was a long time since he'd been with a woman, and while he couldn't wait to take Cass to his bed, he knew he didn't want to rush her.

He found it difficult to understand Cass's concern about Greta's reaction to the news. Surely his ex would be pleased he'd found someone, and that the someone was her best friend.

Time stood still as they sat entwined on the sofa, enjoying their newfound closeness.

It was Cass who pulled away first, extricating herself from Mick's embrace. 'I should get home. I have to work tomorrow. You have, too.'

'You're right.' It was late. Mick stretched his arms above his head. 'You won't change your mind?' he asked, worried she might think differently in the cold light of day.

'No, not now.' Cass kissed him gently on the cheek.

The touch of her lips was amazing, sending waves of desire through him, making him want to… Get a grip, he told himself. You don't want to ruin this. 'Coffee before you go?'

'No, better not. It would keep me awake.'

'I'll take you to your car.'

During the time they'd been trying to head off the reporters, they had always met somewhere in town, Cass and Mick driving there – and leaving – separately. Tonight, Mick had driven Cass to his home. Her car was still parked where she'd left it.

'Tomorrow?' Mick asked, taking Cass into his arms once more before she left his car. 'My place at seven. I'll cook.'

Cass gave him a surprised glance, but said, 'I'd like that,' before kissing him again and sliding out of the car.

*

Mick couldn't stop smiling as he drove back home. To think a stumble on the uneven surface the community had been urging the council to fix, had led to such a change in his fortunes. He could scarcely believe what had happened, but the memory of Cass's lips, the touch of her skin on his, the way she felt in his arms… it was as if they were meant to be together. And to his surprise, she seemed to feel the same way about him.

He was still feeling in good spirits when he arrived home, too wide awake to sleep. He poured himself another glass from the bottle of wine he'd opened earlier and opened his laptop to take another look at the boat he'd put a deposit on earlier in the day.

There it was, looking just as good online as it had in reality. And now, it sported a SOLD sticker. He enlarged the image, contemplating how it would enhance his business. It was fractionally smaller than his existing boat, but that wasn't a bad thing. He'd keep the name, he decided. *Safe Harbour* had a nice ring to it. It would give the passengers confidence they were in good hands, and they would be. He'd contact Len tomorrow to sound him out about taking on the job, and they should be in business by Christmas, all going well with the sale of his dad's house.

His thoughts turned back to Cass and to the following evening. What had possessed him to invite her to dinner? He may have told Jo he'd mastered a few recipes, but he still wasn't much of a cook. But he could do a mean steak on the barbecue. Despite having reduced his intake of red meat, surely one steak wouldn't hurt him, and he could combine it with a healthy salad. Even Jo couldn't complain about that. Jo! Wait till he told Jo. He knew she'd be delighted to hear he and Cass were an item. He suspected Greta would, too, despite Cass's fears to the contrary.

Next morning, he had to pinch himself to believe the previous evening had actually happened. But the two empty wine glasses by the kitchen sink convinced him it hadn't been a dream. He gazed out the window at the view of the harbour, the sea sparkling like diamonds in the early morning light. Life was good.

*

Cass felt guilty as she placed the two coffees on the counter of *Birds of a Feather*. She knew she should say something to Greta about her and Mick. But it was all so new and the urge to keep it to herself was so strong that she remained silent, only responding with a tight smile to Greta's news the reporters were checking out of the hotel, but Ray Morgan was still there. This morning, nothing could spoil her mood. She was still basking in the glow of Mick's kisses and wondering how *he* was feeling this morning, when her phone pinged with a text. Glancing down, she read it quickly.

Thinking of you. Can't wait till this evening. Do you eat steak? xx

Cass's lips turned up in a smile, the glow she'd been feeling intensifying.

'Something important?' Greta raised an eyebrow.

'Not really.' Cass stuffed the phone into her pocket. She wasn't ready to share with Greta just yet. She'd reply to Mick later, when she was in *Sassy's*.

'So,' Greta continued, 'Ray Morgan hasn't left. Has he bothered you again?'

Cass shook her head. 'I think… hope… he got the message.'

'The reporters seem to have killed the story too. Do you think he put them wise?'

'I don't know, but I doubt it. For Ray, any publicity is good publicity, and I'd guess the story amused him.' Cass felt smug in the knowledge her appearances with Mick might have had something to do with it.

'I have some news.' Greta picked up her cup and put it down again. 'Leo and I are going away on a trip.'

Cass's eyes widened. 'What about *Birds of a Feather?*' She knew how Greta hated to leave her shop. She and Leo hadn't even gone on a honeymoon.

'We'll only be gone for two weeks, and Jo has offered to take care of things here. It's school holidays, and she knows the ropes. She used to help out before she went overseas. It'll be the honeymoon we didn't have.' Greta smiled, and Cass suddenly noticed her friend had a glow about her, too.

Two weeks. It would give Cass a reprieve. Maybe, by the time Greta and Leo returned, she would have found the courage to tell her friend about her and Mick. 'Where are you going to?'

Greta smiled again. 'Although Leo has sold his hotels, he's still interested in them. First, we're spending a few days in Manila. He hasn't been back since the earthquake and is eager to see how the reconstruction work is going, and to reconnect with the staff there. Then we're travelling to Paris. I've always wanted to go to Paris. It was top of the list of places I intended to visit before Jo came along and put paid to any travel for me.'

'I'm so glad. I'm sure you'll have a wonderful time. I'll miss you.'

'You'll have Jo. I'm sure she'll be glad of coffee in the morning, too.'

'I guess.' But Cass knew it wouldn't be the same.

*

As soon as she was in *Sassy's*, Cass replied to Mick's text. She couldn't wait to see him again, and although the shop was busy, the day seemed to drag, until finally she was able to put up the *Closed* sign and head home.

Once there, she showered and changed, choosing a dusky pink wool dress which she knew flattered her, and stepping into her highest heels, before taming her hair into a neat style and adding a touch of makeup.

When she walked into the kitchen, Justin was heating up some leftovers, and Hector was winding himself around his ankles in the hope of some titbits.

Her nephew whistled. 'Wow, looking good, Cass. Going somewhere special?'

Cass blushed. 'Just out to dinner.'

'But you don't… Hey, are you going to dinner with Mick? He seemed to be in a particularly good mood today.'

Cass blushed again.

'You make a good couple. I hope…'

'That's enough, Justin. What are you up to tonight?'

'We're all going over to Zack's. His dad and Mel are away and…'

'I hope you're not having a party while they're gone.'

Justin looked guilty. 'Not a party, just a few mates. We're going to play some music.'

'Okay, but be careful. I'm sure Aaron and Mel trust Zack to take care of the place while they're gone.'

'No worries, Cass. We know how to behave.'

'Well, be sure you do.' She had a good idea of what teenagers might get up to when their parents were away. She recalled Vi's story about what happened when Justin had a few friends around. It was what prompted them to banish him to Bellbird Bay. She didn't want to think of Aaron and Mel coming home to a messy house… or worse.

'You have a good time, too,' he said with a cheeky grin.

'Thanks.'

*

Cass was a bag of nerves by the time she arrived at Mick's door and rang the bell. She'd imagined this scenario so often she could scarcely believe it was actually happening. She was about to have dinner with Mick Roberts, in his home, and who knew what might happen before the night was over. She pushed down the worry he'd have changed his mind or that this was a huge mistake as she heard his footsteps coming towards the door.

'Cass, you're looking amazing.' Mick greeted her with a warm hug and a kiss which helped calm her. 'Come in.' He led her into the kitchen where a bowl of salad was sitting on the benchtop along with a platter on which two large steaks were lying in a marinade. 'I'm not a great cook,' he said, 'but I can throw a steak on the barbie.'

'Sounds good to me,' she said, beginning to relax.

'Wine?'

'Please.' Cass gazed at Mick as he opened the bottle of cabernet sauvignon. He looked especially good tonight, in a pair of chinos and a dark blue shirt, the sleeves rolled up to the elbows showing his tanned arms. She swallowed. Somehow, the rolled-up sleeves were a lot sexier than the short-sleeved tee-shirt he wore to work, or was it all in her mind? Was she predisposed to find him sexy tonight? She pictured him naked in bed, his body next to hers, his…

'Cass?' His voice interrupted her daydream. He was holding out a glass of wine.

Cass blushed. 'Sorry, I was miles away. Thanks.' She took the glass and sipped the ruby red liquid, hoping to dismiss the images which were swirling around in her head.

'I thought we could eat outside. The barbecue's there, and I have an outdoor gas heater, perfect for an evening like this. Unless you'd prefer to eat in here?'

'No, outside will be fine.' Cass remembered the wonderful view and hoped it might help dowse the heat the sight of him had stirred up.

The steak was cooked to perfection, and the salad, a beetroot coleslaw which Mick admitted he'd purchased ready-made, complemented it perfectly. Conversation flowed, with Cass feeling as if she'd known Mick for ever. She didn't want the evening to end, sorry when she rose to leave.

'Don't go yet,' Mick said, pulling her into his arms. 'I've been waiting all evening to do this.' His lips found hers and Cass felt her world spinning, as a bolt of desire threatened to overwhelm her. 'I don't want you to leave,' Mick murmured into her hair, his hands stroking her and sending shivers through her entire body.

'I don't want to go,' she whispered, straining against him. Were all her dreams about to come true?

Forty-seven

Next morning, Cass awoke at her usual time. For several moments she lay with her eyes closed, reliving the previous evening. She couldn't believe she'd slept with Mick, though there had been precious little sleep before she'd crept out of his bed and driven home in the early hours of the morning, unwilling to have Justin waken to an empty house. She smiled at the memory of their lovemaking, still enveloped in the glow. Mick was a gentle and experienced lover and had taken Cass to heights of pleasure she'd never known before.

But she couldn't lie here all day. She swung her legs out of the bed, and slid her feet into her slippers, seeing the clothes she'd worn the evening before, lying in a heap on the floor where she'd left them. She picked them up and danced around the room, singing to herself before she entered the shower where she continued to hum the melody which seemed stuck in her head. *Take my Breath Away* mirrored her feelings exactly.

In the kitchen, Hector was standing over his food bowl, only moving slightly to allow Cass to fill it. She filled the kettle to make herself a cup of peppermint tea, and turned on the coffee machine, knowing how Justin liked his morning coffee. It hadn't taken him long to replace the morning tea he'd preferred when he first arrived with coffee. Then she slipped two slices of bread into the toaster and took the jar of ginger, lime and lemon marmalade out of the pantry, making a mental note to order another couple of jars online from The Ginger Factory in Yandina.

By the time Justin appeared, the coffee was ready, and Cass was eating breakfast. These days, he didn't seem to awaken quite as early as he had; Cass put it down to his late nights. He and Zack seemed to have such a full social life, she wondered when the other boy found time to study. But from all accounts, he was doing well at university.

Last night had been wonderful, but she had left in a rush and there had been no time to arrange another meeting, so when her phone pinged with a text, Cass was in no doubt who it was from.

Tonight? xxx

She grinned.

'From Mick?' Justin asked, giving her a wink.

'Maybe. You'll be late if you don't get a move on.'

'Will be off shortly,' he said, draining his coffee and picking up the cheese sandwich he'd put together quickly. 'I'll eat this on the way.'

'On the bike?' Cass asked, but her words fell on deaf ears as Justin left, the front door banging shut behind him.

It was Monday, so no work today, and Greta and Leo were setting off on their trip next day. Cass had wished her friend well yesterday and didn't want to risk bumping into her today, sure her face would give her away.

She was feeling good, so good she decided it was time to speak to her sister, to try to mend fences with Vi. The two hadn't spoken since Vi left for home, and Cass felt bad about it. Now she was happy with Mick, she wanted to be at peace with everyone in her life and, although never close, this last disagreement had driven a greater wedge than ever between her and Vi. She checked the time. It would be around nine in the evening in London. Cass took a deep breath and picked up her phone to call on WhatsApp.

Vi answered straight away. 'Cass, is something wrong? Justin…?'

'Everything's fine, Vi. Justin has just gone to work. I thought we should talk.'

Vi ignored her last comment. 'He's not still working on that boat, is he? Roger's not pleased about it, Cass. He's told Justin if he doesn't change his mind about that and about staying in Australia, he'll stop his allowance. You've poisoned our son against us.'

Cass sighed. 'Vi, can you just stop for a minute and listen to yourself? It's not you talking. You're only parroting your husband. You spent time with Justin when you were here. You must have seen how happy he is. He's almost twenty, capable of making his own decisions. I think you'll find he's no longer dependent on an allowance from his dad.' She remembered Greta's words, and added, 'I know it must be difficult for you to realise he wants his own life, but it is *his* life, Vi. You ought to be proud of him, proud you've raised such an independent young man.' She paused.

There was a moment's silence, then Vi said, her voice breaking, 'You don't understand what it's like for me, Cass. Roger has worked hard in his law practice. It's always been his plan for Justin to join him. This decision of his has made Roger…' Her voice broke.

'Vi, are you all right?'

'I will be, just as soon as Justin is back home.'

'Vi,' Cass said, as gently as she could, 'it's not going to happen. He's already submitted an application to the university and is planning on going up there to have a look around the campus. It's all he thinks about. And he's saving madly to be able to pay for his accommodation. Can't you talk to Roger, help him understand?'

'Talk to him? You don't know my husband.'

Not for the first time, Cass wondered about the state of her sister's marriage. It was none of her business, but she hated to think of Vi being unhappy and bullied. 'I'm sorry, Vi. I really am. I didn't call to talk about Justin… or Roger. I hated the way we parted on bad terms. Now Mum has gone, you and Justin are the only family I have. I want us to be friends. I want you to know I'm here for you if you ever need someone.'

There was no reply, only the suspicion of a sniff.

Then Vi said, 'I don't need friends, Cass. I don't know what I need.'

There was silence again, and Cass realised her sister had ended the call. It hadn't gone the way she'd expected, but it had confirmed her suspicions Vi was under Roger's thumb. She felt sorry for her sister, but there wasn't much she could do from here. If only she could jump on a plane and be there for her, but that wasn't feasible either. It made Cass glad she wasn't in a similar situation, which she might have been if she hadn't left Ray when she did. Ray Morgan and her brother-in-law had a lot in common. Both were men with an inflated idea of their own importance, who liked getting their own way, and bullied anyone who stood up to them. In Ray's case it took the form of stalking. Cass shivered remembering how he'd followed her and tried to force her into resuming their relationship. She was glad she now had Mick to protect her.

Thinking of Mick reminded Cass of his text. She opened it again to send a reply. He answered immediately, making arrangements for them to have dinner at *The Beach House*, Bellbird Bay's premier restaurant. Cass happily agreed.

Forty-eight

For the two weeks Greta had been gone, Cass had been trying to figure out how to pluck up her courage and explain things to her friend. She'd tried to justify her worry to Mick, but once he discovered Greta hadn't blackened his name to her, he couldn't understand her reluctance to tell her best friend they were seeing each other.

Despite this concern, it had been a wonderful two weeks for Cass. She and Mick had met almost every evening, spending time either at his home or in one of the many restaurants in Bellbird Bay. They had even braved the surf club where they'd spoken to Will Rankin and Martin Cooper, and where Mick and Greta's daughter, Jo, had greeted them with a wink and had given her a hug.

They'd also continued to make love, their passion growing as they became more familiar with each other's bodies. Cass couldn't believe how happy she was, and Mick seemed to be, too.

But today Greta would be back, and Cass knew she had to tell her before someone else did.

Cass was trembling with nerves as she balanced the two cups of coffee and pushed open the door to *Birds of a Feather*. 'Welcome back, Greta. Bet you had a wonderful trip. How was Paris?'

'It was incredible.' Greta smiled, then she peered at Cass. 'Jo tells me… you and Mick?'

Cass squirmed. She should have realised her friend would have already spoken to her daughter.

'We have been out together a few times,' she admitted.

'I'm glad.'

Cass stared at her in surprise.

'I've felt bad, ever since Leo and I got back together. I know Mick wanted to reignite our marriage – and I did consider it – but it was too late for us. There was nothing left between us – except for Jo. There'll always be Jo.' She smiled. 'I know I warned you against him, but Jo assures me her dad is a reformed character. If you think you and he can make a go of it, I'd be delighted. He's a good man, Cass, despite all the things I might have said about him in the past.'

'Thanks, Greta. I was worried about what you might think, how you might react. I've always had the impression you…' she swallowed, '… you felt some sort of ownership of him… and you did warn me.'

Greta reddened. 'I'm sorry if I gave that impression. I must admit, for a time, I did hate the idea of seeing him with someone else. I guess it was a hangover from all the women I knew he went around with when we were married. Jo told me I was being silly. It seems she'd been trying to set him up with a woman she works with, unsuccessfully I might add.'

Cass wondered if that was the woman she'd seen him with at the exhibition in the art gallery, the woman who had aroused her jealousy. 'So you really don't mind?'

'No, if it makes you both happy and he doesn't hurt you, then I'm glad. Both you and Mick deserve to be happy. It's odd, I never pictured you two together, but…' she grinned, '… you make a good pair. I guess Justin's pleased?'

'Ecstatic, which is more than I imagine his mother will be when she finds out. But there's no rush to let Vi know.' Cass hadn't spoken to her sister since their last disastrous conversation. She'd made several attempts to call her but there had been no reply, so she could only assume Vi was avoiding her. Justin hadn't been able to reach her either, but he'd told Cass his allowance had been stopped.

'I won't miss it,' he'd said. 'I'm making good money with Mick, and since you refuse to accept any rent from me, I've been able to save most of it.'

'Well, *I'm* happy for you,' Greta repeated. 'I hope you and Mick can be as happy as Leo and me.'

'Thanks.' If Cass had felt good before, she now felt on top of the world with her friend's acceptance 'Now tell me all about Paris. Was it as wonderful as you imagined?'

The next few minutes, while the two women drank their coffee, was taken up by Greta describing the sights and cafés in Paris. 'It was hard to leave and come home,' she finished. 'There was still so much to see. Do you know, there was a group of students staying in the same hotel and they were going to The Louvre every morning, spending time in a different room each day.' She sighed.

'So, when are you going back?'

'I don't know. It's a long way, and we both have commitments here. But Leo says we will make another trip.'

'Lucky you.'

'Maybe you and Mick will go one day, too.'

'Maybe.' Cass didn't think it was likely, though if they did, perhaps she could visit Vi in London, too. She tucked the thought away to consider at another time.

Before Cass left to open up her own shop, Greta said, 'We must have dinner together, you and Mick, me and Leo. Maybe invite Jo and Bryan, too.'

Cass swallowed. 'Maybe,' she said, but she wasn't sure about it. Having dinner with Greta *and* Mick might be going too far, for now, anyway.

She couldn't wait till evening when she was to see Mick again. He was sure to ask her if she'd told Greta about them. Greta's reaction had been such a relief, and her suggestion of dinner a surprise. She wanted to be sure Greta really meant what she'd said before committing to meeting her with Mick… as his partner. The very thought made her knees weak.

*

'I told you Greta would be fine with us getting together.' Mick didn't know why Cass had been so concerned about his ex's reaction to him forming a relationship with her best friend, though she might have imagined he'd break her heart too. He didn't have a good track record. Jo was delighted, trying to take credit for it, saying, 'I told you you'd make a good couple, Dad,' and giving him a big hug. Although not understanding what it was all about, Mia joined in, and they'd all ended up laughing together, making Bryan wonder what was going on. Mick was so glad Jo had found Bryan. He was such a nice guy, and little Mia was a delight. He was looking forward to introducing Cass to them. She already knew Jo, of course.

Tonight, they had arranged to meet at the surf club, and he had a sneaking suspicion Jo and Bryan intended going there too, with Mia.

Mick whistled to himself as he showered and dressed. The business was having a particularly profitable season, the new boat was on order and would be delivered as soon as the money from his dad came in, Dad was settling into his new villa in *Bay Village*, and there was Cass. His face broke into a smile as it always did when he thought of the dainty dark-haired beauty who had captured his heart. How glad he was now that Greta had refused his attempt to renew their marriage. At the time, with Jo returning home, it had seemed an obvious move. But now, he could see it was impossible to revive the past – even if it had worked for Greta and Leo. He supposed what they had together was stronger than what had been between him and Greta, despite their being married and bringing up their daughter together. Had his affairs with other women been a sign he knew that even then? He'd never know. He only knew he'd be faithful to Cass, and never want to look at another woman, if she'd agree to spend the rest of her life with him.

But he was getting ahead of himself. It was early days. Though, despite the fact their relationship was still in its infancy, Mick knew that for him, it was serious. Cass was the woman he wanted to grow old with. His mind went back to the conversation with Martin in the club not so long ago, where his old mate asked him if he wanted to grow old on his own. Back then, it was something he hadn't considered. Now he knew. He didn't. He only hoped Cass felt the same.

There was something else bugging him, niggling away at the back of his mind. It wasn't till he was on his way to pick up Cass and was driving past *The Bay Gallery* that he remembered. It was what Ruby Sullivan had said to him at the opening of Coop's exhibition, something about his fate being in the room and babbling on about crests and troughs. Damn the old woman. She'd been spot on. She really was a witch. But he was on the crest of a wave right now. It should be plain sailing from now on.

Mick was right. No sooner were he and Cass seated on the deck than Jo and Bryan appeared with Mia.

'Can we join you, Dad?' she asked, giving him a hug, while Mia yelled, 'Grandpa Mick!' and put her arms up for a hug, too, before staring at Cass.

'Hello, Cass, I'm pleased to see you.' Jo hugged her, too. 'I think you and Dad are good together.'

Mia was still staring at Cass.

'Mia, this is a friend of mine. Her name is Cass,' he said to the little girl.

'Hello, Cass. I'm Mia. Do you know Gigi?'

'It's what she calls Mum,' Jo said.

'Hello, Mia. I'm very pleased to meet you. Your grandad talks about you a lot. And, yes, I know Gigi. She's a good friend of mine.'

Seemingly satisfied with her response, Mia took Cass's hand and shook it as she'd seen her dad do, while everyone smiled.

Unwilling to risk Jo's disapproval, Mick ordered a non-alcoholic beer and grilled salmon with salad, feeling a touch of envy when Bryan brought back a full-strength beer for himself from the bar and ordered a burger and chips. The women both chose salmon, too, along with white wine, and Mia had the chicken nuggets from the children's menu with a strawberry smoothie.

'I visited Grandad yesterday,' Jo said, while they were waiting for their meals to arrive. 'He seems to be really enjoying his new villa and has met a few people he knows. It was a good move, Dad.'

'Yes. It took a while to convince him, but I think the fall he had gave him a shock. It's a weight off my mind to know he's living in a supportive community.'

'Have you met him, Cass?' Jo asked.

It was Mick who replied. 'Early days, Jo. All in good time. Holidays all over? You're back at school again?'

'Me too,' Mia replied, 'and I've enrolled in Nippers again too.' She grinned.

'I enjoyed being in Nippers too, when I was your age,' Cass said.

Mia looked at her strangely, as if she found it impossible to imagine someone as old as Cass ever being a Nipper.

Their meals arrived before anyone could respond, and the

conversation moved on to discuss the new boat Mick was buying, and his dad's generosity.

*

By the end of the evening, Cass felt she'd been welcomed into Mick's family. It was a strange sensation, as if her life had suddenly changed in a way she could never have imagined, and she was now part of an extended family which would include not only Jo, Bryan and Mia, but also Bryan's parents, Iain and Bev. It was a heady thought.

'Thanks,' she said to Mick as they were driving home. 'Thanks for being you, for having such an accepting daughter, for Mia, too.' She had the feeling it wouldn't be long before Mia found a special name for her, as she had for Greta.

'Thank *you*,' Mick said, turning to smile at her. 'It's no more than you deserve for making me so happy. You've changed my life.'

Forty-nine

It was two weeks since Greta had first mentioned Cass and Mick having dinner with her and Leo, and Cass had finally agreed, sensing her friend wasn't going to accept her refusal for ever.

Now, the day had come, and Greta had popped her head into *Sassy's* before closing time to remind her. 'We'll see you and Mick at seven?'

'We'll be there.'

'It'll be fine, Cass. Mick and I have always remained friends, and there hasn't been anything between us for ages. I know I may have come on a bit strong when I first thought you were getting together, but Jo put me straight... Leo, too.' She chuckled as if remembering something her husband had said to her. 'We'll break out the champagne, make it a celebration.'

Cass smiled, thinking it was a bit early in their relationship for a celebration, but willing to go along with her friend. They were meeting at *The Leonard Family Resort* and she wanted to ask Greta if Ray was still there. Surely he'd be gone by now? It was almost two months since he'd appeared at her door, and she hadn't seen him for some time.

'Going out again?' Justin asked, when he saw her dressed in a new outfit she'd bought from *Birds of a Feather*. When she'd seen Greta unpack the deep blue dress with the handkerchief hemline, she'd been unable to resist it, and she knew it brought out the blue in her eyes. 'Is it okay if I have a few friends around?'

Cass pursed her lips, but she remembered when Justin and a few friends had got together at Zack's parents. There hadn't been any trouble, and Mel reported they'd left the place immaculate – perhaps too immaculate. 'As long as you take care,' she said, knowing she needed to allow him some leeway.

'Thanks, Cass.' He gave her a hug, making her wish once again he was her son, or that she had a son like him.

Cass was feeling flustered when she and Mick walked into the hotel foyer, and seeing Greta and Leo standing there arm-in-arm did nothing to calm her nerves. They all greeted each other with hugs and handshakes and headed into the restaurant. Mick's firm hand on Cass's back gave her confidence, and by the time she was seated at a table by the window, she was feeling more comfortable.

The food, as was to be expected, was delicious and, although Cass felt odd to be toasted with champagne, the meal passed without any problem. While they were waiting for dessert – a decadent-sounding chocolate mousse with marinated cherries – Cass rose to go to the restroom.

Once there, she gazed at herself in the mirror, barely recognising the glowing face smiling back at her. In the few weeks she and Mick had been together, she'd become a different woman. It was as if all the compliments with which Mick showered her had resulted in making her into the beautiful woman he told her she was.

Cass was making her way back to their table when a shadow fell over her. Looking up, her heart jumped. Ray Morgan stood there, a knowing grin on his handsome face. He leant towards her, so close she could smell his aftershave and a faint hint of the whisky he must have been drinking.

'You may have fooled the journalists with your whale-watching guy? But just wait. You'll soon change your mind. You'll realise I'm the one you're meant to be with.'

Shaken, Cass managed to make it back to the table where Mick peered at her. 'What happened, Cass? You look as if you've seen a ghost.'

'Not a ghost. Ray… he was here. He stopped me on my way back.' She glanced over her shoulder and Mick's eyes followed hers, but there was no sign of Ray.

'Ray Morgan?' Greta asked, hearing their conversation. 'Leo, can't you do something? I told Leo about him,' she said to Cass.

'I'm sorry, Cass,' Leo said. 'He's a guest here. I can't force him to go, but I do believe he's due to leave in a few more days. Surely he can't do any more damage in that time?'

Cass tried to smile, but it felt false. Leo had no idea what Ray could be capable of, and she'd never feel safe as long as he was in Bellbird Bay. At least she had Mick by her side. He wouldn't let anything happen to her. But the knowledge he couldn't be with her twenty-four hours of the day was a stark reminder Ray could still torment her.

The mood of the evening was spoiled and, after eating dessert, Cass and Mick chose to leave, thanking Leo for his hospitality.

They were driving past the esplanade, when Cass put her hand on Mick's arm. 'If you don't mind, I think I'd like to take a walk along the beach. It might help me forget about the shock of seeing Ray.'

'Sure, honey. What did he say to get you so upset?'

Cass shook her head. There was no way she was going to repeat Ray's words to Mick. She only wanted to forget them, to forget Ray and enjoy what the future had in store for her and Mick.

One hand carrying her shoes, the other in Mick's, they made their way down to the beach, right to the edge of the water. There, Mick took Cass in his arms. She felt safe there, as if nothing could harm her, as if she'd come home, as if Ray and his malicious words were part of a bad dream.

'Thanks,' she said. 'I needed that. You make me feel so happy.' Cass stood up on her tiptoes and threw her arms around Mick's neck, the roar of the waves drowning out everything else and making her feel as if she and Mick were alone in the world.

'Your place or mine?' Mick asked.

'Unless you want to join Justin and his mates, it had better be yours,' she said, with a laugh. 'I suspect they'll be playing their music till all hours.'

'Does that mean you might decide to stay?'

Cass smiled. The thought had crossed her mind, when Justin asked permission to invite his friends around. It would be the first time she'd spent the entire night with Mick, but she was no longer worried about Justin waking up to find her gone, and the thought of waking up together in Mick's king-sized bed filled her with excitement and a sense of anticipation.

Mick took her silence for agreement and kissed her again, lifting her up so her feet left the ground and making her senses swim.

Fifty

Mick could scarcely believe his eyes when he opened them to see Cass lying beside him, her hair spread out on the pillow, her face so peaceful in repose. He lay staring at her, drinking in the fact she was actually there.

Her eyes opened and she smiled.

'Hey, you. Sleep well?'

'Wonderfully well.' Cass stretched her arms above her head. 'It's so peaceful here.' She had barely finished speaking when the resident kookaburras set up their morning cacophony.

They both laughed.

'Breakfast?' Mick asked.

'Mmm. Maybe later.'

'Works for me.' Mick pulled her into his arms.

It was sometime later, and the sun was streaming in through the window when they disentangled themselves.

'I'm hungry now,' Cass said with a cheeky grin, 'but don't you have to go to work today?'

'No cruises today. I do need some time off. Why don't we have breakfast, then pack a picnic hamper and go to the beach?'

'Sounds good. I'll need to go home first to change… and check what sort of state the house is in. Though I trust Justin, you never know with young people. And I need to check on Hector.'

Mick had yet to make the acquaintance of Cass's cat but had heard a lot about him. He hoped the creature would take to him, as he played a large part in Cass's life. 'Breakfast first. How does bacon with scrambled eggs on toast sound?'

'It sounds delicious.'

Mick had a quick shower and pulled on a pair of khaki shorts and a white linen shirt before heading for the kitchen, leaving Cass to shower and dress.

'Wow, something smells good.' While Cass was wearing the outfit she'd worn to dinner, she had done something different to her hair, and her face, free of makeup, was glowing.

Mick hugged her and kissed her forehead. 'Take a seat. It's almost ready. Coffee?'

'Thanks.' Instead of sitting, Cass went to the window. 'You have an amazing view from here.'

'Yeah.' Mick moved away from the stove and stood behind Cass, wrapping his arms around her and nuzzling her hair. She smelt delicious, of a faint lemon scent which bore no resemblance to his shower gel. 'I love it here. it's like being on top of the world.'

Cass turned towards him. 'I think…'

There was the smell of burning, and Mick quickly went back to rescue the scrambled eggs.

After breakfast, Cass helped Mick pack a picnic basket with bread, ham and a selection of cheeses, all of which he'd bought the day before in anticipation of spending the day with Cass. He added a bottle of wine and some plastic plates and cutlery, and they were ready.

*

There was no sign of Justin when they reached Cass's home, but a large Siamese cat appeared as if from nowhere and wound himself around Cass's ankles before glaring suspiciously at Mick.

'This is Hector,' Cass said. 'Hector, be nice to Mick. He's a special friend.'

The cat didn't move and let out a yowl.

Mick flinched, but he put down a hand to pat the creature which pushed its head into his hand.

'He likes you,' Cass said. 'I'll just fill his bowls, then get changed. Make yourself at home.'

The cat turned his attention to the bowl, now filled with food, and Cass disappeared.

Mick wandered into the living room. It was immaculate, only the odd empty glass sitting on the carpet and the open windows evidence that a group of young people had spent time there. He took the glasses into the kitchen where Hector took one look at him and vanished out through the cat flap.

'Hey, Mick.' A tousled and bleary-eyed Justin walked in. 'Cass back?'

'She's getting changed,' Mick said, feeling as if he was a teenager again and Justin was the adult. He wasn't accustomed to this sort of scenario. 'Good evening?'

'Yeah.' Justin took a carton of milk from the fridge and filled a large glass, downing it in one gulp. He wiped his mouth with the back of his hand. 'Went on a bit. Didn't get much sleep. Might go back to bed.' He disappeared.

'Did I hear Justin?' Cass reappeared, dressed in a pair of jeans and a blue and white striped tee-shirt. She was carrying a navy shirt and looked amazing.

'You did, but he's gone back to bed.'

Cass chuckled. 'It must have been a late night. I'm glad I stayed away.'

'That the only reason?' Mick pulled her into his arms, unable to resist.

'What do you think?' She chuckled again, and kissed him on the lips, before pulling away. 'Ready for that picnic on the beach?'

'Yeah.'

It was only a short drive to Dolphin Beach which, as Mick had hoped, was deserted. It was a glorious day and cursing he hadn't suggested bringing swimsuits and having a swim before lunch, Mick set down the picnic basket in a shady spot and took Cass's hand.

As they walked along in the shallows, stopping every few minutes to kiss, it was as if they were the only two people in the world. What a pity it couldn't always be like this, Mick thought, just as Cass said, 'I wish we could stay here for ever.'

It was with regret that they packed up at the end of the afternoon, but Mick couldn't bear for their time together to end. 'How about dinner at *The Firenze* tonight?' he asked, when they arrived back at Cass's.

'Yes, please.' Cass smiled, and Mick felt as if the sun had come out again.

*

Cass was excited as she dressed for dinner with Mick. Their day together had been perfect, waking up beside him, breakfast prepared by him, then the picnic on the beach after which they'd lain on the sand in each other's arms, regardless of who might see them. But no one had. They'd had the beach to themselves, their own special little piece of paradise.

As she fixed her hair and applied her makeup, wearing a blue linen dress, over which she'd thrown a matching blue wrap patterned with red poppies, Cass wondered if Mick had chosen *The Firenze* on purpose. It was where they had gone for their first dinner together, the dinner at which they had agreed no relationship was possible between them. How ridiculous it seemed, now Cass knew Greta had no problem with their being together, and Mick was convinced Greta hadn't poisoned Cass against him. There was still the issue of Mick's history of womanising, but he had managed to put her mind at rest, reassured her it was all in the past and he was a reformed character. And she believed him. There was no way she'd have allowed him into her life if she hadn't.

'He's a good man, Hector,' she told the cat who had followed her into the bedroom and was now lying on her bed licking his paws, despite knowing he was expressly forbidden to be there. Cass was in such a good mood, she couldn't bring herself to push him off.

This dinner at *The Firenze* was much pleasanter than the previous one. Laughingly, both chose the same items from the menu as before, but this time Mick ordered a bottle of prosecco with the meal. When they finished, there was no question how the evening would end, and back in Mick's home they barely made it inside before they were in each other's arms.

However, unlike the previous night, this time Cass rose to leave at midnight, aware next day she had a shop to open, and Mick had a morning cruise booked. 'I can call a cab,' she said. 'There's no need for you to get up and dress.'

'No way,' Mick said. 'You're not going to run away and leave me like a Bellbird Bay version of Cinderella. I'll drive you. Give me a minute.'

In less than a minute, he had pulled on an old pair of shorts and a tee-shirt, and they were driving through the deserted streets, his hand lying warmly on her thigh, and Cass filled with a sense of wellbeing.

When they stopped at her door, she turned to meet his kiss, feeling as if all was right with her world. 'My turn to cook for you tomorrow,' she said, running her fingers through the hair at the nape of his neck.

'I can't wait,' Mick replied, kissing her one more time, before she slid out of the car.

As Cass stood waving him goodbye, before turning into the house, she experienced a huge upsurge of pleasure, and Ruby Sullivan's words came back to her. Maybe the old woman had been right. Maybe her time had come, and she was going to get her wish, her own happy ever after.

Fifty-one

Mick couldn't believe his luck. He felt jubilant. It was as if all his Christmases had come at once. He found himself smiling for no reason and whistling as he went about his daily tasks. Even Justin had noticed the happy mood which no number of difficult passengers could dent.

All day, thoughts of Cass kept intruding on what he was doing. He was glad when the day was over, and he could go home. On the way, he stopped to buy a bottle of wine and a bunch of flowers, determined not to arrive at Cass's emptyhanded. He wondered how the evening would end. They had never made love in Cass's bed, probably because of Justin's presence, but maybe tonight… Even if they didn't, it was enough she had invited him to dinner. It was a definite step forward in their relationship – and Hector seemed to like him.

Mick was driving past the esplanade, smiling to himself at the sight of *Sassy*'s. Even in the dim light he could see Cass's new window display, the base of which mimicked a beach scene.

Suddenly he noticed what appeared to be an accident. A woman was leaning over the figure of a man who was lying on the ground. As he watched, she raised her hand as if asking for help. He recognised her. It was Brenda Collins. A dart of guilt stabbed Mick. He hadn't spoken to the woman or contacted her, since his call to let her down as gently as he could. She'd been very nice about it, but he could tell from her voice she was disappointed, that she'd hoped for more.

Checking the road was clear, Mick hit the brakes, jumping out and crossing the road as soon as the car stopped. 'What's happened?'

he asked, recognising the figure lying on the ground. It was Brenda's brother. He wasn't moving.

'Oh, Mick! I'm so glad to see you,' Brenda said, tears streaming down her cheeks. 'We were making our way back to the car when Andy seemed to stumble and fall. He hit his head, and I can't get him to respond. I was… my phone's dead.' She held up her iPhone. 'Can you…?'

Mick pulled out his phone and dialled 000. 'Ambulance,' he said and, glancing around, gave the location. It was the same spot where Cass had stumbled, where he'd taken her in his arms and…' He pulled his mind back to the present. 'It shouldn't be long,' he said, worried there was no sign of movement from Brenda's brother.

'You don't think he's…?' Brenda said, her voice trembling with fear. 'Andy's all I have in the world. He has a weak heart, and I've always tried to take care of him. I should have…'

'Shh.' Mick took Brenda in his arms to offer what comfort he could. 'Whatever has happened to your brother isn't your fault. The council should have fixed this footpath. The uneven surface is a danger to everyone who walks along it. He…'

Just then, there was a groan from the man lying on the ground. Brenda dropped to her knees again. 'Andy, can you hear me? Don't try to move. The ambulance will be here soon.'

No sooner had she spoken than the sound of a siren split the air, and an ambulance appeared and stopped nearby. The paramedics immediately got to work, checking Andy out and attaching him to a drip before loading him into the ambulance.

'Will you be all right now?' Mick asked Brenda.

'Could you…?' she asked, her eyes filled with tears.

Mick thought of the evening he had planned, then looked at Brenda's woebegone face and knew he had no choice. 'Give me a minute,' he said, pulling out his phone again, and pressing Cass's number on speed dial. It was busy. He glanced at Brenda, at the ambulance which was about to leave. He'd have to send a text. He quickly typed, *Have had an emergency. Won't make dinner. So sorry. Forgive me. Will come when I can. Explain later. xx*, and pressed *Send*. Then he turned back to Brenda. 'I'll follow the ambulance and meet you at the hospital.'

Brenda met him at the entrance to Emergency. 'They've taken him in to be examined. They said they'll do a brain scan and... Oh, Mick, what will I do if...?'

Mick pulled her into his arms again, patting her back as he used to with Jo when she was a child. 'Try not to worry,' he said, knowing it was probably an impossibility, 'with luck, all will be well and Andy will be sitting up talking to you in no time.'

'Will you stay?' Her eyes were wide with fear.

'Of course I will.' Mick mentally dismissed any hope of getting to Cass's later and made up his mind to stay at the hospital until Brenda had news of her brother one way or the other. He hoped the news would be good but feared the worst. He reached for his phone to contact Cass again, but it wasn't in his pocket. It must have slid out in the car. He cursed silently. There was no way he could leave Brenda to fetch it. He just hoped Cass would understand.

*

Cass had set the table in the dining room, and the meal she'd carefully prepared was ready to go into the oven. Her phone rang as she stepped out of the shower. Hoping it was a wrong number – she didn't have time for a long chat – Cass sighed when she saw it was her sister on the line.

'Hello, Vi,' she said, wishing her sister had chosen a better time, the memory of their last conversation clear in her head. What did Vi want now?

'Cass.' She paused. 'I'm sorry I haven't been in touch, and I'm sorry about our last conversation. I resented your comments about my marriage, the suggestion all wasn't well with Roger and me. You were right. I refused to acknowledge it for ages, but I've finally accepted the truth. He cares more about his law practice than he does about me, and he blames me for Justin's decisions. I've decided to leave him.'

Cass gasped. This was the last thing she expected to hear from her super-conventional sister. 'What will you do? Where will you go?'

Cass took a seat on the bed as Vi laid out her plans to rent a small apartment in a neighbouring suburb and institute divorce proceedings, finishing with, 'I'll be much better on my own than staying with Roger.'

This was a shock coming from the woman who had always despised Cass's lack of a partner. Cass didn't know what to say.

'There's no need for you to say anything, to tell me how much you care,' Vi continued. 'I know you've never liked Roger. But would you tell Justin for me? His phone's always either busy or off. I don't think he wants to speak to me, and I don't want to give him this news in a text or an email.'

Trust Vi, Cass thought, asking her to tell Justin. 'Okay, I can do that. Do you want me to ask him to call you?'

'Would you?' For the first time Cass could remember, her sister was pleading with her.

'Of course I will.'

When the call ended, Cass sat for a few moments staring at her phone. How bizarre life was. Just as she had found happiness with Mick, her sister was leaving her husband of over twenty years. She noticed a text from Mick and smiled. But when she read it, her expression changed. *An emergency? What sort of emergency? Had Mick been hurt?*

Hector pushed open the bedroom door and tried to leap up onto the bed beside her. 'Not now, Hector.' Cass pressed Mick's number, but the call went to voicemail. Undecided what to do, she pulled on the outfit she'd laid out earlier, but the sense of anticipation she'd felt when she chose the black and white patterned dress had disappeared. She went into the kitchen and poured herself a glass of wine, putting the food she'd prepared into the fridge till she knew what was happening, then going into the living room and turning on the television.

After flicking through the channels and finding nothing to hold her attention, Cass turned it off again and picked up a book. But her mind was in a whirl, trying to imagine what might have happened to prevent Mick from coming to dinner as planned. She relived the past few days and weeks in her mind. *Had something happened to Mick's dad?* According to Justin, who was out with his friends again, the tours had gone well today, and Mick had been in a particularly cheerful mood. She'd have to be patient and wait for his explanation.

It was late. There had been no further word from Mick, and Cass was tired of trying to contact him. She was on her third, or maybe fourth, glass of wine, when her phone pinged with another text. She opened it eagerly. But it wasn't from Mick. Her heart dropped when she saw the sender. *Why was Ray Morgan contacting her? Hadn't he heard her when she told him she didn't want to see or hear from him again?* She read the message.

See what your friend, Mick, gets up to when you're not around. I would never let you down like this.

There was an attachment.

Cass's eyes widened at the photo of Mick holding another woman in his arms, a woman she recognised as the one she'd seen him with at the art gallery all those weeks ago, the woman he'd said worked beside Jo and who he wasn't interested in.

Fifty-two

Cass hadn't slept. She'd tossed and turned, picturing Mick with this other woman, the woman he'd dismissed as being one of Jo's failed attempts at matchmaking. And just as she'd been feeling superior to her sister, secure in her own burgeoning relationship. It served her right. Had he been seeing this woman all the time? He couldn't have been, but what other explanation could there be? Should she have paid more attention to Greta's warning?

After a shower, which did little to improve her mood, Cass dressed and made her way to the kitchen where Justin was eating breakfast as usual.

'I fed Hector,' he said.

'Thanks, Justin. Have you heard anything from Mick?' Surely if there had been an emergency which would prevent him working today, Justin would have heard.

'No. Did something happen last night?'

Cass had been in bed when she heard Justin come home at around midnight. She shook her head and busied herself making coffee. This wasn't a morning for herbal tea. She was about to take it over to the table with a slice of toast she doubted she'd be able to swallow, when her phone rang. It was Mick, the call she'd been waiting for. But, for some reason, she was reluctant to answer, the photo Ray had sent her flashing into her head.

'Not going to answer?'

'Not now.' Cass slid the phone into her pocket and took a sip of coffee.

Determined to try to remain positive, Cass bought two coffees in *The Bay Café* as usual, but when she pushed open the door *to Birds of a Feather* to be greeted by Greta's smiling face, she faltered.

'How was last night?' Greta asked. Cass had confided in her the day before and shared her plans to cook dinner for Mick.

'It… it didn't happen. Mick was otherwise engaged.'

'What do you mean?'

'Oh, Greta! He texted me to say he couldn't make it due to some emergency, then I received this.' She opened her phone to reveal the photo Ray had sent. 'It looks as if Mick has gone back to his old tricks. I fell for his promise it was all in the past, but…' She felt her eyes moisten and blinked rapidly.

'I don't believe it.' Greta peered at the photo. 'Isn't she the woman he was with at the gallery, Jo's friend?'

'Yes. I recognised her straight away. He told me there was nothing between them, but it doesn't look like it, does it?'

'There might be an explanation.'

'You think?' Cass stared at the photo again as if by doing so she could change the image.

'Have you spoken to him?'

'No. He rang this morning, but I couldn't face talking to him. I'm not ready to hear his lies.'

'Oh, Cass!' Greta hugged her. 'I'm so sorry. I wouldn't have this happen to you for the world. I was sure Mick was a reformed character, that he'd put all this behind him. You need to talk to him. There might be a good explanation,' she repeated, but didn't sound hopeful.

'His text came just after my sister called to tell me she'd left her husband,' Cass said with a wry grin. 'And I was feeling smug that my life was happier than hers.' As she spoke, she remembered she hadn't told Justin about his mother's call. She'd do it tonight and try to persuade him to call her. Now she had a shop to open and needed to put a smile on her face for her customers.

To Cass's surprise, the day went more quickly than she expected. There were no more calls from Mick; she'd turned off her phone. Greta was right. They needed to talk, but she wasn't ready to hear his excuses just yet. She needed time to think. After closing *Sassy's*, instead of going straight home, she crossed the road to the beach, taking off her shoes before stepping down onto the sand.

Wandering along the edge of the ocean, her feet in the water, the sound of the waves in her ears, Cass felt better than she had all day. She was glad the beach was deserted. It helped her thinking process, but her thoughts were going round and round in circles. There was no denying the fact Mick had his arms around another woman. They were in a passionate embrace. The photo proved it. Greta said there might be some explanation, but what explanation could there be? When Mick was supposed to be having a romantic dinner with Cass, he was in the arms of another woman, playing Cass for all kinds of a fool.

She made her way back to the esplanade to the shrieking of the rosellas which always flew over at this time of night, filling the sky with their wings, and took a seat on a bench to put her shoes back on.

'You got my message?'

Cass looked up. 'Ray! What are you doing here?'

'I tried your shop, but it was closed. I had to see you. I'm leaving Bellbird Bay tomorrow. My leave's over. I have to be back in the studio on Monday. I wanted to… I needed to show you what this guy was like. I knew that…'

A dreadful thought occurred to Cass. 'You were following Mick too?'

'And I was proved right. He doesn't deserve you. Now you know what he's like, you're free to follow me to Sydney. I'd never be unfaithful to you. I never…'

'Ray! You were married.' The memory of her shame made her want to throw up. She'd been young and foolish, crazy to think she loved this man. How could he imagine she'd turn to him, no matter what Mick might have done?

'I was a lot younger back then, flattered by your attention. But I don't love you now. My life is here in Bellbird Bay, and I have no intention of leaving.' *Even if there's no future for me with Mick; even if I spend the rest of my life alone.*

'You'll regret it.' But Ray seemed finally to accept her words and, to Cass's relief, walked off.

Cass turned on her phone to see several missed calls from Mick. It rang almost immediately. It was Mick again. This time she answered.

*

Mick had gone through the day in a blur. He'd called Cass several times, only to reach her voicemail. Was she avoiding him? He wanted to ask Justin how she'd been this morning but was too embarrassed to put the young man in what might be a difficult position. This was something he and Cass had to work out between themselves. Surely she wasn't upset about him cancelling dinner?

When he'd texted Cass from the roadside, waiting for the ambulance, he'd intended to go over later to explain, sure she'd understand. But, once he arrived at the hospital, Brenda pleaded with him to stay until they knew how her brother was. He should have contacted Cass again. It was bad luck his phone was in the car, and Brenda was in no condition to be left alone. The hospital had been slow to get the results which revealed Andy had suffered a violent blow which could have proved fatal but was out of danger. It had been after midnight when he finally returned to his car, too late to call Cass.

Now he was home, he took out his phone again. If Cass didn't reply this time, he intended to go around, break down her door if necessary. He needed to find out what was wrong, why she was avoiding him. He pressed her number.

'Hello?' Cass's voice was faint, and he could hear the roar of waves in the background. *Where was she?*

'Cass, thank God. I've been trying to call you all day. Is everything all right?'

'It depends what you mean. Is it all right that you cancelled dinner with me, that you went straight to another woman's arms? I don't think so.'

Mick had never heard such a bitter note in Cass's voice before. 'What do you mean?'

'Don't try to deny it. You were seen.'

Mick racked his brain. *What was she talking about?*

'I thought you'd changed, Mick Roberts. I was wrong. A leopard never changes its spots.'

Leopard... spots. What was the woman talking about? Had she gone mad? 'Where are you?'

'On the esplanade.'

'Don't move. I'm on my way.' Without stopping to think, Mick rushed outside into the car, and drove directly to the esplanade. Cass was sitting on one of the benches facing the beach. She was hunched over and looked as if she might be crying. 'Cass?'

She looked up, her eyes red, her face blotched with tears.

Mick sat down beside her and tried to take her hand.

She pulled it away.

'I don't know what you've heard,' he said, 'but it's not true. Last night, I was on my way to dinner with you, when I saw two people. There had been an accident. I went to help, and…'

'I saw you,' she said, 'Ray sent me a photo of you and her. I know who she is.'

'Ray? Ray Morgan? What does he have to do with it?'

'He saw you with her in your arms, took a photo and sent it to me.' Cass took out her phone to show a photo of him with Brenda in his arms.

Mick stared at the image in astonishment. It must have been taken when he was comforting Brenda. He had to admit it did look suspicious. But it wasn't what happened. The photo had been carefully cropped – maybe even photoshopped – to make it look as if they were in a passionate embrace. No wonder Cass was distraught, had ignored his calls. But surely she couldn't believe…?

'It isn't… I didn't… It didn't happen. It's not what it looks. I can explain. Cass, you need to listen to me,' he said as she began to rise.

'I'm sorry, Mick. It seems to me it's very much the way it looks. I'm only sorry it took me so long to discover how wrong I'd been. I should have listened to the little voice in the back of my head, the one that said you couldn't be trusted, you were a womaniser and always would be, I should have paid attention to Greta's warnings, but I hoped… Goodbye,' she said, her voice breaking, as she rose and hurried away.

Mick wanted to race after her, force her to listen, but he knew it was useless. A flash of anger welled up threatening to choke him. He'd like to wring Ray Morgan's neck. What did the man think he was doing poisoning Cass against Mick? Did he hope she'd turn to Ray for comfort? Surely he knew Cass better than that, but perhaps not. The man was so full of himself, he probably thought it's exactly what she would do. He was tempted to go over to *The Leonard Family Resort* and… But common sense prevailed. It might give Mick pleasure to take his anger out on the man who caused it, but it would only result in another headline, and more publicity for the breakfast show host.

Wearily, Mick made his way home, determined that somehow, he'd make Cass listen to him. Although consumed with anger at her for believing Ray over him, he loved her too much to leave things like this.

Fifty-three

It had been two weeks since Cass had left Mick sitting on the esplanade, and he was no further forward, despite trying to call her and even going round to her house several times. But no matter what he tried, Cass refused to speak to him. He couldn't believe she didn't trust him enough to listen to an explanation. The only thing he hadn't tried was turning up at *Sassy's*, and he was loath to do that. It was her place of work, and she didn't deserve to have him confront her there, no matter how much he wanted to.

One piece of good news was that Ray Morgan had left Bellbird Bay. He was back on the breakfast show acting as charming as ever, no doubt ruining someone else's life, careless – or perhaps proud – of the chaos he'd created in Mick's.

Tired of spending his evenings alone thinking about Cass, Mick decided to go to the surf club. He'd been avoiding the place, unwilling to answer the questions about him and Cass he knew he'd be subjected to. They'd been so happy. He'd hoped to spend the rest of his life with her and was convinced she felt the same way. How could a photo, a moment comforting a distressed friend, have changed everything?

As soon as he reached the top of the stairs, he saw Jo and Bryan at the bar with Bev and Iain. He was about to retreat when little Mia caught sight of him.

'Grandpa Mick!' she yelled, running over to almost cannon into him.

'Hello, sweetie.' Mick picked her up and gave her a hug.

'Are you having dinner with us, too?'

By this time, Jo had joined them. 'I didn't know you were coming here tonight, Dad. We're about to go out and find a table on the deck. You'll join us?'

Knowing how impossible it would be to refuse, Mick nodded and, putting Mia back on her feet, went across to the bar with them.

Once they had drinks, the group made their way to the deck where they pushed two tables together, before choosing their meals. Mia insisted on sitting beside Mick, and Jo was on his other side, making it impossible to ignore her.

As the evening progressed, the conversation revolved around a project Iain had recently undertaken, and some improvements Bev was planning for the garden centre. There wasn't a lot Mick could contribute, so when Mia became restless and begged to be allowed to go to the play centre designed for children, he volunteered to take her.

'You don't need to stay, Dad,' Jo said, 'it's well supervised. Mia will be fine on her own.'

When he returned, Bryan was involved in a discussion with Bev and Iain, and Jo pulled Mick aside.

'Brenda told me what you did for her,' she said. 'Your Good Samaritan act. She only came back to work today. Her brother's home now and expected to make a full recovery. It's all thanks to you.'

Mick shrugged. 'Hardly. I only did what anyone would have. I just happened to be passing.'

'Well, Brenda credits you with saving Andy's life.'

At what cost?

'What's happening with you and Cass?' Jo nudged him. 'She's not with you tonight.'

'It's over.' Saying it aloud made it real. Until now, Mick had been trying to pretend he could work things out, but he had to accept Cass's decision, difficult as it might be.

'What? But I thought… What happened?'

Mick didn't reply immediately, then said, 'Some sleazebag took a photo of me with Brenda and doctored it to make it look as if me and Brenda were more than friends.'

'But surely you explained what had happened?'

Mick sighed. 'I tried, but Cass didn't want to listen. I guess my past has caught up with me. I led your mother a pretty dance. Cass is her best friend. Why should she believe I've changed?'

'Oh, Dad! I'm sorry. I was sure you and she…' She gave Mick a hug.

'Hey, you two, why are you looking so serious?' Bryan asked, the conversation at the other end of the table having come to an end. 'Mick, Jo tells me you're buying another boat, becoming quite the entrepreneur.'

'Not exactly, but yes, I'm planning to expand. The market's there, and I'm coming into a bit of money from my dad. I've put a deposit down on a vessel up in Pelican Crossing and hope to be able to take possession before Christmas.'

'Good for you, Mick,' Bev said. 'I can imagine how you're feeling. When I decided to grow the garden centre and add a café, I knew it was a bit of a risk, but did it anyway. It could have been a flop, but it wasn't. It was the same when I started up *Pandanus Weddings* and look how successful it has been. You'll be the owner of a whole fleet of whale-watching boats before you know it.'

'I doubt it, Bev. I think I'll be satisfied with two.' He managed a chuckle, the first since he'd spoken with Cass.

'I think it's time we were off. It's getting close to Mia's bedtime.' Jo sent a silent signal to Bryan.

'I'll collect her and meet you at the foot of the stairs,' he said, rising. 'Night, Dad, Bev, Mick.'

'It's probably time we left, too,' Iain said. 'An early night won't do us any harm. Mick?'

There was no good reason for Mick to stay. The cat was out of the bag about Cass now, and he had no desire to stay and drink alone.

'Why don't you come back with us for coffee, Dad?' Jo said, her eyes filled with concern for him. 'You can read a story to Mia. She's a good reader – better than I was at her age, I'm sure – but she still loves to have a bedtime story read to her.'

'Thanks, honey. I'd like that.' For some reason Mick didn't want to be alone. Although he'd lived happily on his own for years, since he'd stopped seeing Cass, he'd become miserable in his own company, dejected at the thought that this was how it was going to be from now on.

But he wasn't alone. He had Jo and Bryan and little Mia, and he wouldn't be surprised if, before long, there was another baby on the way. He had a family. He was loved. And, if there was to be no future with Cass, he would have to make do with what he had, which was more than many others.

Fifty-four

Another Monday morning. Cass turned over in bed and tried to go back to sleep, but the bright light streaming in through the white plantation shutters and the screech of a cockatoo in the tree outside her window forced her awake.

Thankful Justin had already left for work, Cass lingered over her cup of peppermint tea and wondered how she would fill her day. It had never been a problem for her before Mick. These days she counted time as before and after Mick, while realising how foolish she was being. It had been *her* decision to end their relationship and she didn't regret it, but sometimes, like now, she wished things could have been different. But, having been let down by one man in the past, she wasn't going to set herself up for that to happen again. Better to cut it out now, before she became too involved.

But that was the problem, she thought, as Hector pushed his way onto her lap, she had become involved, and she couldn't regret it, couldn't regret the wonderful times they'd had together, the nights of passion, the… She stopped herself remembering. It only caused her pain.

But the day stretched out before her and she had no plans, other than to stay away from the harbour where she might bump into Mick, and to avoid anywhere that might remind her of him. She glanced out the window. It was a glorious day, the sort of day she'd normally want to spend on the beach. Why not? Why should she let the fact she and Mick had walked along the beach stop her from having a swim, then relaxing on the sand with a book. She could have lunch at *The Bay Café*, check out the window of *Sassy's* to see if she could figure out how she could improve it, then come home and take a nap. She hadn't been sleeping well since Ray sent her that photograph and needed to catch up.

Having made the decision, Cass showered and dressed in a pair of loose linen pants and shirt over her swimsuit, popped a towel, book, bottle of water and sunscreen into a small backpack and set off.

At the beach, Cass chose to set her towel down as far away from Will Rankin's surf school as possible. She didn't want to risk a conversation in which she was asked about Mick, and she had no idea how many people knew they'd been together and now weren't.

The water was perfect. Cass swam out between the flags, then turned on her back and floated, gazing up at the clear blue of the sky. There wasn't a cloud in sight. Out here like this, it was easy to believe everything in life was good, almost impossible to imagine anything could possibly go wrong. But it had. Damn Ray Morgan! But would it have been better not to know, to carry on with her relationship with Mick, ignorant of the fact he was seeing other women – one other woman in particular? He'd joked about his daughter's attempts at matchmaking. Just how many women had Jo introduced him to?

Back on the sand, Cass dried herself and dressed, then settled down with her book. But today, the one chosen by the book club she'd reconnected with – *That Bligh Girl* by Sue Williams – failed to hold her attention. She packed up, headed across to the café and chose a seat at one of the sun-bleached wooden tables from where she could watch the passers-by.

A cup of cappuccino and a focaccia filled with ham, cheese and pickles soon put her in a better frame of mind, and she wandered over to *Sassy's* to examine her window display with a critical eye.

'It looks good. Makes me want to refresh my beach wardrobe.'

Cass turned to see Libby Holland standing behind her. 'Thanks, Libby. I'm trying to work out how I can improve it before the next lot of tourists arrive.'

'It looks perfect to me, but I'm no designer of window displays. I only know that black and white swimsuit is very tempting. I may pop in tomorrow and try it.'

'Please do.' Cass smiled. *Sassy's* was one thing that would never disappoint her, or let her down, and she loved her customers, loved helping them choose beachwear which made them look and feel good.

'I'm glad you've come back to the book club,' Libby continued. 'We missed you when your mum was ill. I was sorry to hear of her passing.'

'Thanks.' Cass never knew what to say when people offered their condolences. They meant to be kind, but it brought it all back – the visits to the nursing home, her mother's final days, and Vi.

Clearly seeing Cass's discomfort, Libby changed the subject. 'How are you going with this month's book? Are you enjoying it?'

'Funny you should mention it, I was trying to read it on the beach, but had difficulty concentrating. I don't think it was the book. The author writes well, and I have enjoyed other books by her.'

'Perhaps not a beach read.'

'Perhaps not.'

'Well, I won't keep you. I can see Adam coming out of *Bay Books*. He was signing copies of his latest Jay Bolton book. I got bored watching him and wandered off. We're having lunch at the surf club. Have you eaten? You're welcome to join us.'

'Thanks, I have.' People were so kind, but these days, Cass preferred to be alone, afraid of breaking down if she was with someone who knew she had been seeing Mick and wanted to know what happened and offer sympathy. She didn't want to be an object of pity. She gave a sigh of relief when Libby walked off, watching enviously as she was greeted by her husband with a hug and a kiss. Bellbird Bay seemed to be full of couples who'd met and married in later life. Why couldn't it happen to her? She thought it had, but… She shook her head. No use crying over spilt milk as her mother would have said. Picturing her mother didn't make her sad any longer. Instead, she was able to remember the happy times, and enjoy her memories.

*

Back home, Cass showered and changed before settling down for the afternoon nap she'd promised herself. She awoke a couple of hours later, still feeling sleepy, but after sluicing her face with cold water, she was refreshed.

There was a text on her phone from Justin to tell her he was meeting Zack and wouldn't be home till late, so she fed Hector and pulled a frozen meal out of the fridge, as she didn't feel like cooking.

Cass had finished eating, poured herself a glass of wine and was settling down to make another attempt at the book club book when there was a loud knock at the door. Putting down the book with a sigh, she went to the door and peered through the peephole expecting it to be Mick. He'd come to the door several times already, and she'd refused to open it. Seeing him again, speaking to him, would only make it harder.

It wasn't Mick. It was Jo.

Cautiously, Cass opened the door, glancing left and right to make sure Mick wasn't hanging around.

'I'm on my own, if that's what you're worried about. Can I come in?'

Cass led Jo into the kitchen where Hector, who had been washing himself by the back door, scampered off.

'Oh, you have a cat. I love cats,' Jo said.

Cass stood silent. *Why was Jo here? Had Mick sent her?*

'Dad doesn't know I'm here,' she said, as if reading Cass's mind. 'He'd probably be furious if he knew, but I can't sit back and watch him mope – if a grown man can mope. Mind if I take a seat?'

'Of course not.' Where were Cass's manners? Jo was a guest in her house. 'Would you like tea, coffee?'

'Herbal tea would be lovely.'

While she was making two cups of lemon and ginger tea, Cass was wondering why Jo was here. It had to be something to do with Mick. Was he ill? Greta hadn't said anything about him. But Cass had made it very clear to her friend that anything to do with Mick was out of bounds.

She placed the two cups on the table and sat down opposite Jo.

Jo gave a sigh. 'It seems I'm destined to sort out my parents' love lives. Dad said you won't listen to him, so here I am.'

Sort out...? 'What do you mean?'

Jo leant her elbows on the table. 'Dad told me about Brenda and about the photo.'

Cass stiffened. If Jo was here to plead her dad's case, she was out of luck.

'I can understand your reaction. I'd probably have done the same in your position. But it wasn't how it looked.'

Cass put up one hand to silence her. If she was just going to repeat what Mick had said… But she hadn't really allowed Mick to say anything, she realised.

'Hear me out. It's not just from Dad I heard this. I teach with Brenda. She only came back to work this week and she told me what happened. Evidently, Andy – that's her brother – stumbled and fell when they were walking along. He hit his head. Dad saw them. I think he may have been on his way here at the time?' She raised one eyebrow.

Cass nodded, wondering what was coming next.

'Brenda was in a state, as you can imagine. Dad stopped and went over to see if he could help. He called an ambulance and managed to comfort her. That's probably when the photo was taken.' She glanced at Cass.

Cass swallowed. Could this be true? In the photo, Mick and Brenda were definitely in each other's arms. For the first time she wondered if it might have been doctored in some way. She wouldn't put it past Ray.

Jo continued, 'Brenda didn't want to be left alone, so Dad stayed with her till they knew Andy was going to be all right. He was badly injured. He's only just got back home. Dad says he tried to contact you but couldn't.'

'Oh!' Cass wanted to believe Jo, but it all seemed too neat, too prepared. She remembered how she'd ignored Mick's calls, turned her phone off.

'And I suppose you want me to say everything's fine now, and your dad and I can carry on as before as if this never happened?'

'Well…' Jo looked embarrassed. 'I thought, maybe, once you knew what had happened… Dad's really broken up about it. I've never seen him so upset, not even when Mum told him about her and Leo. He really cares for you, Cass. He was so happy when the two of you were together. You're good for him.'

He's good for me, too.

But Cass didn't know if she could go back and risk being hurt again. 'Thanks for coming to tell me,' she said.

Jo rose. 'Can I tell Dad…?'

'No! I need time to think about what you said. It's not as simple as you seem to believe. Your dad has a history, one I decided to ignore, but there are some things… Thanks,' she said again.

When Cass returned to the kitchen after seeing Jo out, she looked at the two cups sitting on the table and realised neither of them had touched their tea.

Fifty-five

After another sleepless night, during which Cass couldn't stop thinking about Mick, wondering if she'd been too quick to make assumptions and should have allowed him to explain, she woke up to the sound of Hector scratching on her bedroom door. She swung her legs out of the bed and opened the door. 'What's up, Hector? Are you hungry? Hasn't Justin fed you yet?' Cass had become accustomed to Justin taking care of Hector's bowls each morning.

She pulled on her bathrobe and made her way through to the kitchen. There was no sign of her nephew. Yawning, Cass filled Hector's food and water bowls before returning to shower and dress ready for work. By the time she returned, Justin was sitting at the table.

'Sorry, Cass. Late night. I overslept.' He grinned, looking surprisingly bright for someone who hadn't come home till after midnight.

The resilience of the young.

Cass looked at her phone, willing it to ring. But the iPhone which had buzzed repeatedly with calls from Mick was now frustratingly silent. If she wanted to speak with him, she'd have to make the first move, and Cass wasn't sure she was ready to do that.

'See you later. I'll be home tonight,' Justin said, putting his dirty dishes in the dishwasher before he left for work. To Cass's surprise, he'd taken the news of his parents' splitting without surprise, only saying, 'Maybe Mum will be happier on her own.'

'No worries.' She loved the way Justin had fitted seamlessly into her life, making Bellbird Bay and her house his home. It was what annoyed his parents so much, though, perhaps now she had taken the plunge to leave Roger, Vi might understand Justin's decision better. Cass could only hope. She'd hate it if they were estranged for long. Everyone needed their family, even her sister.

The sun was beaming down on Cass as she carried the two coffees from *The Bay Café* to *Birds of a Feather*. It was going to be another hot day, but Cass was oblivious to the weather, her mind still filled with what Jo had told her.

'Morning,' she said, handing Greta a coffee.

'Morning.' Greta peered at her. 'You look as if you haven't slept.'

'Thanks.' Cass took a sip of coffee. She'd tried to camouflage the dark circles under her eyes, but clearly not well enough to fool her friend.

'I'm sorry. Jo told me she'd been to see you.'

Cass felt her stomach lurch. *Was nothing private in this town?* She should have known Jo would speak to her mother. She was worried about her dad. It was only natural, but…

'She was only trying to help. She loves her dad. Whatever he might or might not have done, he's always been there for her.'

'I know, Greta.' Cass sighed. She took a gulp of coffee enjoying the caffeine rush.

Greta hadn't finished. 'It was Jo who managed to get Leo and me back together when I doubted him. If she hadn't… there would have been no wedding. Leo would have gone off on a tour of his hotel chain and might never have come back to Bellbird Bay.'

'I know,' Cass repeated. She remembered Greta's anguish when she thought Leo didn't care for her. *Had she made the same mistake about Mick?*

'I know it's not my place to tell you what to do, but Mick's a good man, his heart's in the right place, and with the right woman… Oh, Cass!' She pulled Cass into a hug. 'I only want you both to be happy, as happy as Leo and I are.'

Cass pulled herself out of the hug. 'Thanks,' she said, before leaving to open up *Sassy's*, knowing she had some serious thinking to do.

The day passed slowly, giving Cass plenty of time to consider her options. Should she make the first move to contact Mick, or would she be setting herself up for yet another disappointment? Could she believe Jo? Her eyes went to her phone so many times during the day, but she couldn't bring herself to make the call.

It was late afternoon when the shop door opened and to Cass's shock, the woman who had been in the photo walked in, followed by Martin Cooper. The woman stood awkwardly just inside the door.

'Cass,' Martin said, clearly uncomfortable at being there.

Cass looked from one to the other. *What was this about?*

'Hello,' the woman said. 'We haven't met. I'm Brenda Collins. I teach with Jo Roberts. She told me a story about a photograph of her dad and me. It seems I need to clear something up, so, on Jo's advice, I contacted Martin…' She gestured to where Martin was standing. 'I have no idea when or why the photo was taken and can only imagine it was to cause trouble. Jo told you the truth. My brother was badly hurt, and I was in a terrible state. If Mick hadn't appeared when he did, I don't know what we'd have done. If I'd known it was going to cause so much trouble…' She bit her lip. 'I can only say sorry. Mick and I had a few dates, and I'd hoped it would lead to something, but he was very clear he didn't feel the same way.'

Cass gulped. It was exactly what Jo had told her and confirmed Mick's account of his dates with Brenda. There was no reason for all three of them to be making it up. 'It's good of you to come and tell me,' she said. *But what was Martin Cooper doing here?*

'Brenda asked me along,' Martin said. 'Can you show me the photo?'

Hesitatingly, Cass took out her phone and scrolled to the image. *What good was this going to do?*

Martin examined the photo for a few moments. 'Ah, I see what he's done.' He turned the screen to face Cass. 'If you look here…' he pointed, '… and here, you can see where someone has manipulated the image to make it look as if…' He glanced at Cass's puzzled expression. 'If you know what to look for, it's easy to see where the original has been altered, but most people wouldn't notice. It's a good job.'

Cass stared at the photo which had haunted her, unable to see what Martin was referring to. But she believed him. Martin Cooper was a world-famous photographer. He knew what he was talking about. It had never occurred to her Ray might have altered the image of Mick and Brenda to make her believe… She shook her head. *How desperate was he?*

Cass looked across at Martin and Brenda. 'Thanks. I've been a fool.'

'Not at all,' Martin said. 'It's an expert job. The guy who did this must be a professional.'

Cass swallowed. Ray Morgan wasn't a photographer. He wouldn't know how to do this, but he'd have contacts who did. The bastard! And for what? To try to persuade her to leave Mick and go back to him? Well, he'd been successful with the first part.

'Thanks, Brenda,' she said again. 'And thanks, Martin, for taking time to show me what I should have realised for myself.' She had a lot to thank Jo for, too.

'No worries,' Martin said. 'Happy to help.' He left.

'I hope everything works out for you and Mick,' Brenda said. 'He's a good man and deserves to be happy. You seem like a nice woman. Jo tells me you and her mum are good friends. You must have known both her parents for a long time.'

'Yes.' *Almost all my life.* 'Thanks for coming,' she said again.

Brenda had barely left when Greta stepped in. 'Was that Jo's friend I just saw, the one you said was in the photo – and Martin Cooper?'

Cass sighed again. Greta didn't miss much. She must have seen Brenda and Martin arrive and both of them leave.

'Did she confirm Jo's story?'

Cass nodded. 'And Martin said the photo had been altered to make me think… Oh, Cass, Ray played me for a fool and I fell right into his trap.'

'Well, now you know, what are you going to do about it?'

Cass glanced at her phone again. Should she…?

'You can't do this by phone. Mick's afternoon cruise will be finished. Why don't you close up and go to see him? You two need to talk.'

Greta was right. This wasn't something to be resolved over the phone. She and Mick needed to talk face-to-face. But could she risk it?

'You know I'm right. Don't leave it till it's too late.'

What if it already was?

*

Cass's heart was in her mouth as she drove to the harbour. Her head was telling her she was mad to risk being hurt again, but she decided to follow her heart which was urging her to give Mick another chance. When she parked, she could see Mick and Justin standing on the deck talking. As she watched, Justin left, jumping on his bike and riding off. Mick turned to go into the cabin.

Her stomach churning, her mouth dry, Cass stepped out of the car and made her way towards the whale-watching boat, remembering her first trip on it, before she and Mick had got together. She almost turned back before she reached the gangplank but forced herself to continue. There was the sound of music coming from the cabin, an old melody she remembered from her teenage years. Mick wouldn't have heard her. It wasn't too late to change her mind. The cabin door was open. Tentatively she knocked.

Mick swung round, his eyes widening with surprise when he saw Cass, his lips turning up in the smile which made her heart leap. 'Cass, what are you doing here?'

'I… I…' Cass stuttered. Now she was here, she didn't know what to say. The sight of Mick wearing a navy singlet and pair of disreputable khaki shorts took her breath away. She was flooded with warmth, the sound of her own heartbeat thrumming in her ears. 'I…' she began again.

'How about a cuppa? Take a seat.' Mick's eyes held the warm glow Cass remembered.

'Thanks.' She sank gratefully onto a nearby bench seat and watched as he boiled water and dropped two teabags into mugs without speaking.

'Now,' Mick said, handing Cass a mug and taking a seat next to her, 'what's this about? I've tried to contact you so often, I finally gave up. I assumed you didn't want to speak to me, that you'd made up your mind.'

'I had,' Cass said in a small voice. She was gripping her mug tightly in both hands. 'I was hurt. I lashed out. It wasn't fair of me. I should have listened to you.' She took a deep breath. 'I've come to say I'm sorry, so sorry. I was wrong. I should have listened to you, believed you. Can you ever forgive me? I'll understand if you can't. I'm not sure if I would, if I was you. But when Jo…'

'Jo? What has she done?'

'Nothing. Well, she did come to see me, to explain what had happened, how you'd only been helping Brenda and her brother. I was a fool to believe anything Ray Morgan told me. I have no excuse, apart from the fact I'd been let down before. But that isn't any reason for believing… for refusing to allow you to explain.' Cass paused to draw breath. She stared at Mick, hoping to see some sign he might be willing to forgive her.

'My Jo did that?' Mick shook his head and gave a chuckle. 'Who'd have thought she'd go that far to get me matched up.'

Cass's breath caught. *Did he…? Was he going to…?*

Mick put down his mug and edged closer. 'I've never stopped caring for you, Cass. I was devastated when you refused to listen to me, angry too. I wanted to punch the bastard for what he did, but it wouldn't have made you change your mind. Of course I can forgive you. I've never stopped thinking about you, remembering…'

Mick's arm went around Cass's shoulders. His free hand took the mug from her hands and placed it on the floor. Then his lips were on hers and her world spun out of control.

There were tears in Cass's eyes when he released her, tears of joy. What a fool she had been to endanger what they had together on the word of a charlatan like Ray Morgan. What had she been thinking? In truth, she hadn't been thinking straight. The sight of the photo of Mick and Brenda had brought back the memory of the day Ray proudly announced his wife's pregnancy on breakfast television and destroyed her hopes for a future with him. Mick was nothing like Ray. She knew now he would never hurt her.

Cass snuggled into Mick's arms, secure in the knowledge it was where she belonged. How could she ever have thought otherwise? She breathed in the aroma which always surrounded him, a mixture of saltwater, oil and sweat. It was so familiar to her she wanted to weep again, to hold onto this man who was so forgiving, so loving, so… sexy. A flash of desire shot through her, so intense it made her gasp.

'I've missed you so much,' Mick muttered into her hair, 'missed holding you, missed…'

'Me, too.' Cass couldn't believe how close she'd come to throwing all this away.

Mick pulled her into his arms again, and suddenly they were lying together on the narrow bench seat in each other's arms, finding a release of the pent-up passion of the time they'd been apart.

'I think we need to go somewhere more comfortable, don't you?' Mick said, sometime later.

Suddenly aware of the hardness of the bench on which they were lying, Cass began to laugh. 'I think you may be right,' she said.

Mick took her hand, and they moved as one towards the jetty and Mick's car, unable to bear being parted as they headed to Mick's home and his king-sized bed to consummate their reunion yet again.

Fifty-six

2 months later

'She's beautiful, Mick.' Cass stared at the boat sitting at the edge of the marina, the name Safe Harbour painted on her side in red.

'Glad you think so. It's too late to change my mind.' Mick pulled Cass back against him, his hands around her waist, and nuzzled her neck. 'We could change her name, call her after you… or Jo. We have a lot to thank her for.'

'No, I think it's a perfect name for her.'

They had driven up to Pelican Crossing, leaving early that morning and accompanied by Justin. The young man was to drive the Toyota Landcruiser back to Bellbird Bay, while Cass and Mick would sail the new boat down the coast. It had taken longer than Mick expected for his dad's money to come through, so it was now closer to Christmas than he'd predicted.

Cass had been bubbling with excitement ever since she awoke in Mick's arms, something she now did every morning, either at her own home or at Mick's. They had already had conversations about which of the two they would make into their permanent home, but hadn't decided. Until Justin left for university, it was important he could still regard Cass's house as his home. And Vi was coming to spend Christmas with them.

That had been the most surprising piece of news. When the call came asking if she could come to visit, if she'd be welcome after everything she'd said, Cass was so surprised, it took her several moments to formulate a reply. She knew her sister had found it difficult to adjust to the single life after leaving Roger, but she had purchased a small apartment in a neighbouring suburb and seemed to be finding her feet and making a fresh start.

Justin was very laid back about his parents' divorce, telling Cass he doubted if he and his dad would ever see eye-to-eye, but agreed his relationship with his mother had improved. This was likely due to her acceptance of his decision to live and study in Australia, having listened to Cass's oft-repeated advice that continuing to disagree with Justin was a sure way to alienate him for good.

Now, happy in her relationship with Mick, and looking forward to reuniting with her sister, Cass was able to anticipate the festive season with a sense of expectation she never had before.

'Ready?'

Cass turned to face Mick. She'd been so lost in thought, she hadn't noticed Mick preparing the boat for their trip.

'Ready,' she said with a smile. She seemed to be smiling a lot these days. Mick made her so happy.

As they made their way slowly down the coast, Mick pointed out the pods of dolphins which followed them part of the way just as if they were guiding them. It was peaceful out here on the ocean, the seabirds whirling above them, the lapping of the waves against the side of the boat, and the sun beaming down on them. Cass wished they could stay here for ever.

'Happy?' Mick asked, leaving his post at the steering wheel to give Cass a kiss. 'No regrets?'

'So happy,' she said, throwing her arms around his neck and returning his kiss. 'You're the best thing that ever happened to me. For so long I watched other women finding their happy ever after and wondered if it would ever be my turn. You were worth waiting for.'

Mick opened a bottle of champagne and filled two glasses. 'To us, and our future together,' he said, raising one glass and handing the other to Cass.

'To us,' she said, knowing she would never be alone again. With Mick, she had found her own happy ever after.

The End

If you've enjoyed Cass and Mick's story, a way you can say thank you to me is to leave a review on Amazon and/or Goodreads. A few words will suffice, no need for a lengthy review. It will mean a lot to me and help other readers find my books.

I've loved writing my Bellbird Bay series and I know many of you have loved it, too. So, it's with mixed emotions that I'm moving on to a new series – though this might not be the last you see of the Bellbird Bay community.

The new series will be set in Pelican Crossing, a fictional town somewhere on the Queensland coast, the town where Mick went to buy his new boat in this book. The first book in the series, currently titled Pelican Crossing, features Poppy Taylor, the widow who owns and manages the restaurant *Crossings*.

Poppy Taylor has always been content with her life in *Pelican Crossing*, but as she watches her youngest daughter get married, she can't help but feel that there's something missing. Never would Poppy have predicted the dramatic transformation that occurs as she reunites with an old love and makes a choice that will reshape everything.

Cam Mitchell has always felt a strong attraction to Poppy, and when she reveals her plans to make changes in her life, Cam sees it as his chance to finally reveal his feelings. But Cam's hopes are crushed when he discovers Poppy's past love is back in the picture.

Cam becomes increasingly sceptical of the man from Poppy's past – a feeling that escalates when he uncovers his shocking plans for Pelican Crossing.

With their town now at risk, Cam and Poppy must work together to save their home and find their own happy ending. But will their feelings for each other be enough to overcome the obstacles in their way?

For fans of small-town romances and heartwarming stories of second chances, *Pelican Crossing* is a must-read. A captivating tale of love, loyalty, and the fight to protect what matters most.

You can order here https://mybook.to/RestaurantinPC

From the Author

Dear Reader,

First, I'd like to thank you for choosing to read *Happy Ever After in Bellbird Bay*. I hope you've enjoyed this trip to Bellbird Bay as much as I've enjoyed writing it.

I'm really enjoying writing about my fictional town in the part of Queensland where I live and populating it with characters who I hope you will come to love. I'm thrilled at the number of my readers who tell me they want to live there. It's the ninth book in this series, but like the others, can be read as a standalone.

If you'd like to stay up to date with my new releases and special offers you can sign up to my reader's group.

You can sign up here

https://mailchi.mp/f5cbde96a5e6/maggiechristensensreadersgroup

I'll never share your email address, and you can unsubscribe at any time. You can also contact me via Facebook, Twitter or by email. I love hearing from my readers and will always reply.

Thanks again.

Acknowledgements

As always, this book could not have been written without the help and advice of a number of people.

Firstly, my husband Jim for listening to my plotlines without complaint, for his patience and insights as I discuss my characters and storyline with him, for his patience and help with difficult passages and advice on my male dialogue, and for being there when I need him.

John Hudspith, editor extraordinaire for his ideas, suggestions, encouragement and attention to detail, and for helping me make this book better.

Jane Dixon-Smith for her patience and for working her magic on my beautiful cover and interior.

My thanks also to early readers of this book – Helen, Maggie and Louise for their helpful comments and advice.

And to all of my readers, reviewers and bloggers. Your support and comments make it all worthwhile.

About the Author

After a career in education, Maggie Christensen began writing contemporary women's fiction portraying mature women facing life-changing situations, and historical fiction set in her native Scotland. Her travels inspire her writing, be it her trips to visit family in Scotland, in Oregon, USA or her home on Queensland's beautiful Sunshine Coast. Maggie writes of mature heroines coming to terms with changes in their lives and the heroes worthy of them. Maggie has been called *the queen of mature age fiction* and her writing has been described by one reviewer as *like a nice warm cup of tea. It is warm, nourishing, comforting and embracing.*

From the small town in Scotland where she grew up, Maggie was lured to Australia by the call to 'Come and teach in the sun'. Once there, she worked as a primary school teacher, university lecturer and in educational management. Now living with her husband of over thirty years on Queensland's Sunshine Coast, she loves walking on the deserted beach in the early mornings and having coffee by the river on weekends. Her days are spent surrounded by books, either reading or writing them – her idea of heaven!

Maggie can be found on Facebook, Twitter, Goodreads, Instagram, Bookbub or on her website.

https://www.facebook.com/maggiechristensenauthor
https://twitter.com/MaggieChriste33
https://www.goodreads.com/author/show/8120020.Maggie_Christensen
https://www.instagram.com/maggiechriste33/
https://www.bookbub.com/profile/maggie-christensen?list=about
https://maggiechristensenauthor.com/

www.ingramcontent.com/pod-product-compliance
Lightning Source LLC
Chambersburg PA
CBHW022042290426
44109CB00014B/945